Citizenship, Nationality and Access to Public Service Employment

Europa Law Publishing, Groningen 2001

Citizenship, Nationality and Access to Public Service Employment

The Impact of European Community Law

Dr. J.E. Beenen

First edition

Europa Law Publishing is a publishing company
specializing in European Union Law.
For further information please contact Europa Law
Publishing via email: info@europalawpublishing.com
or visit our website at: www.europalawpublishing.com.

Typeset in Scala and Scala Sans
Graphic design by G2K Designers, Groningen/
Amsterdam

NUGI 698
ISBN 90-76871-04-3
British Library Cataloguing-in-Publication Data
A catalogue record for this book is available from the
British Library

'[Open government is] a contradiction in terms, you can be open or you can have government'

(From the TV-series 'Yes, Minister' by Sir Antony Jay and Jonathan Lynn)

Preface

Discrimination on the grounds of the nationality of workers is prohibited in the EC Treaty, apart from a limited number of exceptions laid down in Article 39 (ex Article 48) EC. This thesis focuses on one of those exceptions, namely the public service exception which is laid down in paragraph 4 of Article 39 (ex Article 48), the trend towards an increasingly narrower interpretation of this exception by the European Court of Justice in Luxembourg and the consequences thereof in both European and national legislation. My investigation of the public service exception would not have been possible without the advice and guidance of Professor J.B.J.M. ten Berge and Professor R. de Lange. I would like to take this opportunity to thank them for their support.

This study could not have been completed without the help of others. I would first of all like to thank Professor D.M. Curtin, Professor H.R.B.M. Kummeling, Professor K.J.M Mortelmans, Professor R.J.G.M. Widdershoven and Professor G.J.M. van Wissen (University of Amsterdam) for their willingness to sit in the evaluation committee. In addition I would like to thank the following people for supplying me with invaluable information: Dr. Friedrich Fröhlich from the *Bundesministerium für Finanzen* of the Republic of Austria; Professor Olli Mäenpää from the University of Helsinki, Finland; Staffan Ingmanson of the *Rättsvetenskapliga Institutionen* of Umeå University in Sweden; Professor Dr. Günter Frankenberg from the *Institut für Öffentliches Recht* at the Johann Wolfgang Goethe Universität, Frankfurt am Main, Germany; Dr. Roberto Caranta of the University of Turin, Italy; Pierre Neyes, Director of *l'Administration du Personnel de l'Etat* of Luxembourg, Professor Dr. Faustos de Quadros, Ms Carla Sequeira and Mr Luis Reis of the Law Faculty (European Institute) of the University of Lisbon, Portugal; and Professor Christopher Forsyth of Cambridge University, United Kingdom. Thanks also go to Mr. P. Morris, who edited the manuscript.

Specials thanks are due to my family for their continued support during the years it took to finish this thesis: mum, dad, Mirjan and Michel. Also thanks to my friends and colleagues at the G.J. Wiarda Institute, with a special mention going to 'de zolder', Erik Kraai, Ann-Sophie VandenBerghe, Sebastiaan Princen, Monica Wirtz and Renaat Hoop, for all the laughs. Thanks also go to my friends Piet-Hein and Patrick, Mary and Ian, and Gene. Last but not least: Taffy, your support has been invaluable. You encouraged me and lifted my spirits when needed. Thank you.

Nanda Beenen
January 2001

Table of Contents

CHAPTER I

Introduction

1 Central problem

In 1982 the Court of Justice of the European Communities ruled in the case *Commission* v. *Belgium*[1] that the jobs of shunters, drivers and plate-layers with the Belgian National Railway, as well as joiners and gardeners with the City of Brussels, were not covered by the so-called public service exception of Article 39 (4) (ex Article 48 (4)) of the EC Treaty. The result of this ruling was that access to these jobs could no longer be restricted to only Belgian nationals because they did not 'involve direct or indirect participation in the exercise of powers conferred by public law and duties designed to safeguard the general interests of the state or of other public authorities'.[2] Nationals from other EC Member States should also be allowed to apply for and be appointed to these jobs. According to Article 39 (ex Article 48) EC, discrimination on the basis of nationality was forbidden for posts not covered by the public service exception or any of the other exceptions laid down in that Article. Non-nationals, at least those from other EU Member States, should have access to these posts on a par with Belgian nationals.

This was the first important case dealing with the public service exception before the European Court since the entry into force of the EC Treaty. Since then, eight more cases have directly dealt with the public service exception as such, and other cases have done so indirectly. Over the years the trend has been towards an increasingly narrower interpretation of Article 39 (4) (ex Article 48 (4)) EC. In the last of these cases, *Commission* v. *Greece*[3] in 1996, the Court decided the following posts were not covered by the public service exception: public, semi-public or municipal undertakings and companies distributing water, gas and electricity, the public health service, teaching posts in nursery, primary and secondary schools and higher education establishments and universities, transport services, posts for scientific and non-scientific staff in public establishments conducting research for non-military purposes, postal and telecommunications services, radio and television broadcasting services, and musicians' posts at the Athens Opera and in municipal and local orchestras.

As we can see, the public service exception as laid down in Article 39 (ex Article 48 (4)) of the EC Treaty and as interpreted by de European Court has a significant impact on national policy covering access to public service employment. A very broad category of public service posts have to be opened up to EU citizens who are not nationals of the Member State in question. The question is whether there are any posts left which are in fact still covered by the exception

---

1 Case 149/79 (II), [1982] ECR 1845, paras. 8-10, which was a follow-up to the original case 149/79, [1980] ECR 3881.

2 Case 149/79, [1980] ECR 3881, para. 10.

3 Case C-290/94, [1996] ECR I-3285.

and, if so, which posts are they and on the basis of which criteria are they covered by the exception?

What will become clear in this book is that, although the public service exception is interpreted narrowly, there are still posts which are covered by the exception, a number of which are named by the Court in its case law. Examples of covered posts are: supervisors and night watchmen in public buildings, the former because they have some degree of authority and the latter because they would have access to possible confidential plans.[4] Also posts with research bodies advising the state on scientific and technical matters can be covered.[5] These are the only categories of posts which the European Court decided were covered by the public service exception and mentioned in its case law. Other posts which might be covered by the exception have not been laid before the Court and as a result it has proved quite difficult to decide which posts are in fact covered by the public service exception. The Court has mainly focussed on posts which are *not* covered by the exception and has adopted a case-by-case approach which means that drawing more general conclusions from the case law is difficult.

One conclusion that can be drawn from the case law is that by 1996 a number of countries[6] had still not fully complied with Community legislation as far as the public service was concerned. The question is whether this was the case because they were unwilling or unable to comply, or whether the non-compliance had other causes, such as difficulty with the definition of the Article provision or the Court's interpretation of it.

The aim of this book is to, firstly, discover in detail how the European Court of Justice has interpreted the public service exception as laid down in Article 39 (4) (ex Article 48 (4)) EC. The question which follows on from this is how this interpretation of the exception has influenced national legislation in the EU Member States.

The main questions which will be dealt with in this thesis are, therefore:

1 How does the Court of Justice of the European Communities interpret the public service exception as laid down in Article 39 (4) (ex Article 48 (4)) EC? And how does this interpretation of 'public service' relate to other interpretations of state entities or emanations of the state in other areas of European law?
2 In which form are nationality requirements laid down in the national legislation of the EU Member States?

---

4 Case 149/79 (II), [1982] ECR 1845, paras. 8-10.

5 Case 225/85, *Commission* v. *Italy*, para. 9.

6 Besides Greece, these were Luxembourg (case C-473/93) and Belgium (case C-173/94). These three cases were joined, [1996] ECR 3207ff.

3 Has the interpretation by the European Court influenced national legislation dealing with nationality requirements for the public service within the Member States? And, if so, in what way?
4 Is national legislation, after possible changes due to the European Court's case law, in compliance with Community law? (Since it has not been possible to investigate the national legislation of all 15 Member States, this question will be dealt with for a number of Member States only.)
5 If it transpires that there are Member States whose national legislation is not in compliance with Community law, what are the reasons for this non-compliance?
6 Should there be changes to the text of the public service exception as laid down in Article 39 (4) (ex Article 48 (4)) EC? If so, what should these changes be?
7 What does the future hold for the public service exception within the ever more integrated European Union?

In this thesis I have not investigated the possibilities of enforcement of the public service exception, either at a Community or a national level. I will, of course, discuss the infringement procedures brought by the European Commission against a number of Member States, but I will not move beyond a description of those cases as needed for the definition of the public service exception as laid down in Article 39 (4) (ex Article 48 (4)) EC. Although I will make a number of suggestions regarding the public service exception and its future, possible improvements to this provision are not the prime focus of my thesis. What I wanted to achieve was a greater knowledge and understanding of what the public service exception entails, both at a Community and at a national level. I wanted to discover what forms the exceptions have taken in national legislation and what, if any, differences may be found, and what may be the result of different systems of incorporating nationality requirements for posts in the public service.

2 Structure of this thesis

This thesis consists of two parts. Part I will deal with the Community level of legislation which is of importance when looking at the public service exception of Article 39 (4) (ex Article 48 (4)) EC. It will discuss Community legislation which is pertinent to the public service exception, and more broadly, I will look at the provisions dealing with free movement of workers within the European Union and the citizenship-rights provisions as laid down in the EC Treaty. There is also an in-depth look at the provision dealing with the public service exception in the EC Treaty: Article 39 (4) (ex Article 48 (4)). A separate chapter will investigate two other areas of Community law which also deal with the concept of the state and compare those with the public service exception.

Part 2 will look at national legislation in a number of Member States. First of all there will be a general survey comparing different systems of public service exceptions laid down in the national legislation of a number of EU Member States. The next three chapters will pay specific attention to three Member States, namely the Netherlands, Belgium and the United Kingdom.

Part 1 of this thesis starts with Chapter 2 entitled *Free Movement of Persons within the European Union*. It will describe the possibilities for EU citizens to move to a Member State other than their own and to settle and work there. It will also look at the exceptions to free movement within the EU, one of which is the public service exception of Article 39 (4) (ex Article 48 (4)) EC.

Chapter 3, *Citizenship*, will consider citizenship in general and European citizenship in particular. It will look at the rights introduced into the EC Treaty by the Maastricht Treaty which was signed in 1992. In these first two chapters we will see that the provisions of the EC Treaty are no longer geared solely towards economic rights and rights which are linked to pure economic goals.

Chapter 4, Article 39 (4) EC: *The Public Service Exception*, will look at the public service exception itself in great detail. It will describe the case law of the European Court in the cases dealing specifically with Article 39 (4) (ex Article 48 (4)) EC. It will consider the Court's narrow and functional interpretation of the exception and investigate other possible interpretations, such as the institutional approach favoured by a number of Member States. This Chapter will analyse the Court's approach and compare it with the exception to the provisions dealing with the right of establishment and the freedom to provide services as laid down in Article 45 (ex Article 55) EC. This provision excludes activities which are connected with the exercise of official authority from the principle of freedom of establisment and provision of services.

Finally, in this first part of the thesis in Chapter 5, entitled *The Concept of the State in Two Other Areas of European Law*, I want to side-step and look at two other areas of Community law in which the definition of 'the state' or state authorities plays a crucial role. These two areas are: the direct effect of directives and public procurement. In this chapter I will briefly investigate whether or not there is one single definition for what constitutes 'the state' or 'state bodies' for the purposes of Community law. If this is not the case and there are in fact several such definitions, I will look at the reasons behind this phenomenon.

Part 2 of this thesis then goes on to look at the national level of legislation. It considers how nationality requirements for the public service are laid down in national legislation in the Member States and in which way, if any, Community legislation or case law from the European Court have influenced the legislation of the Member States at the national level.

First of all, Chapter 6, *Access to Public Employment in a Number of EU Member States; a General Study,* looks at how nationality requirements are laid down in a number of European Union Member States. The information required to write this chapter was acquired through setting up a survey with pertinent questions about national public service exceptions, which was sent to experts in all Member States. Unfortunately, I was unable to obtain the necessary information about all the Member States, but this Chapter still gives an intriguing overview of the differences and similarities in national legislation dealing with nationality requirements for the public service.

Chapter 7, *Access to Public Service Employment in the Netherlands,* Chapter 8, *Access to Public Service Employment in Belgium,* and Chapter 9, *Access to Public Service Employment in the United Kingdom,* take a deeper and more extensive look at the nationality requirements for the public service in these three countries. It would have been ideal to be able to do this for all 15 Member States of the European Union, but time did not permit this. The choice of these three countries was made based on both practical reasons and interesting features within the legal systems in these countries. First of all, the practical reasons, which were mainly based on language ability (English and Dutch being the main languages spoken in these countries), connections in these countries and access to information. However, my choice for the UK was also based on the fact that the Anglo legal system is in many ways different from that in the rest of Europe, which made it interesting to study. Belgium was in itself an interesting country to include in my research as the first and most important case[7] dealing with the public service exception of Article 39 (4) (ex Article 48 (4)) EC was an infringement case brought by the European Commission against Belgium in 1979 and it is also the only country which has had two such cases brought against it by the Commission, namely again in 1994.[8]

As we will see in these three chapters, which look at the public service exception as laid down in national legislation, there are differences in emphasis when it comes to various parts of the public service, such as official posts, office holders (political or otherwise), civil servants and contractual employees. This is a result of the way in which the national provisions deal with nationality requirements for the public service, as well as the way in which the public service itself is organised and has grown over the centuries. I have focussed on the posts within the public service for which I have found that nationality requirements exist and I have investigated those. Since the various countries use different methods of excluding non-nationals from certain posts and also have

7 Case 149/79, *Commission* v. *Belgium,* [1980] ECR 3881.

8 Case C-173/94, [1996] ECR I-3265.

different traditions and customs of dealing with this matter, the contents of the three chapters are in some ways quite different. Certain posts are covered in one chapter and not, or to a lesser extent, in another. This may be because one State does not apply a nationality criterion, or because there is no legislation dealing with nationality restrictions, either because they are deemed unnessecary or because the access of nationals only to the post in question is considered to be self-evident. As a result, the definition of 'public service' as investigated in this thesis is not identical for each of these chapters.

The last chapter of this thesis is Chapter 10, *Summary and Conclusions,* which will try to distil the most important findings of this thesis and suggest possible improvements as far as the public service exception as laid down in Article 39 (4) (ex Article 48 (4)) EC is concerned, as well as improvements in the access to public service policy in the EU Member States. Lastly, this chapter will look at what the future might have in store for the public service exception.

CHAPTER 2

Free Movement of Persons within the European Union

1 Introduction

This book concerns access to public service employment within the Member States of the European Union. Before we can look at the specific provision dealing with access to public service in the EC Treaty, namely Article 39 (4) (ex Article 48 (4)), I want to look at the broader topic of free movement of persons within the EU. This is necessary because the public service exception, which constitutes the main topic of this study, is an exception to this basic principle of free movement of persons, which is laid down in EC legislation.

According to the EC Treaty, freedom of movement is one of the rights of EU citizens. According to Article 18 (ex Article 8a) EC every citizen of the Union has the right to move and reside freely within the territory of the Member States, subject to the limitations and conditions laid down in the EC Treaty and adopted secondary legislation in this field.[1] In this Chapter the conditions and limitations dealing with the free movement of persons within the EU will be discussed, in so far as they are relevant to the topic of access to public service employment.

2 Free movement of persons within the EU

Title III of the EC Treaty deals with the free movement of persons, services and capital. In Chapter I the provisions dealing with the free movement of workers are laid down. It is not unexpected that the first persons within the European *Economic* Community (as it then was) to be given the right of free movement were the workers. The principal aims of the Treaty were, after all, economically based. Over the last decade, however, the group of persons entitled to free movement has grown and now includes: pensioners, students and persons who are and will not be a burden on their host State.[2]

In this book I will focus on the free movement of workers laid down in Articles 39 (ex Article 48) to 42 (ex 51) EC.

2.1 Article 39 (ex Article 48) EC

Article 39 (ex Article 48) EC states in paragraph 1 that free movement for workers shall be secured within the Community. Paragraph 2 then goes on to state that this entails the abolition of all discrimination based

---

1 Article 18 is one of the rights of the citizens of the European Union as incorporated into the EC Treaty by the Amsterdam Treaty. These citizenship rights are discussed in more detail in Chapter 3.

2 Directives 90/364-366, OJ 1990 L 180/26, 28 and 30.

on nationality. As such, Article 39 (ex Article 48) is an extension of the basic prohibition of discrimination on the basis of nationality which is laid down in Article 12 (ex Article 6) EC.[3]

2.1.1 Non-discrimination on grounds of nationality

Paragraph 2 of Article 39 (ex Article 48) EC prohibits discrimination on grounds of nationality. Discrimination can take three forms. Firstly, direct discrimination, that is to say, rules which specifically provide for a different treatment of non-nationals. Secondly, there is indirect or covert discrimination,[4] i.e. rules which, although based on a criterion which appears to be neutral, in practice lead to the discrimination of non-nationals.[5] Thirdly, there is reverse discrimination, which occurs in situations where a Member State discriminates against its own citizens in favour of foreign nationals. This can occur because in certain cases a Member State's own nationals are not in a position to challenge the compatibility of national legislation with Community law because a relevant intra-Community factor is not present, i.e. there has been no relevant crossing of Community borders in their case, which placed them at a disadvantage.

The first two forms of discrimination fall within the scope of Community law and are forbidden. The third one, reverse discrimination, is not. Because the intra-Community factor is absent, the Court has decided that it has no jurisdiction in these cases and leaves it up to the individual Member States whether or not to remedy such forms of discrimination. The idea behind this being that if the national legislation puts a Member State's own nationals at a severe disadvantage it can and often will remedy this by adopting national measures.

As a result of the Court's interpretation that reverse discrimination is not within its jurisdiction, the principle of non-discrimination, as established by the EC Treaty and interpreted by the ECJ, is far from securing total equality among Union citizens. Despite its progressive and flexible interpretation, as manifested

---

3 The first part of Article 12 (ex Article 6) EC reads: "Within the scope of application of this Treaty, and without prejudice to any special provisions contained therein, any discrimination on grounds of nationality shall be prohibited."

4 In *Allué & Coonan*, case 33/88, [1989] ECR 1591, the Court stated in paragraph 11 that 'the principle of equal treatment [...] prohibits not only overt discrimination based on nationality but all covert forms of discrimination.' In *Allué & Coonan* the Court referred to its judgment in case 41/84 *Pinna* v. *Caisse d'Allocations Familiales de la Savoie*, [1986] ECR 1, which prohibited covert discrimination in the area of social security for migrant workers.

5 Also in the case *Allué & Coonan*, the Court held that the principle of non-discrimination forbids any disguised forms of discimination based on nationality.

in the *Cowan* case,[6] the Court finds a constitutional limit to this prohibition because it will only apply it to the scope of application of the Treaty. Therefore, an individual claiming equal treatment must establish that he falls within an area covered by the Treaty before he can rely on Community legislation.

Although there is the main principle of non-discrimination on the basis of nationality, there are also a number of explicit Treaty derogations to this principle. Some of these derogations are based on the protection of public policy, public security or public health.[7] Furthermore, the principle of non-discrimination is not applicable to those situations where nationality is considered to be a prerequisite for the exercise of certain rights or functions from which Member States may legitimately exclude Union citizens other than their own nationals. These are situations covered in particular by Article 39 (4) (ex Article 48 (4)) and Article 45 (ex Article 55) EC. The Court has repeatedly confirmed that certain functions with the objective of safeguarding a State's general interest imply the existence of a particular relation of solidarity or loyalty with the State as well as the reciprocity of rights and duties which are the foundation of the nationality link.[8]

The entry into force of the TEU, which introduced the concept of Union citizenship,[9] has not altered this situation and the aforementioned Articles remain unchanged. Any change derived from the introduction of the concept of Union citizenship will, therefore, have to be brought about by the Court's interpretation of the already existing legislation in the light of the existence of Union citizenship.[10]

---

6 Case 186/87, *Cowan* v. *Trésor Public*, [1989] ECR 195. The Court ruled that the prohibition of non-discrimination is also applicable in cases where it concerns recipients of services who are nationals from one Member State while they are in another Member State, such as tourists.

7 See below, paragraphs 3.2ff.

8 Case 149/79, *Commission* v. *Belgium*, [1980] ECR 3881, and case 66/85, *Lawrie-Blum*, [1986] ECR 2121. See also below, paragraph 3.5.

9 See Chapter 3.

10 This is, for example, the opinion of Wouters, for whom it seems reasonable to expect that the Court will further narrow the scope of Articles 39 (4) (ex 48 (4)) and 45 (ex 55) EC now that the provisions for citizenship have given a clear dimension to the EC Treaty. See: Wouters, J., 'European Citizenship and the Case-Law of the Court of Justice of the European Communities on the Free Movement of Persons', in Marias, E., (Ed.) *European Citizenship* (European Institute of Public Administration, Maastricht, 1994) p. 49.

2.1.2 The definition of a worker in EU law

Article 39 (ex Article 48) declares that workers are entitled to freedom of movement within the Community. The Treaty did not provide a definition of the term 'worker' and it was therefore up to the Court to decide this matter. As a result we will have to distil its meaning from the Court's case law.[11]

The definition of a worker is important as it determines the scope of Article 39. If the term 'worker' has a broad meaning, then it means that the prohibition of discrimination is applicable widely. This also has consequences for the application of the public service exception. After all, the exception need only be applied where it concerns 'workers' as defined in Article 39 (ex Article 48) EC. Should certain categories of workers, e.g. civil service employees, not be considered workers within the meaning of this Article, then for those categories the public service exception would be a moot point.

The first case dealing with the definition of a 'worker' within Community law was *Levin* v. *Staatssecretaris van Justitie*.[12] A British national was refused a permit to reside in the Netherlands because the Dutch authorities considered the income from her work to be inadequate for her to live on. The question which was referred to the Court asked whether Article 39 (ex Article 48) covers a person whose activity yields an income less than the minimum required for subsistence under the legislation of the host state. In this case the Court insisted that the notion of 'worker' has a Community law content. The Danish and Dutch submissions opined that national criteria governing minimum wages and minimum hours of work should apply. The Court concluded that the notion of a worker should possess a uniform Community meaning in order to preclude the use of different interpretations at the national level. To allow Member States to decide what constitutes a worker would open the door to unilateral modifications of the scope of Community law. The Court proceeded to state that the definition cannot be too narrow because of the need to secure economic development referred to in Articles 2 and 3 EC. Such objectives would be undermined if Article 39 (ex Article 48) excluded those pursuing part-time work, for such activity is 'an effective means of improving [...] living conditions'.[13]

What is required is only that the work involves 'the pursuit of effective and genuine activities to the exclusion of activities on such a small scale as to be regarded as purely marginal and ancillary'. Once this test has been satisfied, 'the

---

[11] For a description of the development of Article 39 (ex Article 48) EC and the pertinent case law, see also: Craig, P. and de Búrca, G., *EU law: Text, Cases and Materials* (2nd edition), (Oxford University Press, Oxford, 1998) pp. 664ff.

[12] Case 53/81, [1982] ECR 1035.

[13] Ibid., para. 15.

motives which have prompted the worker to seek employment in the Member State concerned are of no account and must not be taken into consideration'.[14]

The Court's insistence on the concept of worker as a Community law concept is an important element in securing uniform protection of the rights of free movement for workers throughout the Community.[15]

In *Steymann* v. *Staatssecretaris van Justitie*[16] the Court grappled with a case of a wage/work bargain. The individual involved was a German national living in the Netherlands. He joined the Bhagwan Community, a quasi-religious commune. In return for the commune providing for all his basic needs such as food and a place to live, he worked for the commune as a plumber and participated in the commune's commercial activities. The Court decided that a migrant must be able to show an economic activity within the meaning of Article 2 of the Treaty to claim the status of a worker. It accepted that this individual's participation in the commune, though not part of the economic mainstraim, was nevertheless work that was genuine and effective and an essential means of participating in the commune's goal of self-sufficiency. It was to be viewed as work for which services are provided in return by the commune. The German national was awarded the status of worker according to Community law.

In *Bettray* v. *Staatssecretaris van Justitie*[17] the Court had to consider whether participation in a Dutch Social Employment Law scheme granted the status of worker. It decided that it did not. The scheme was designed to rehabilitate those handicapped for various reasons (drug addiction in Mr Bettray's case) and make it possible for them to participate in normal economic activity in due course. Suitable employment in accordance with the needs and abilities of the individual was found for those participating in the scheme. The idea behind the scheme was to help the participants to ultimately be able to function in a normal work environment again. The participant in such a scheme was not within the scope of Community law according to the Court as it could not be regarded as an effective and genuine economic activity since it constituted merely a means of rehabilitation or reintegration for the persons involved.[18] [19]

In *Lawrie-Blum* v. *Land Baden-Württemberg*[20] the Court decided that a trainee teacher conducting lessons for a few hours a week would be classified as a

---

14 Ibid., paras. 17 and 22.

15 Weatherill, S. & Beaumont, P., *EC law* (Penguin Books, London, 1993) p. 483.

16 Case 196/87, [1988] ECR 6159.

17 Case 344/87, [1989] ECR 1621.

18 Ibid., para. 17.

19 For a contrary viewsee: O'Leary, S. 'The Free Movement of Persons and Services', in Craig, P. and de Búrca, G. (Eds.), *The Evolution of EU Law* (Oxford University Press, Oxford, 1999), p. 395.

20 Case 66/85 [1986] ECR 2121.

worker if the activities counted as 'effective and genuine'. The defending *Land* submitted that the activities were part of the training period that was merely preparatory to qualification as a teacher and did not constitute work as such. The Court found the fact that the work was part of a training period of no relevance as long as the work in question was performed under the conditions of an activity as an employed person. The Court stated that '[t]he essential feature of an employment relationship [...] is that for a certain period of time a person performs services for and under the direction of another person in return for which he receives remuneration'.[21]

From the Court's case law we can surmise that it is not necessary that the work is continuous, nor that it is full-time. However, the Court has taken this point even further, by ruling that a national from a Member State need not even be working at the material time in order to be entitled to rely on Article 39 (ex Article 48). It is sufficient that a person is in the course of preparing to be a worker (as was the plaintiff in *Lawrie-Blum*, who had moved from England to Germany in order to work as a trainee teacher) or that he had been a worker and remained in the country in which he worked in order to pursue studies related to his previous experience.[22] More significantly, the judgments in *Levin*[23] and *Adoui & Cornuaille*[24] refer to rights of those who 'intend to carry out work' or 'wish to seek work'. As a result of these decisions (potential) workers must be given a reasonable period of time in which to find work. However, they are not allowed to claim benefits of any kind in the host state during that time.

This line of interpretation was underlined in the *Antonissen* case.[25] In this case the Court decided that Member State were allowed to require a non-national to leave its territory if he has not found employment there after six months, *unless* he can show he is continuing to seek work and has a genuine chance of being employed. The Court held that Article 39 (3) (ex Article 48 (3)) must be interpreted as specifying, in a non-exhaustive way, certain rights benefitting nationals of Member States in the context of the free movement of workers. These rights include the possibility for nationals of a Member States to move freely to and stay within the territory of other Member States for the purposes of seeking employment.[26]

---

21 Ibid., para. 17.

22 Case 39/86, *Lair* v. *Universität Hannover*, [1988] ECR 3161.

23 Case 53/81, [1982] ECR 1035.

24 Joined Cases 115 and 116/81, *Adoui & Cornuaille* v. *Belgium*, [1982] ECR 1665.

25 Case C-292/89, *T* v. *Immigration Appeal Tribunal ex parte Antonissen*, [1991] ECR I-745.

26 Mancini, G., 'The Free Movement of Workers in the Case-Law of the European Court of Justice', in Curtin, D. and O'Keeffe, D. (Eds.), *Constitutional Adjudication in European Community and National Law* (Butterworth (Ireland) Ltd., Dublin, 1992), p. 69.

A finding that an individual does not satisfy the Community law requirements to qualify as a worker is not always fatal to the ability of that individual to rely on Community law. Although there are persons other than workers who have the right of free movement under Community law. The worker, however, is in an uniquely favoured position in claiming a broad array of social rights which are available under the national laws of Member States. Access to such benefits is dependent on being able to cross the *Levin* threshold.[27]

2.1.3 The rights contained in Article 39 (ex Article 48) EC

The bare Treaty provisions offer relatively little specific elaboration on the basic right of freedom of movement within the Community. Article 39 (2) (ex Article 48 (2)) specifies the 'abolition of any discrimination based on nationality between the workers of the Member States as regards employment, remuneration and other conditions of work and employment'. This is an extension of the basic Treaty rule forbidding any discrimination on grounds of nationality within the scope of the Treaty, which is contained in Article 12 (ex Article 6) EC. In Article 39 (3) (ex Article 48 (3)) the scope of the rights is expanded. It states that a worker shall have the right (subject to exceptions considered below):

a to accept offers of employment actually made;
b to move freely within the territory of Member States for this purpose;
c to stay in a Member State for the purpose of employment in accordance with provisions governing the employment of nationals of that state;
d to remain in the territory of a Member State after having been employed there (within certain restrictions as laid down in Community law).

A simple example of impermissible discrimination is provided in the case *Commission* v. *France*.[28] The *Code du Travail Maritime* set a three-to-one ratio for the employment of French merchant seamen as opposed to non-French crew. This was a form of direct discrimination based on nationality and, therefore, it violated the fundamental rule of free movement, which entails the abolition of all direct (and most forms of indirect) discrimination based on nationality. For similar reasons, in *Commission* v. *Greece*[29] restrictions on the ownership of immovable property that applied to migrants from other Member States, but not to Greeks, were held to be incompatible with the Treaty.

---

[27] I.e., the requirement that the work involves 'the pursuit of effective and genuine activities to the exclusion of activities on such a small scale as to be regarded as purely marginal and ancillary'. See above.

[28] Case 167/73, [1974] ECR 359.

[29] Case 305/87, [1989] ECR 1461.

2.2 Secondary legislation

The scope of the free movement rights is closely linked with the notion of labour as a factor of production in the liberalisation designed to create a common market. It is obvious that the provisions were initially created to serve economic objectives. Article 39 (ex Article 48) only concerns itself with the workers. It does not provide for associated rights. For example, Article 39 (ex Article 48) EC does not include the right of workers to bring their families with them to live in the host state or to obtain access to social benefits made available to the hosts nation's own workforce. However, Article 40 (ex Article 49) provides for the adoption of measures which help to progressively bring about the freedom of movement for workers. According to Weatherill and Beaumont '[t]hese are measures that can be viewed as contributions to market integration, but the fact of conferral of rights on individuals also locates them in the more general sphere of social policy'.[30]

2.2.1 Regulation 1612/68

Regulation 1612/68[31] expands in Part One the worker's right to free movement. In three titles it deals with Eligibility for Employment (Articles 1-6), Employment and Equality of Treatment (Articles 7-9) and Workers' Families (Articles 10-12).

The first title elaborates on the basic Treaty rules of non-discrimination between nationals of different Member States in respect of access to employment. In principle, jobs are equally open to nationals of all Member States. Article 3 (1) of the Regulation envisages that conditions of linguistic competence may be permissible as requirements in a particular post, even though the practical effect may be to exclude non-nationals. This is an example of a justified form of indirect discrimination. The Court in *Groener*[32] was prepared to accept that Irish-language competence could be a requirement for a college lectureship. However, it insisted that any such conditions must apply to national and non-nationals alike. The conditions must also be proportionate both to the desired end result and in the way in which they are applied.

The second title covers equality in the conditions of employment. The broadest provision is Article 7 (2), which stipulates that the migrant 'shall enjoy the same social and tax advantages as national workers'. This provision has been

---

30 Weatherill & Beaumont, p. 485.

31 Regulation (EEC) No. 1612/68 of the Council of 15 October 1968 on the freedom of movement for workers within the Community, OJ Sp. Ed., 1968 (II), p. 475.

32 Case 379/87, [1989] ECR 3967.

interpreted by the Court to cover equal availability of benefits arising outside the contract of employment. In *Ministère Public* v. *Mutsch*[33] a roofer who was a Luxembourg national resident in a German-speaking municipality of Belgium found himself before a criminal court after an 'extended pub crawl'.[34] A Belgian citizen would have been entitled to choose to use the German language. Although the matter was not directly linked to the contract of employment, the Court held this to be irrelevant. It held that Article 7 (2) of the Regulation covers advantages that are 'generally granted to national workers primarily because of their objective status as workers or by the virtue of the mere fact of their residence on national territory'. Mutsch had to be given the same advantages. This wide interpretation was considered essential by the Court to bring about labour mobility, which is a fundamental Community objective. The Court held that the choice of language before a court on the same conditions as nationals is an important element in the integration of a migrant into the host country.

The European Court has consistently held that the equal treatment rule as laid down in Article 7 of Regulation 1612/68 prohibits both direct and indirect (or covert) discrimination. In the case of *Commission* v. *Greece*[35] the Court decided that Greek legislation which rendered it impossible for employment in the public service of another Member State to be taken into account for the purposes of calculating pension rights and salary scales was in breach of Article 39 (4) (ex Article 48 (4)) EC and Article 7 of Regulation 1612/68. Although the wording of the legislation was 'neutral', its effect was to discriminate indirectly on the basis of nationality.[36] The fact that there might be practical problems comparing employment in a foreign public service with that in the national public service, this did not justify the overall refusal to take these periods into account.[37]

Article 7 (4) declares that discrimination results in 'any clause of a collective or individual agreement or of any other collective regulation concerning eligibility for employment, remuneration and other conditions of work or dismissal' being null and void. Article 8 of the Regulation extends the rule of equality to membership of and participation in trade unions. Article 9 of the Regulation provides specific rules on equal access to housing, a matter that could just as easily be accommodated under the broad terms of Article 7 (2).

Both Article 7 (4) and Article 8 demonstrate that the prohibition of discrimination on grounds of nationality extends beyond the employment relationship and into the private sphere. The Court confirmed this in *Walrave and Koch* v.

---

33 Case 137/84, [1985] ECR 2681.

34 Ibid., Opinion AG Lenz, p. 2682.

35 Case C-187/96, [1998] ECR I-1095.

36 Ibid., para. 13.

37 Ibid., para. 22.

UCI[38] by saying that even rules originating from private bodies have to respect the equal rights of migrant workers where they regulate employment and the provision of services in a collective manner. The Court reached this conclusion both in view of the need to extend the impact of this basic Community law principle and in order to preclude inequalities in the application of Community law between states flowing from variations in the scope of the public sector.[39]

Community law does not interfere concerning the way in which such advantages are conferred on a national level. It provides only that the objective is achieved by means that do not lead to (direct or indirect) discrimination based on nationality. This may require a host state to apply its rules in a manner that reflects the migrant's distinct situation. *Sotgiu* v. *Deutsche Bundespost*[40] involved a separation allowance payable to those working away from their place of residence. A higher allowance was made to those working away from a place of residence in Germany than to those whose residence was outside Germany at the time they were first employed. The difference was based solely on residence and not on nationality, but this would in practice lead to discrimination based on nationality (i.e. indirect or covert discrimination), which led the Court to conclude that the scheme did not comply with Community law unless there were objective grounds that justified it. Direct discrimination is never allowed, but indirect discrimination is open to objective justification. In this case an objective justification might be shown, the Court suggested, if the higher allowance was being paid because those living away from home in Germany were expected in due course to move their place of residence. The final resolution of the compatibility of such a scheme with Community law lay with the national court under the preliminary reference procedure.

It is important to appreciate that the focus of these provisions is equality of treatment between migrants and workers who are nationals of the host state. The Regulation does not establish a minimum set of rights for migrants that is uniform throughout the Community. The rights of a migrant in each individual Member State are those which the nationals of the host state already enjoy and these inevitably vary from state to state. In order to improve standards and to achieve a common set of social advantages a more ambitious legislative commitment is required. That would encroach on the field of social policy, however.

The third title of Regulation 1612/68 encompasses the provisions which deal with the different classes of family members who may obtain rights as a result of their relationship with the worker. Article 10 (1) gives the spouse, descendants who are under 21 or dependent, and dependent relatives in the ascending line

---

38 Case 36/74, [1974] ECR 1405, especially paras. 17 and 21.

39 There is, however, no form of direct control that the Commission can exercise over a private party acting in violation of Article 39 (ex Article 48) EC.

40 Case 152/73, [1974] ECR 153.

the right to migrate with the worker and install themselves in the host state.[41] Article 10 (2) only requires that Member States 'shall facilitate the admission' of other family members if they are dependent on the worker or 'living under his roof in the country whence he comes'. Article 10 (1) and (2) are subject to Article 10 (3), which requires that the worker has available for his/her family housing which is 'considered normal for national workers' in the area where he or she works.[42]

Article 12 states that children of the worker residing in the host state have to be given the same access to 'general educational, apprenticeship and vocational training courses' as children of nationals. These rights ensue irrespective of the nationality of the family member. They depend on the status of the worker only. In that sense they are derivative rights.

2.2.2 Directive 68/360

Rights of entry, residence and equality of treatment are conferred on workers directly by the Treaty. Directive 68/360[43] elaborates on these basic free movement rights. It focuses on administrative matters. The free movement rights are directly effective and must be respected by national authorities, including the courts. However, the privileged status of being a worker must be proved. Directive 68/360 sets out the documentation that a host state may demand of the migrant in order to prove his case. Failure to obtain the relevant documents may be subject to penalties imposed by the national authorities. However, the Community law principle of proportionality is also applicable here and a breach of administrative rules should lead to appropriate penalties. The Court has made it clear that the failure to respect rules concerning proof of status cannot be punished by a denial of the status itself. The result of the principle of proportionality is that a fine may be lawful under Community law, but deportation is not.

Article 3 of the Directive requires that workers and their family members covered by Regulation 1612/68 are admitted to the host state 'simply on production of a valid identity card or passport'. Additional formalities, such as visas, cannot be required, except where family members are third-country nationals.

---

41 'Dependence' is a factual matter. There is no need to determine why a person has to be supported by the worker; Case 316/85, *Centre Public* v. *Lebon*, [1987] ECR 2811.

42 This condition applies only to the initial taking up of residence and cannot be reapplied thereafter; case 249/86, *Commission* v. *Germany*, [1989] ECR 1263.

43 Council Directive of 15 October 1968 on the abolition of restrictions on movement and residence within the Community for workers of Member States and their families (68/360/EEC), OJ Sp. Ed., 1968 (II), p. 485.

According to Article 4, Member States have to grant the right of residence to workers on production of certain documents, namely the document with which he legally entered the territory of the host state and a confirmation of engagement from the employer or a certificate of employment. Family members also have to produce the document of entry, and additionally documents which prove their family relationship and/or dependency upon the worker.

2.2.3 Regulation 1251/70

Regulation 1251/70[44] deals with the right of a worker to remain permanently in the territory of a Member State after having been employed there. As is the case with other extensions of the basic free movement right, this right can be seen as both an aspect of promoting the mobility of labour within the common market and as an facet of conferring rights in the social sphere on individuals.[45] Article 2 lists the three different categories of workers which have the right to remain. These are: (a) the worker who has reached pensionable age, (b) the worker who has to cease work due to permanent incapacity and (c) the frontier worker. Different qualifying periods apply to each of these three categories and relate to employment and/or residence before the accrual of the right. The worker's family members (as defined by Article 10 of Regulation 1612/68) also have the right to remain permanently once the worker is qualified to remain and they retain that right even after the worker's death.

2.2.4 Regulation 1408/71

The Court has always underlined that the objective of the free circulation of workers can only be attained if a migrant does not have to fear losing social security benefits guaranteed under the law of a Member State.[46] Regulation 1408/71[47] is the source of the Community's rules on social security

---

44 Regulation (EEC) No. 1251/70 of the Commission of June 1970 on the right of workers to remain in the territory of a Member State after having been employed in that State, OJ Sp. Ed., 1970 (II), p. 420.

45 Weatherill & Beaumont, p. 492.

46 E.g. case 100/63, *Kalsbeek* v. *Bestuur der Sociale Verzekeringsbank*, [1964] ECR 565; case 24/75, *Petroni* v. *ONPTS*, [1975] ECR 1149.

47 Regulation (EEC) No. 1408/71 of the Council of 14 June 1971 on the application of social security schemes to employed persons, to self-employed persons and to members of their families moving within the Community, OJ Sp. Ed. 1971 (II), p. 416. Amended and up-dated by Regulation 2001/83, OJ 1983 L 230/6 and by Regulation 1249/92, OJ 1992 L 136/28.

entitlement for workers ('employed persons'). It also covers the self-employed and the family members of both employed and self-employed persons.

However, a 'worker' or employed person for the purposes of this Regulation has quite a different meaning to that which the Court applies to Article 39 (ex Article 48). Under Article 1 (a) of the Regulation a beneficiary has to be 'insured, compulsorily or on an optional basis, for one or more of the contingencies covered by the branches of a social security scheme for employed or self-employed persons'. This shows that it is insurance rather than the pursuit of 'effective and genuine activities'[48] that determines the applicability of the Regulation. This means that individuals other than migrant workers and their family members, for instance holiday-makers, may be entitled to benefit from equal treatment in social security matters.[49]

More generally, Article 42 (ex Article 51) of the Treaty provides the basis for the adoption of measures in the field of social security. These measures are divided into two categories, namely arrangements to secure (a) the aggregation, for the purpose of acquiring and retaining the right to benefit, of all periods under the laws of several countries, and (b) the payment of benefits to persons resident in the territories of Member States. The two types of measurement are supplemented in Regulation 1408/71 by specific expressions of the principle of non-discrimination on the grounds of nationality.[50] In addition, Directive 79/7[51] requires equality on the grounds of sex.

3 Exceptions to free movement

As we shall see, the right to free movement is limited by public interest criteria. In Article 39 (3) and (4) (ex Article 48 (3) and (4)), respectively, it is laid down that the right may be limited 'on grounds of *public* policy, *public* security or *public* health' and does not apply to 'employment in the *public* service'. The same holds true for activities connected with the exercise of official authority according to Article 45 (ex Article 55).[52]

Article 39 (ex Article 48) contains two separate sets of exceptions to the basic principle of free movement for workers. The first can be found in Article 39

---

48 The so-called 'Levin threshold'. See: case 53/81, *Levin* v. *Staatssecretaris van Justitie*, [1982] ECR 1035; see paragraph 2.1.2.

49 E.g. case 44/65, *Hessische Knappschaft* v. *Maison Singer et Fils*, [1965] ECR 965.

50 Article 3.

51 Council Directive of 9 February on the implementation of the principle of equal treatment for men and women as regards access to employment, vocational training and promotion, and working conditions (76/207/EEC), OJ 1976, L 39/40.

52 Mancini, p. 74.

(3) (ex Article 48 (3)), namely: 'limitations justified on grounds of public policy, public security or public health'. Secondly, in Article 39 (4) (ex Article 48 (4)), 'employment in the public service' is excluded. The justified limitations under Article 39 (3) (ex Article 48 (3)) resemble those under Article 30 (ex Article 36) EC[53] which relate to the free movement of goods. As is the case in all provision which encroach upon one of the fundamental freedoms laid down in the EC Treaty, the provisions as laid down in paragraphs 3 and 4 of Article 39 (ex Article 48) EC are subject to a narrow interpretation so as not to damage the *effet utile* of Community law.[54]

In the *Royer* case,[55] the Court of Justice made it clear that the exceptions contained in Articles 39 (3) (ex Article 48 (3)) and 46 (1) (ex Article 56 (1)) were not to be regarded as a condition precedent to the acquisition of the right of entry and residence but rather as providing the possibility, in individual cases where there was sufficient justification, of imposing restrictions on the exercise of a right derived directly from the Treaty. This line of interpretation was followed in the *Pieck* case,[56] where the Court held that the restrictions on free movement under Article 39 (3) (ex Article 48 (3)) could not justify administrative measures requiring formalities at the border other than the production of a valid identity card or passport. This is an application of the proportionality principle.

In the *Rutili* case,[57] the Court considered what was meant by the expression 'limitations justified' in Article 39 (3) (ex Article 48 (3)) of the EC Treaty. It held that only those limitations which fulfilled the requirements of the law, including those contained in Community law, were permissible with regard to, in particular, the rights of nationals of Member States, to freedom of movement and residence. The application of these limitations is subject to judicial control:[58] such control covers not only legislative measures but also individual decisions taken in application of these measures.[59]

Community law has severely restricted Member States' discretion concerning these limitations to free movement. As is the case with derogations from this fundamental principle, the scope of these limitations is to be narrowly interpreted, which also means that their scope cannot be unilaterally determined by each Member State without being subject to control by the Institutions of the Community, most notably the Commission and the Court. It is clear that these

53 'The provisions of Articles 28 and 29 shall not preclude prohibitions or restrictions on imports, exports or goods in transit justified on grounds of public morality, public policy or public security [...]'.

54 Weatherill & Beaumont, p. 494.

55 Case 48/75, *Royer*, [1976] ECR 497, para. 29.

56 Case 157/79, *Pieck*, [1980] ECR 2171, para. 9.

57 Case 36/75, *Rutili*, [1975] ECR 1219, paras. 23-24.

58 Case 41/74, *Van Duyn*, [1974] ECR 1337, para. 7.

59 Case 36/75, *Rutili*, [1975] ECR 1219, paras. 17-21.

derogations may not be invoked where there is no factual basis for their application.[60] The important requirement of proportionality must also be satisfied.[61]

3.1 Directive 64/221

Directive 64/221[62] elaborates the nature of the public policy, public security and public health derogations from the principle of free movement of workers contained in Article 39 (3) (ex Article 48 (3)) of the Treaty. The provisions laid down in this Directive limit the a Member State's competence to implement these exceptions. For a start, they may not be invoked to serve economic ends.[63] As to the derogations based on public policy or public security, measures 'shall be based exclusively on the personal conduct of the individual concerned' and, more narrowly still, cannot be taken on the grounds of previous criminal convictions alone.[64] The public health exception is narrowed down by Article 4 of the Directive, which makes clear that only certain named[65] diseases or disabilities can justify refusal of entry or of the renewal of a first residence permit. Articles 6 to 9 impose procedural safeguards on the exercise of these exceptional powers. These rules reflect the idea that these provisions are not designed merely to promote the working of the common market, but that they also give rise to rights bestowed on individuals who require protection.[66]

3.2 Public policy

The exception based on public policy is contained in Article 39 (3) (ex Article 48 (3)), but to interpret it one should look at Directive 64/221.[67] As we have seen in the previous paragraph, Article 3 of the Directive has the effect of substantially enhancing the Treaty formula of Article 39 (3) (ex Article 48 (3)) by providing that the national measures adopted in the name of public order must be based on the 'personal conduct of the individual' to whom they are to apply.

60 See, case 260/89, *ERT*, [1991] ECR I-2925, para. 25.

61 See case 36/75, *Rutili*, [1975] ECR 1219, para. 32.

62 Council Directive of 25 February 1964 on the co-ordination of special measures concerning the movement and residence of foreign nationals which are justified on grounds of public policy, public security or public health (64/221/EEC), OJ Sp. Ed., 1963-4, p. 117.

63 Article 2 (2).

64 Article 3 (1) and (2).

65 In the Annex to the Directive.

66 Weatherill & Beaumont, p. 495.

67 See the previous paragraph.

Consequently, measures adopted with a general preventative purpose or to serve as examples to others will be unlawful under Community law.[68]

Against a general thematic background of hostility to obstacles to free movement a not entirely consistent line of case law has developed on the interpretation of primary and secondary Community law in this area. We will look at the European Court's case law on the subject of the public policy exception below.

Bonsignore[69] is among the least conservative of the Court's judgments. Bonsignore was an Italian national resident in Germany. He was arrested in Germany and charged with manslaughter and the illegal possession of firearms. After being found guilty and sentence having been passed, the German authorities deported him. They did so by applying a national measure which was regarded as a general deterrent. The measure did not have the necessary link with the personal conduct of the person in question. The Court held, as a result, that the measure was incompatible with Article 3 of Directive 64/221. The reservation contained in Article 39 (3) (ex Article 48 (3)), the Court declared, was an exception which had to be narrowly interpreted. The concept of 'personal conduct' meant that deportation could only be allowed if the accused person had specifically and directly breached public order and security.

Van Duyn v. *Home Office*[70] concerned a challenge to a decision to refuse entry into the United Kingdom to a Dutch woman wanting to move to the UK to work as a secretary for the Church of Scientology. An Article 234 (ex Article 177) EC reference was made by the High Court after the UK authorities had refused her entry, claiming that the activities of the sect were socially harmful. As we have seen, Article 3 (1) of the Directive declares that action must be based exclusively on personal conduct. The question that the High Court wanted answered was whether membership of the sect could in itself be classified as personal conduct. The Court started by stating that the provision was directly effective and could therefore be pleaded before national courts. It then went on to declare that 'present association, which reflects participation in the activities of the body or organisation as well as identification with its aims and designs' could amount to personal conduct.[71] The idea behind this statement being that membership of a particular group was a voluntary act on the part of an individual. This is a wider definition of personal conduct than was to be found in previous cases. The next question which the Court had to address was whether Van Duyn's conduct in the circumstances was sufficiently threatening to one of the interests recognised by Article 39 (3) (ex Article 48 (3)). The United Kingdom considered Scientology to be contrary to the public good, but had not taken any legislative steps to ban it.

---

68 Mancini, p. 74.

69 Case 67/74, *Bonsignore* v. *Oberstadtdirektor der stadt Köln*, [1975] ECR 297.

70 Case 41/74, [1974] ECR 1337.

71 Ibid., para. 17.

Indeed a British national would not have been punished for accepting the very job offered to Van Duyn. The Court declared that Article 39 (3) (ex Article 48 (3)) is to be interpreted narrowly and is not at the unilateral disposal of a Member State, but at the same time conceded that the circumstances in which recourse to public policy may arise will inevitably vary from state to state. It decided that where a state views an activity as socially harmful and has taken administrative measures against it, it is able to rely on the public policy exception even where it does not consider it 'appropriate in the circumstances' to outlaw the activity for its own nationals.[72]

On two accounts the Court's decision in *Van Duyn* gives Member States a generous measure of discretion in acting to repress conduct. The decision allows a Member State to control an activity which it claims to be socially harmful, but which has not been shown in practice to be dangerous. Over and above this, it allows steps to be taken against nationals of other Member States in circumstances where no comparable measures are taken internally. The Court's reasoning in allowing this in *Van Duyn* was that absolute equality of treatment between migrants and a Member State's own nationals is impossible, since a state cannot deny entry or residence to its own nationals. The Court concluded that this difference could justify the refusal of freedom of movement by migrants where nationals were not restricted. This analysis, however, can be classified as evasive.[73] The United Kingdom had not even taken less repressive measures against its own nationals involved with the cult. This seems to be a form of discrimination based on nationality, which is not unacceptable under Community law.

However, the Court seemed to quickly recover from what many people consider as an anomalous judgment in the *van Duyn* case with its decision in the *Rutili* case,[74] where it held that the derogation could only be invoked where there was a 'genuine and sufficiently serious threat to public policy'. The limitations placed by Directive 64/221 in respect of the control of aliens was a manifestation of a more general principle, enshrined in the European Convention on Human Rights,[75] that no restrictions should be placed on the rights secured other than such restrictions as are 'necessary for the protection of those interests in a democratic society'.[76]

Since its lenient judgment in *Van Duyn*, the Court has significantly clamped down on Member States' discretion in matters such as these. It did so both by

---

72 Ibid., para. 19.

73 Weatherill & Beaumont, pp. 496/497.

74 Case 36/75, *Rutili*, [1975] ECR 1219, paras. 29 and 32.

75 Articles 8, 9, 10, 11 and Article 2 of Protocol No. 4.

76 Handoll, J., *Free Movement of Persons in the European Union* (Wiley & Sons, Chichester, 1995) pp. 229/230.

defining more carefully the type of threat that must be posed by the personal conduct and by requiring that the threat be effectively combated whatever its source. So in *R* v. *Bouchereau*[77] a French national convicted in the United Kingdom of possession of drugs wished to rely on Community law to avoid deportation. The Court was asked to rule on the scope of the United Kingdom's permissible reliance on the Article 39 (3) (ex Article 48 (3)) exception. The Court relied on Article 3 (2) of Directive 64/221 to state that a previous criminal conviction is of itself not a basis for repressive measures. A previous conviction could only be relevant insofar as it is evidence of personal conduct that forms a threat to public policy. This indicated that a propensity to re-offend must be shown. The Court suggested that previous conduct might be sufficient,[78] but it did not elaborate on the point and stated that it would apply only in exceptional circumstances.

The Court went on to consider the nature of 'public policy' itself. It referred to *Van Duyn* as an authority for the proposition that a narrow view of what constitutes public policy must be taken, but that, at the same time, its definition also depends on circumstances prevalent in particular states at particular times. However, in *Bouchereau*, and without further reference to *Van Duyn*, the Court established a test which was considerably more restrictive that anything found in that decision. Public policy is only infringed by a 'genuine and sufficiently serious threat to the requirements of public policy affecting one of the fundamental interests of society'.[79] This requires more than mere criminal behaviour and most certainly would not cover mere membership of a marginal cult.[80]

Rezguia Adoui and Dominique Cornuaille v. *Belgium*[81] involved the Belgian authorities who tried to deport two French prostitutes because of their profession. In Belgium prostitution was not in itself unlawful, although connected activities, such as soliciting, were prohibited. The Court referred to its own finding in *Van Duyn* that strict comparability between the measures taken by a state against its own nationals and against migrants is not possible, because a state cannot deport its own nationals. However, the Court added that such a difference could not be used to justify arbitrary discrimination. The Belgian authorities were not allowed to expel foreign prostitutes if they did not at the same time apply equally severe repressive measures or other genuine and effective measures to Belgian prostitutes in an effort to combat prostitution. The Court repeated the formulation in the *Bouchereau* case concerning the scope of public policy. Although this test is rather imprecise and vague, through it the

77 Case 30/77, [1977] ECR 1999.

78 Ibid., para. 29.

79 Ibid., para. 35.

80 Mancini, p. 76.

81 Joined cases 115 and 116/81, [1982] ECR 1665.

Court definitely shows a much firmer commitment to non-discrimination than it did in *Van Duyn*.[82]

Looking at the case law in this paragraph it is easy to see the trend towards an increasingly restrictive interpretation of 'public policy'. *Van Duyn* was the least restrictive of the cases and left the door open to arbitrary discrimination. In *Bonsignore* it was established that in order to justify a restrictive measure, there had to be a real threat to public order. *Rutili* and *Adoui* eloborated on this principle by requiring that the values detrimentally affected by the conduct of a foreign worker had to be universally held. The most restrictive case is *Bouchereau*, which identified in very narrow terms the values which merit a Member State's reliance on the public policy exception as laid down in Article 39 (3) (ex Article 48 (3)) EC. It was not enough, the Court held, that the measure had been adopted in reaction to the 'perturbation of the social order which any infringement of the law involves'. Public policy is infringed only by 'a sufficiently serious threat [...] affecting one of the fundamental interests in society'.[83] One could say that the Court has come a long way since *Van Duyn*.

3.3 Public security

The Court of Justice has yet to rule in a case where the scope of the public security derogation from the rules of free movement of persons is the main issue. However, there is another area of Community law which also has an exception to one of the basic principles of Community law based on protecting public security. According to Article 30 (ex Article 36) of the EC Treaty the provisions on the free movement of goods do not preclude prohibitions and restrictions on imports and exports when they are justified on grounds of (amongst many others) public security.

As a result, some guidance as to the possible scope of the public security exception may be found in the *Campus Oil* case,[84] which considered the concept of public security in the context of the Article 30 (ex Article 36) public security exception. In that case, which concerned national measures which Ireland claimed were necessary to ensure the security of oil supplies,[85] the Court held that petroleum products were of fundamental importance to a country's existence: not only its economy, but above all its institutions, its essential public services and even the survival of its inhabitants depended upon them. As a

---

82 Weatherill & Beaumont, p. 497.

83 Case 30/77, [1977] ECR 1999, para. 35.

84 Case 72/83, [1984] ECR 2727, paras. 34-35.

85 In order to support Ireland's one and only oil refinery importers of petroleum were required to buy up to 35 percent of their total needs from this refinery at a price set by the responsible Minister.

result, the Court allowed Ireland's reliance on the exception, although it still had to abide by the demands of the principle of proportionality.

According to Handoll,[86] 'the public service derogation presupposed a threat to a country's existence which is, perhaps, more direct than that covered by the public policy derogation'. Examples of the activities which may be covered are: terrorism, spying and other forms of subversion. This is an area where a great deal of discretion is left to the Member States. National security is an area where the Court of Justice is unlikely to trespass to any great extent. However, drawing a parallel with the application of the derogation as encorporated in Article 30 (ex Article 36), the same exception based on public security in Article 39 (3) (ex Article 48 (3)) is most probably subject to the principle of proportionality as well.

3.4 Public health

When it comes to a threat to public health the Members States are allowed to refuse entry to a Community worker. However, it is not up to them to decide what constitutes a threat to public health. Refusing entry or a refusal to issue a first residence permit can only be justified in relation to diseases or disabilities that are listed in the Annex to Directive 64/221.[87] The exception can only be relied upon when an individual first enters a Member State and wants to make use of his right of residence: any such disease or disability occurring after the issue of a first residence permit cannot justify expulsion nor the refusal to renew the permit.[88]

3.5 The public service exception

The exceptions to free movement in Article 39 (3) (ex Article 48 (3)) are followed by another exception, which is encorporated in paragraph 4. It is the so-called public service exception and it provides that the principle of non-discrimination on the grounds of nationality does not apply to employment in the public service. This provision, however, does not itself define the concept of public service. Neither does Article 45 (ex Article 55), which excludes activities connected with the exercise of official authority from the scope of the provisions dealing with the freedom of establishment. It was therefore left to the Court of Justice to define the scope of these exceptions.

We will look at Article 39 (4) (ex Article 48 (4)) in more detail in Chapter 4.

---

[86] Handoll (1995), p. 231.

[87] Article 4 (1).

[88] Article 4 (2).

4 Conclusions

Free movement of workers is one of the four basic principles within the European Union, the other three being free movement of capital, goods and services. This free movement of labour was essential in order to create an economic community in which workers were free to work anywhere within the territory of the Community. Nowadays, not only workers in employment or seeking employment are free to reside in Member States other than their state of origin, persons such as pensioners, students and others also have such a right as long as they are not a burden on the host Member State. This shows that the European Union is no longer pursuing purely economic goals.

The main focus of this Chapter is Article 39 (ex Article 48) of the EC Treaty. It forbids discrimination against workers on grounds of nationality. This includes both direct and indirect discrimination. As such, the provision lays down the principle of the free movement of workers. As it does not contain a definition of the term 'worker', it was up to the European Court to define the term.

The Court decided that the term should have a *communautaire* meaning as it should not be up to the individual Member States to define such a term which is crucial to the *effet utile* of the provisions dealing with the free movement of workers. According to the Court what was required was that the work involves 'the pursuit of effective and genuine activities to the exclusion of activities on such a small scale as to be regarded as purely marginal and ancillary'.[89] This is a fairly broad definition of the term worker and as such the provision of Article 39 (ex Article 48) EC has a broad scope of effectiveness. The Court sought to give the provision maximum effect within the text of the EC Treaty.

Article 39 (ex Article 48) EC only concerns itself with workers and with access to employment. Secondary legislation extends the rights given to workers (and to their immediate family), such as the right to reside, social and tax advantages which are equivalent to those enjoyed by workers having the Member State's own nationality.

The right to free movement is not an unlimited right. Article 39 (ex Article 48) also lays down exceptions to free movement. These are based on public interest criteria. Article 39 (3) and (4) (ex Article 48 (3) and (4)), respectively, state that the right to free movement may be limited 'on grounds of public policy, public security or public health' and does not apply to 'employment in the public service'. This chapter has investigated these exceptions and the conclusion is that the Court has tried to maximise effectiveness of the basic principle of free movement of workers. This can be seen from the narrow interpretation of the exceptions laid down in paragraph 3 of Article 39 (ex Article 48) EC. As a result

[89] Case 53/81, *Levin*, [1982] ECR 1035, para. 17.

of this narrow interpretation of these exceptions it is not surprising that, as we shall see in Chapter 4, the public service exception laid down in paragraph 4 of Article 39 (ex Article 48) EC is also narrowly interpreted.

CHAPTER 3

Citizenship

1 Introduction

In the first part of this chapter I consider the concept of citizenship, which will also require dealing with the concept of nationality. What do these two concepts mean? What is the difference between the two? We need to have a clear understanding of what these concepts denote before we can look more closely at European Union citizenship in the second part of this chapter.

2 The concepts of citizenship and nationality

In the next few paragraphs I want to look at the two concepts of citizenship and nationality. Although these two concepts are often considered to be synomyms, they are in fact two different concepts.

2.1 Citizenship

The concept of citizenship has become a popular one over the last few years. With the inclusion of this term in Article 17 (ex Article 8) of the EC Treaty (as amended by the Treaty on European Union) it is a concept which is at the heart of the European Union. But what does it mean?

Looking at its historical roots, it is clear that the concept of citizenship has rather a long history. It first appeared in Greek antiquity and has since covered a broad scope of meanings. The etymological roots of the term refer to the inhabitants of a city. The 'city' (*polis*), however, here signifies not so much a physical location, but the emergence of a new ethic of cooperation. As Everson and Preuss put it: '[i]n its ancient Greek origins the city, and hence citizenship, replaces the familial and tribal bonds of the individuals and creates a mode of "civic" cooperation.'[1] Citizenship starts to transcend the boundaries of the 'natural' groups of the family, the clan and the tribe and is the result of a political organisation of a social group, rather than one based on family links. The essence of citizenship is here the notion of the shared fates of individuals who are bound together by the more abstract ties of common religion,[2] common habits and traditions, and also of common laws.[3]

---

1 Everson, M. and Preuss, U., *'Concepts, Foundations, and Limits of European Citizenship'*, ZERP-Diskussionpapier 2/95, pp. 48/49.

2 Weber, M., *Economy and Society: An Outline of Interpretive Sociology* (University of California Press, Berkeley/Los Angeles/London, 1964). p. 946.

3 Riesenberg, P., *Citizenship in the Western Tradition. Plato to Rousseau* (The University of North Carolina Press, Chapel Hill/London, 1992), p. 20.

By definition, the inclusion of certain individuals also means the exclusion of others. There can be no 'us' if there is no 'them'; no sense of belonging to a certain group, if there are not several groups. Citizenship, therefore, first and foremost denotes a status of social belonging. It is thus 'an exclusive status, setting boundaries between "ins" and "outs"'.[4]

The concept of citizenship not only defined who was part of a particular community, but also, and most importantly, who was not. Not belonging to such a community could be based on physical boundaries, the fact that the individual did not live in the territory of the community itself, but also on social boundaries, differences between classes in a society, for instance. Slaves, for example, being the property of their masters could never be members of the community they lived in. They had no rights and were therefore not a member of the community, i.e. not a citizen. The same would often hold true for other groups in the community: women and children, for example.

After the French Revolution, the concept of citizenship was constructed around Rousseau's idea of self-determination, primarily in developing the principle of equality of individuals. Everyone should be in a position to expect that all will receive equal protection and consideration in his or her inviolable integrity as a unique individual, as a member of an ethnic or cultural group and as a citizen, that is, as a member of a political community.[5] The idea of popular sovereignty signified the transformation of authoritarian into *self-legislated* power. The social contract was no longer thought of as a historical pact; it provided an abstract model for the very way in which political authority is constituted and legitimated.[6]

The one element that binds all the different meanings of citizenship together seems to be the notion of an individual's membership of a political community, whatever form that community may take. For a long time citizenship only meant, in the language of the law, political membership. It is only recently that the concept has been extended to cover the status of citizens defined in the terms of civil rights. Today the expression 'citizenship' is not only used to denote membership of a state (i.e. a political community), but also to denote a status defined by civil rights.

As a result of democratic rights, the modern citizen is both the governor and the governed. In a republic,[7] the force of arms, and all the powers of public

---

4 Preuss, U., 'Problems of a Concept of European Citizenship', 1 *European Law Journal* (1995), p. 269.

5 Habermas, J., 'Citizenship and National Identity', in Steenbergen, B. van (Ed.), *The Condition of Citizenship* (Sage, London, 1994) p. 24.

6 Habermas, p. 24.

7 Even a political community formally headed by a monarch, such as the Netherlands is called a republic. This is because its citizens ultimately determine the course of events and not the monarch.

authorities, such as political decision-making, government and the administration of justice, are exercised by citizens and their fellow citizens, through a form of elected government.

In order to practise this dual role of governor and subject, citizens must display 'a minimum of autonomy, sound judgement and loyalty'.[8] As stated above, it is evident that, given these requirements, citizenship was not always granted to everyone. Historically, the supreme indicator that proved the fulfilment of the three requirements was the possession of property, in particular landed property.[9] From the characteristics that citizens should possess, as listed above, we can see that those who formally or materially in their way of life or for subsistence have to rely on the arbitrary will of others,[10] cannot be proper citizens. The same holds true for individuals who are incapable of reasonable observation and judgment. If someone is not allowed to make, or capable of making, his or her own decision as a citizen, then loyalty cannot be expected of them as subjects. They must be allowed to have a stake, however small, in the running of their state.

Conditions for citizenship, like the ones mentioned above, have always existed. Traditionally, the maintenance of and control over the admission to citizenship was performed by the state. In this century, however, the state not only maintains the conditions of citizenship, it also assists individuals aspiring to citizenship to overcome any obstacles to admission. Governments help individuals to develop themselves as citizens. They foster the formation of people into independent and competent citizens.[11]

Modern republics strive for citizenship for all people, including those who do not own landed property or do not pay a certain amount of taxes, which historically were reasons for exclusion from full citizenship. They do so by providing welfare facilities that protect the less well-off from having to give up their independent political judgment. Social security and welfare assistance can, therefore, be seen as the functional equivalents of property as a prerequisite for modern citizenship, because without it not all its subjects would be proper citizens, as they could very easily lose their independence. The same is true for arrangements that help to provide the so-called lower classes in society with the access to knowledge, culture and organization that are necessary for the effective practice of citizenship in modern society.[12]

---

8 Gunsteren, H. van, 'Four Conceptions of Citizenship', in Steenbergen, B. van (Ed.), *The Condition of Citizenship* (Sage, London, 1994), p. 36.

9 Van Gunsteren, pp. 36/37.

10 Such as slaves, and women before they had equal political and social rights.

11 Van Gunsteren, pp. 37/38 and 45.

12 Ibid., p. 37.

A distinctive feature of modern citizenship rights is that they are legally constituted rights, which means that they are defined and enforced by public authorities. They are laid down in legislation and can be enforced through the courts. Consequently, 'citizenship rights - as distinct from merely non-legal or simply conventional rights - [have] extra political importance, social value, and thereby sociological significance.'[13]

Equality of legal status seems to be an agreed characteristic of modern citizenship. Along these lines Meehan[14] argues that the basic element of citizenship, from which capacities for full participation arise, is to live under the rule of law. That is to say, under a system where laws and offences are known and can be enforced; a system where there is predictability and certainty that offences will be punished, but that punishment for breaches can follow only from the application of the due process of law. In such a system rights cannot be removed without a legal basis to do so.

So what are the characteristics of modern citizenship? The classical account of the process of the creation of modern citizenship is that by Marshall.[15] In his theory the personal status of a citizen results from acquiring three levels of rights. The first group are known as the 'civic rights'. These rights give an individual a basic legal equality before the law, i.e. that each individual is equal before the law and there there are no differences between, for example rich and poor, or between people of different descent. The second set of rights are the 'political rights', which enable an individual to participate in the exercise of national sovereignty. An individual who is excluded from exercising political rights is not a full citizen. Finally, there are 'social rights'. These are the rights which have come into their own with the development of the modern welfare state. According to Marshall, the attainment of these social rights mark the final stage of the development into citizenship.[16] Once an indivual has gained all these rights, according to Marshall he has full citizenship.

Marshall's theory of citizenship concerns the relations maintained between the individual and the community. Since World War II this community is primarily to be understood as being the nation state.[17] Modern national citizenship determines an individual's relationship to his nation state. The modern nation state defines its authority and sovereignty along territorial lines. That is to say, its claim to obedience is (with a few exceptions) based on physical control over its territory. However, the modern constitutional state has developed

---

13 Close, P., *Citizenship, Europe and Change* (Macmillan, London, 1995), p. 55.

14 Meehan, E., *Citizenship and the European Community* (Sage, London 1993), p. 123.

15 Marshall, T., *Citizenship and Social Class* (Cambridge University Press, Cambridge, 1950).

16 Closa, C., 'The Concept of Citizenship in the Treaty on European Union', 29 *Common Market Law Review* (1992), p. 490.

17 Everson/Preuss, p. 39.

'beyond the physical limitations of its authority and developed non-physical boundaries of its power, for instance when it claims respect for the symbols of its stateness (e.g. the flag, head of state) outside its territorial boundaries (a claim which is supported by international law).'[18]

The legal and political entitlements of citizenship can be made clearer by contrasting the citizen with a denizen, metic or subject. A denizen may be described as 'a lawfully resident foreigner with the same basic rights of political participation as a native or naturalised citizen.'[19] A metic has fewer rights than the denizen, being a 'resident foreigner with legal status, but enjoying only some of the rights of citizenship, rather than all.'[20] Finally, a subject is not necessarily a foreigner. He can have the same nationality as a citizen. The lives of both a citizen and a subject are regulated by legislation passed by the same political authority. The difference between a subject and a citizen is that a subject has no rights to participate in lawmaking. A subject is thus someone who is governed without participating in the process of electing the governing authorities.

Within a Community context we see that migrants have, until recently, been treated as metics. Their economic and social activities were ruled by regulation commonly applicable to them and EU nationals. Before the ratification of the Maastricht Treaty, they did not have any basic political rights in their new places of residence, except in those countries which already had specific arrangements.[21]

With the emergence of new supranational organisations such as United Nations after the Second World War and the EEC, Euratom and the ECSC in Europe in the 1950s, nation states became more and more interlinked and interdependent. National citizenship is no longer seen as the only form of citizenship. A notable theme within recent literature has thus been the development of various concepts of 'earth citizenship'.[22] The idea behind such concepts is that the population of the earth as a whole is responsible for the survival of the planet. With the diminishing global resources, the interrelatedness of global economies, etc., the belief has arisen that the entire world population as a whole should shoulder the responsibilities for the preservation and sharing of these resources, leading to mutual interdependence. Such increased interdependence between nation states can ultimately be seen as a challenge to the linkage of citizenship to the nation state.[23]

---

18 Ibid., pp. 60/61.

19 Meehan, p. 18.

20 Ibid.

21 Ibid., p. 21.

22 See: Stewart, F., 'Citizens of Planet Earth', in Andrews, G. (Ed.), *Citizenship* (Lawrence & Wishart, London, 1991), pp. 65-75.

23 As an aside: the latest medium where the concept of citizenship has surfaced is the Internet, where the 'citizens' of this worldwide, interconnected medium are known as 'netizens'.

Some authors take up this point and they question the continued ability of the nation state to function as the unit which is most capable of guaranteeing citizenship and the rights connected with it.[24] There are doubts whether the nation state in a modern world which is characterised by mass-migration and increased economic, political and environmental interrelatedness can still deal with these complicated matters without having to refer to supranational organisations. In the modern world many decisions taken by one nation state will have a direct or indirect effect on other nation states. Therefore, it is often vital that there is communication and cooperation between nation states, if only to avoid major conflicts. Institutions such as the European Union can play a vital role here.

2.2 Nationality

The concept of nationality derives from the idea of the nation, which, in turn, derives from the Latin verb '*nascere*' (to be born). According to this etymology, nationality is an undetermined attribute of a person. It is assigned at birth, rather than something which is gained on merit or status. It is, therefore, not surprising that nationality did not, initially, convey any political meaning, but inferred only a person's provenance. The concept of nationality secured a continuity with a certain ancestry. It also maintained a link with the geographical area in which this ancestry had always been connected, in other words, the area of birth.[25]

Historically, for instance in Roman times, nations were defined as 'communities of people of the same descent, who are integrated geographically in the form of settlements or neighbourhoods, and culturally by their common language, customs, and traditions, but who are not yet politically integrated in the form of state organization.'[26]

Progressively, however, the concept of nation evolved to embody a more transcendent meaning which referred to something other than the sum of many concrete and precise individuals born or linked to a certain geographical area. The fundamental continuity and identity through time was established as the most basic characteristic of a nation. In time nationality came to express the link with one political community (in most cases the bearer of sovereignty) in particular, aside from any other political communities. Transcendence and differentiation now became the basic characteristics of the nation.[27]

---

24 Everson/Preuss, p. 39.

25 Closa (1995), p. 488.

26 Habermas, p. 22.

27 Closa (1995), p. 489.

The relevance of the transcendent component in the determination of the nationality bond was established by the *Nottebohm* case.[28] The International Court of Justice established that: 'nationality is a legal bond having as its basis a social fact of attachment, a genuine connection of existence, interest and sentiments, together with the existence of reciprocal rights and duties'. Consequently, the Court argued, 'the individual upon whom it is conferred is in fact more closely connected with the population of the State conferring nationality than with that of any other State'.

Nationality nowadays 'represents a legal relation between an individual and a state according to which the individual is subject to the public authority and the legal order of that state.'[29] The determination of nationality is regarded by nation states as an exercise of state sovereignty because it is one of the primary means by which a state defines itself and who are its subjects.[30]

2.3 The differences between the concepts of citizenship and nationality

Conceptually the terms nationality and citizenship are not synonymous,[31] even though today in most countries of the world nationality is often regarded as identical to citizenship. In most modern nation states every person holding the nationality enjoys the rights and is burdened with the duties of citizenship of that state. And conversely, every citizen is the national of that state.

For reasons of conceptual and terminological clarity, we should note the distinction between nationality and citizenship. Under present-day conditions this differentiation has for the most part lost its practical significance, whereas it is of major conceptual relevance.

At the dawn of the modern constitutional state there was great discrepancy between the two categories of nationality and citizenship. Nationality had the meaning of being subject to the government of a particular state and thus served as a demarcation against foreigners ('them' versus 'us'). The term citizen referred to social status within the political organisation: only those who were neither slaves, nor minors or women (or in other words, those who owned possessions or status which enabled them to lead an independent life), qualified

---

[28] *Nottebohm* case, *Liechenstein* v. *Guatemala*, [1955] ICJ 15, p. 23.

[29] Everson/Preuss, p. 10.

[30] O'Leary, S., 'Nationality Law and Community Citizenship: A Tale of Two Uneasy Bedfellows', 12 *Yearbook of European Law* (1992), p. 354.

[31] Everson/Preuss, p. 10.

for the status of citizen. Only this rather small group had a stake in the political organisation and was entitled to participate in the legislative process.

From the definitions above we can see that nationality conveys a position of passive submission on the part of a subject to the state. On the other hand, citizenship denoted an active status of participation in the shaping of the political organisation. In its early beginnings the concept of citizenship was socially and politically exclusive, differentiating between those who were allowed to participate in the shaping of the political organisation and those who were not. Only a minority of subjects were allowed to participate in the shaping of the political organisation. However, as a result of democratic development during the last two hundred years or so, the concept has become increasingly inclusive through a continual process wherein the initial property, status and gender qualifications were abolished. The age requirement also decreased over time, so that today almost all adult nationals enjoy the status of citizenship.[32]

The growing together of the two concepts of nationality and citizenship equalised the political status of all denizens of a country and abolished one important internal division within society. This inclusive effect, however, which realised the democratic nation state's ideal of a congruence of nationality and citizenship made it more difficult for non-national residents to acquire the status of a national, as this was the key to simultaneously becoming a citizen of that state. By granting an individual nationality, the state would also have to give him all the rights that come with full citizenship.[33]

As we have seen in the previous paragraph, nationality was described by the International Court of Justice in the *Nottebohm* case,[34] as a 'legal bond having at its basis a social fact of attachment, a genuine connection of existence, interests and sentiments, together with the existence of reciprocal rights and duties'. Nationality characterises the relationship between a state and an individual *externally*. Citizenship, on the other hand, implies the rights and duties applicable in the *internal* legal order.[35] However, nationality does not only affect the external bond between subject and state, because citizenship often depends on having the nationality of a state. Nationality therefore has an effect on the internal bond between the state and an individual by defining who is in fact a citizen.

The essence of citizenship has been defined as 'the constitutional arrangements made for participation by a defined category of individuals in the life of

---

32 Preuss, p. 269.

33 Ibid.

34 *Liechtenstein* v. *Guatemala*, [1955] ICJ 15 at 23.

35 O'Keeffe, D., 'Union Citizenship', in O'Keeffe, D. and Twomey, P. (Eds.), *Legal Issues of the Maastricht Treaty* (Chancery Law, London, 1994), p. 91.

a state'.[36] Participation in the life of a state denotes the possession of political rights. According to states, (national) political rights can affect national sovereignty and these rights are, as a result, not readily available to non-nationals. Other, more fundamental rights, such as equality before the law, are more easily conferred on non-nationals.

As we have seen, nationality and citizenship are two different concepts which serve different functions. Nationality is the legal concept which defines the legal membership of an individual to a state. Citizenship may or may not ensue from nationality. However, more often than not nationality is the starting point for citizenship, but, once again, is not the same as citizenship.

3 Citizenship of the European Union

3.1 Characteristics of EU citizenship

Article 18 (ex Article 8a) EC states that any person holding the nationality of a Member State is a citizen of the Union. From the wording of this Article we can see that citizenship of the Union cannot be independently acquired, but only through acquisition of the nationality of one of the EU Member States. In other words, individuals who are not nationals of a Member State are not to be considered citizens of the Union, and as a consequence, these third-country nationals are in principle excluded from (and only exceptionally, i.e. when specifically provided for, included in) the catalogue of rights of citizenship.

The possibility of repealing Union citizenship is not addressed anywhere and the only possible way in which to lose Union citizenship and the rights thereby attached is by losing the nationality of a Member State (if this loss is not compensated by the acquisition of the nationality of another Member State). Citizenship of the Union may be characterised, therefore, as a *derived* condition of nationality of a Member State.

The term 'citizenship' is part of Community law. One would expect that this term is therefore defined according to an agreed European-wide concept. This is in fact not the case. Among the different Member States there are differences in the definition and interpretation of the concept of citizenship. This is because, as we have seen above, the concept of citizenship is not a purely legal one and it has its roots in the political and social culture of a state. As a result a comparative analysis of the notion of citizenship throughout Europe demands a broader approach than the comparison of mere legal rules on nationality.[37]

---

36 Evans, A., 'Nationality Law and European Integration', 16 *European Law Review* (1991), pp. 198/199.

37 Everson/Preuss, p. 11.

Competence as to the determination of nationality is jealously guarded by the Member States. They see decisions concerning the acquisition and loss of their nationality as being an essential part of their sovereignty as a nation state. The main instrument used to back up this assertion has been the Declaration on Nationality of a Member State annexed to the Maastricht Treaty of 1992, whereby the IGC declared that 'wherever in the EC Treaty reference is made to the nationals of the Member States, the question whether an individual possesses the nationality of a Member State is settled solely by reference to national law of the Member State concerned'.

There are two implications of this Declaration. Firstly, it lays down a code belonging to the sphere of international law. It does not bring about a specific Union definition. A further result of the wording of this Declaration is that it could eventually lead to forms of unequal treatment for some categories of individuals, depending on how nationality is determined in their home state, since it is nationality alone which determines EU citizenship.[38] The purpose of the Declaration is to confirm that, from the point of view of Community law, it is the Member States who control which of their nationals may enjoy rights under Community law. It is something which the individual Member States still value highly as a sign of their sovereignty in this matter and will not give up easily.

Most of the Member States of the European Union[39] are also Parties to the Strasbourg Convention on Reduction of Cases of Multiple Nationality and Military Obligations in Cases of Multiple Nationality,[40] which aims to minimise cases of dual citizenship with the rule that the original citizenship must be renounced where a new citizenship is acquired when the applicant is an adult and freely applies for new citizenship either by naturalisation, registration or recovery. Those with more than one nationality are only required to carry out military service in one country. Being parties to this Convention, Member States seem to be opposed to the principle of sharing nationality.

The nationality provisions concerning Union citizenship respect the exclusive competence of the Member States in this area. Although this may produce anomalies, nevertheless, because of the attitude of the Member States, reinforced by the *Micheletti* judgment[41], it seems unlikely that Community legislation or the case law of the Court will alter the competence of the Member States

---

38 Closa (1995), pp. 510/511.

39 As of 28 March 2000, only Greece, which does not allow the renunciation of Greek citizenship, has not signed this Convention among the fifteen EU Member States.

40 Council of Europe, ETS No. 43, 6 May 1963.

41 In case C-369/90, *Micheletti*, [1992] ECR I-4239, the Court held that the definition of conditions governing the acquisition and loss of nationality were, according to international law, matters which fell within the competence of each Member State, whose decision must then be respected by the other Member States.

in this area. It is only as a result of the success of the Union and of the internal market, accompanied by a slightly increasing bundle of rights attached to Union citizenship that change in this area is possible. This will not happen until the nationality of the Member States starts to become increasingly irrelevant in a real European community. Only when the relationship between a Member State and its citizen is overshadowed by that between the citizen and the Union will that competence as to nationality be less guarded by Member States.[42] However, that will not happen overnight and can only ever come about if and when European citizens really see the European Union as a (political) community of which they are a vital part.

This exclusive competence on the part of the Member States is rather at odds with the division of competence in other areas of Community law. Normally, in Community law concerning the free movement of persons, the Court has held that the concept of, for example, a 'worker', is a Community concept, which cannot be defined by reference to national law, but instead must be interpreted in the light of Community law, as otherwise it would be subject to unacceptable variations in its interpretation.[43] Nevertheless, as regards nationality, the possession of which is an absolute requirement for entitlement to fundamental Community rights such as the free movement of persons,[44] the Member States are deemed to have exclusive competence.

We can conclude that the conditions for acquiring European Citizenship are not uniform within the framework of the Union and depend for the most part on the conditions for acquiring the nationality of a Member State. This lack of uniformity in the application of Community law regarding the acquisition and the loss of European Citizenship could lead to unequal treatment among the citizens of Europe.

The TEU provisions, as they now stand, do not provide for the possibility of extending Union citizenship to third-country nationals legally resident in the Community by firmly linking the acquirement of Union citizenship to the possession of Member State nationality.[45] As we have seen in paragraph 2.1, the inclusion of certain groups, defined by nationality, inevitably has the exclusion of others as its result.

---

42 O'Keeffe (1994), pp. 91/92.

43 See Chapter 2, paragraph 2.1.2.

44 Article 39 EC does not specify that the workers to which it refers must have the nationality of a Member State but it is generally interpreted in this way. In case 238/83, *Meade* v. *Caisse d'Allocations familiales de la Region Parisienne*, [1984] ECR 2631 the Court arguably so held. The Treaty articles on freedom of establishment and freedom to provide services, on the other hand, do refer to nationals of the Member States.

45 O'Keeffe (1994), p. 92; for the position of third-country nationals within the EU see also: Staples, H., *The Legal Status of Third Country Nationals Resident in the European Union* (Kluwer, The Hague, 1999).

The status of citizen of the Union does not imply a privilege with a view to acquiring nationality or national citizenship of a Member State. However, some of the regulations regulating citizenship of the Union may in practice undermine the procedural mechanisms which some Member States may have used as technical mechanisms for minimising naturalisation.

There are several entitlements which provide the basis for opting for nationality through naturalisation; the one that is directly affected by the TEU provisions is naturalisation through residence (*ius loci*). Member States grant the possibility of acquiring nationality or citizenship of that state to foreigners who were not born within the national borders and with no family or ethnic connection with the State providing, among other things, that they can demonstrate residence in the national territory during a qualifying period, often coupled with some sort of integration test. The residency periods are of different duration in each Member State,[46] reflecting either particular circumstances, or beliefs (or both) corcerning the desirable duration of residence to create a bond of attachment, which could ultimately lead to becoming a 'full member' of the society of residence. At the time, the European Parliament proposed to harmonise the duration of the residence period required in order to apply for naturalisation, which would do away with differences in protective attitudes.[47] On 1 March 2000 the Council of Europe's European Convention on Nationality[48] came into force. It provides for a 10-year residency period before naturalization.[49] However, at present Austria is the only EU Member State to have ratified this Treaty.[50]

The granting of work and/or residence permits has been a time-honoured method for states to control residence, because it restricts the opportunities to apply for naturalisation through *ius loci*. However, the discretionary use of this instrument is no longer available for Member States when it comes to citizens of the Union. Since EU citizens now often have a right of residence under EU law, it can be argued that the residence requirement has been deprived of its potential deterrent effects on naturalisation for Union citizens.[51]

---

46 For example, the qualifying periods are five years for Belgium, France, Ireland, the Netherlands and the United Kingdom; six years in Portugal; seven years in Denmark; ten years in Italy and Spain, and fifteen years in Germany.

47 The EP suggested in a proposal for a resolution that third countries' residents with residence periods longer than five years must have the right to apply for the nationality of the host Member State. PE Doc. A 3-0284/92.

48 Council of Europe, European Treaties, ETS No. 166, Strasbourg, 6 November 1997.

49 Article 6, para. 3.

50 All other EU Member States except Belgium, Germany, Luxembourg and Spain have signed, but not yet ratified the Treaty.

51 Closa (1995), p. 516/517.

Most authors seem to agree that citizenship of the Union has not replaced nationality, but has, rather, created an additional circle of rights for nationals from Member States. A distinctive characteristic of citizenship is additionality: citizenship of the Union adds to the first group of nationality rights enjoyed within a Member State a second set of new rights, based on Community law, enjoyed in any Member State. The rights embodied by the notion of citizenship of the Union are strictly limited, even though there is provision for their further enlargement. This limitation creates a difference with national citizenship: Union citizenship is a concept whose scope is limited to the effects expressly mentioned in the Treaty and which is therefore distinct from the general character of national citizenships.[52] Citizenship of the Union, as laid down in the TEU, is a guarantee for the enjoyment of certain rights, the exercise of which no longer depends on which Member State nationality an individual possesses.[53]

3.2 Historical development of European Citizenship

European citizenship occurred as an inevitable consequence of the completion of the internal market in 1992. It is well known that the free circulation of the factors of production was the necessary prerequisite for the effective functioning of the Common Market. Thus the Treaty establishing the European Economic Community provided for certain economic rights, such as the free movement of persons, capital, and goods and services, and the right of establishment. These economic rights were supplemented by various social rights, such as the right to equal pay for men and women.

However, the mere provision of these rights in the EEC Treaty (as it then was) could not lead to the creation of a real supranational civil society. The Member States of the Community, for instance, in the early stages of the EEC remained adamant that the EEC Treaty did not differ from a standard international treaty[54] within the framework of which the States were the sole subjects of the law. If this view was correct, then nationals could not assert subjective rights protected by the courts.

However, the European Court of Justice did not agree with this view. Had it done so, the course of European integration would have been very different indeed. In place of what is well known today as a real European civil society, there would have been a complex of horizontal inter-state relations where nationals would have lacked any genuine Community rights and, in principle, would

[52] Ruzie, D., Citoyenneté et nationalité dans l'union européenne. Paper for the 2nd ECSA World conference: *Federalism, Subsidiarity and Democracy in the European Union*, Brussels 5-6 May 1994, p. 10.

[53] Closa (1995), p. 494.

[54] See e.g. the observations of the Dutch Government in case 26/62, *Van Gend en Loos*, [1963] ECR 1.

have been deeply dependent on the goodwill of their own nation states. In fact, as is well known, the European Court took another approach concerning this major issue. As Advocate General Roemer stated in his Opinion in the *Van Gend en Loos* case, anyone familiar with Community law knew that the Community did not merely consist of contractual relations between a number of States considered as subjects of the law of nations.[55] The Community was competent to enact laws which directly created rights in favour of the citizens of Member States.[56] In giving its famous judgment in this case, the Court of Justice held that the objective of the EEC Treaty was to establish a Common Market, the functioning of which was of direct concern to interested parties in the Community.

Hence the EEC Treaty was more than an agreement which merely created mutual obligations between the contracting States.[57] This view, according to the Court, was confirmed by the Preamble of the Treaty which referred not only to the governments, but also to the peoples of Europe. In conclusion, the Community, according to the Court, constituted a *new legal order* of international law, the subjects of which comprised not only Member States, but also their nationals [JEB: emphasis added].[58] Community law, therefore, concluded the Court, was not only imposing obligations on individuals but was also intended to confer rights upon them.

The decision of the Court in the *Van Gend en Loos* case paved the way for the creation of a genuine European civil society, over and above the individual Member States.[59] Within the framework of this new European civil society the nationals of Member States could exercise the economic and social rights conferred upon them by the Treaty and secondary legislation based thereon without having to wait for their Member State to act first. It was the case law of the Court of Justice regarding the four fundamental freedoms on which the Community is based which determined the interpretation of these rights.[60] The Court held that fundamental rights were enshrined in the general principles of Community law.[61] According to the Court this was a result of the common constitutional traditions of the Member States,[62] and subscribing of all to inter-

55 Case 26/62, *Van Gend en Loos*, [1963] ECR 1, p. 20.

56 Ibid.

57 Ibid., 12.

58 Ibid.

59 Marias, E., 'From Market Citizen to Union Citizen', in Marias, E., (Ed.) *European Citizenship* (European Institute of Public Administration, Maastricht, 1994), p. 3.

60 Ibid., pp. 1-3.

61 See: case 26/69, *Stauder* v. *City of Ulm*, [1969] ECR 419, case 11/70, *Internationale Handelsgesellschaft GmbH* v. *Einfuhr- und Vorratstelle Getreide*, [1970] ECR 1125, and case 222/84, *Johnston* v. *Chief Constable of the RUC*, [1986] ECR 1651.

62 Ibid.

national treaties such as the European Convention on Human Rights and the European Convention for the Protection of Human Rights and Fundamental Freedoms.[63] The Court also decided that a failure to respect the obligation of political neutrality by Community nationals cannot justify their expulsion from a Member State.[64]

The inclusion of citizenship of the Union in the EC Treaty means that some citizenship rights will be governed mainly by Community legislation and the *acquis communautaire* is applicable. The exercise of citizenship rights will be through the involvement of Community institutions. Furthermore, legislation will on the whole be directly applicable and the European Court will have jurisdiction over it.[65]

The introduction of citizenship of the Union into the EC Treaty has implied the generalisation of the rights of residence and movement, the constitutionalisation of the right of petition and the establishment of a clear legal foundation for regulating voting in local and EP elections regarding residence.

Originally, the main goal of the Community was the integration of the economies of the Member States, and consequently the rights of individuals (primarily the right of equal treatment of all participants of the market irrespective of their nationality) were tailored according to the functional requirements of *economic* integration. In the meantime, the development of the Community has clearly gone beyond this 'functional integration' of the economies of the Member States. The somewhat narrow conception of individuals as workers or self-employed persons has been considerably widened. Individuals now also have numerous social rights. Three Council directives issued in 1990 so broadly define the right of a person who is a national of a Member State to reside in any other Member State that almost every citizen of a Member State is entitled to move to and reside freely within the territory of the Member States irrespective of his or her economic status.[66]

That nation states constitute a problem within the difficult developement towards a European Union is not so much due to their claims to sovereignty than to another factor, namely that democratic processes have up to the present day only functioned within national borders. The political public sphere has traditionally been fragmented into national units.[67] This is the way it has always been and the way people see the political sphere as operating. The question

---

63 See case 4/73, *Nold* v. *Commission*, [1974] ECR 491.

64 See case 36/75, *Rutili* v. *Minister of the Interior*, [1975] ECR 1219, CMLR 1976-I, 140.

65 Closa, C., 'The Concept of Citizenship in the Treaty on European Union', 29 *Common Market Law Review* (1992), p. 1158.

66 Council Directive Nos. 364/90, 365/90 and 366/90, all of June 28 1990, in OJ 1990, L 180, pp. 26/28/30 respectively.

67 Habermas, p. 29.

arises whether there can ever be such a thing as a true European citizenship, so long as people do not identify with the European Union as a (political) community of which they are a part.

Obviously, in practice, the most serious obstacle to a true European citizenship is the lack of a common European language and culture. Thus, unlike in most federal states Community citizenship is not likely to supersede national citizenship or to make it a status of minor importance frequently verging on mere irrelevance; rather, both statuses will co-exist, representing two different principles of political organisation.

The future development of the concept of citizenship of the Union will be shaped to a considerable degree by the Members State's notions as to what citizenship is supposed to be as held in the Member States. Therefore, an analysis of the meaning of citizenship in the different Member States is a precondition for the understanding of the potential meaning of European citizenship.[68]

3.3 Citizenship in the EC Treaty

In the next few paragraphs the provisions dealing with EU citizenship as laid down in the EC Treaty will be examined.

3.3.1 Introduction

Although the notion of European citizenship was not entirely new,[69] it was not until the Treaty on European Union was signed at Maastricht on 7 February 1992 that 'citizenship of the Union' was formally established in a Community legal text.

As we have seen in the previous paragraph, although the term 'citizenship' is part of Community law and hence suggests a presumption that it can be defined according to a Community concept, this is not the case. In this and the next few paragraphs we will look at the Articles in the EC Treaty (as amended by the TEU) that define European citizenship.

The preamble to the TEU states that the High Contracting Parties 'resolved to establish a citizenship common to nationals of their countries'. In Article 2 (ex Article B) TEU, under the heading of Common Provisions, one of the objectives of the Union is stated to be 'to strengthen the protection of the rights and interests of the nationals of its Member States through the introduction of a citizenship of the Union'.

---

68 Everson/Preuss, p. 31.

69 See above paragraph 3.2.

The EC Treaty provisions on Union citizenship are remarkable, because at the time they were introduced by the Maastricht Treaty in 1992, they were one of the few provisions in that Treaty that explicitly refered to the Union. With the coming into force of the Amsterdam Treaty more references to the Union have been introduced.

Union citizenship is established by Article 17 (ex Article 8) of the EC Treaty. The inclusion of the Union citizenship provisions in the EC Treaty means that 'Union citizenship' becomes a concept of Community law which may be interpreted and applied by the European Court of Justice. The characteristics of Union citizenship can thus be changed by judicial interpretation or legislative action, either under Article 22 (ex Article 8e) or under other EC Treaty provisions.

A result of incorporating the provisions in the EC Treaty is that the provisions on Union citizenship are not applicable to the areas covered by the second and the third pillars of the European Union, namely the Common Foreign and Security Policy or Cooperation in the fields of Justice and Home Affairs (since the entry into force of the Amsterdam Treaty also: Police and Judicial Cooperation in Criminal Proceedings) even though these areas form a constituent part of the Union. These provisions are not part of Community law and they contain no reference to Union citizenship.[70]

As we have seen, citizenship of the Union is possessed only by those persons who hold the nationality of one of the Member States. This means that third-country nationals by definition do not enjoy the rights of Union citizenship granted in Part Two of the EC Treaty. An inclusive citizenship per definition means the exclusion of others, in this case it is the exclusion of third-country nationals.[71] Nevertheless, the segregation of Union citizens and third-country nationals is not as clear-cut as it might at first seem.[72] Certain categories of third-country nationals possess rights under the EC Treaty which are identical in substance to citizenship rights. Many of these rights have been bestowed through Association Agreements with third countries, but some are laid down in the provisions themselves.[73] Additionally, there are cases where the national legislation of a Member State gives rights to third-country nationals on a par

---

70 Handoll, J., *Free Movement of Persons in the European Union* (Wiley & Sons, Chichester, 1995), p. 268.

71 See: D'Oliveira, H., 'European Citizenship: Its Meaning, its Potential', in Monar, J., Ungerer W. and Wessels, W. (Eds.), *The Maastricht Treaty on European Union: Legal Complexity and Political Dynamic* (European Interuniversity Press, Brussels, 1993), p. 84.

72 See: Staples (1999).

73 E.g. Article 21 (ex Article 8d) EC: the right of petition and the right to appeal to the Ombudsman is not restricted to EU citizens. See paragraph 3.3.2(e).

with their own nationals, or if not their own nationals, then with EU citizens.[74] There seems to be a trend away from strict nationality requirements and towards residency requirements for the granting of many citizenship rights, except those which are deemed to be directly connected with national sovereignty. One could say, and some authors do, that the privileged position given to Union citizens under the EC Treaty provisions is, in some respects, more apparent than real.[75]

Even though the concept of citizenship means an upgrading of the status of individuals under Community law, it by no means overrides the dominance of the concept of nationality of each Member State.[76] Union citizenship is clearly additional to, and also dependent on, the possession of national citizenship. The importance of national citizenship rights continues both within and outside the Union framework. Within the Union framework, the constitutive elements of national citizenship, namely exclusive citizenship rights in national and regional elections, as well as access to public office at a national level, continue to be essential for the democratic process as long as such decision-making power is vested in the Member States themselves.

It is therefore clear that national citizenship remains crucial as long as the most important decisions are taken by the Member States. Nevertheless, the fact remains that the Community legal order is independent from those of the individual Member States. It has its own institutions, legislation and structures. This means that the EU citizen can relate to and feel part of the Community not only through the Member State of his own nationality, but also more directly, through the enjoyment of directly effective rights laid down in European legislation and case law, and his involvement, through the election of the European Parliament, in the decision-making process at a Community level.[77]

3.3.2 The rights of citizens of the Union

The rights of the citizens of the Union are laid down in Part Two of the EC Treaty in Articles 17-22 (ex Articles 8-8e).

---

[74] For instance, the Netherlands has granted voting rights in national elections to all non-nationals (with certain residency requirements) and not just EU citizens.

[75] Handoll (1995), p. 269.

[76] Closa (1992), 1137.

[77] Handoll (1995), p. 311.

3.3.2(a) Article 17 (ex Erticle 8) EC: establishing Union citizenship

Article 17 (ex Article 8) EC establishes the concept of citizenship of the Union and states in paragraph 1 that '[e]very person holding the nationality of a Member State shall be a citizen of the Union'. Under Article 17 (2) (ex Article 8 (2)) of the EC Treaty, citizens of the Union are to enjoy rights conferred by the Treaty and are to be subject to the duties imposed thereby. This provision means that the content of Union citizenship goes beyond the bundle of specific rights set out in Part Two of the Treaty.

As the EC Treaty and secondary measures stand, Article 17 (2) (ex Article 8 (2)) may be thought to have only cosmetic significance. It does not create or confer new rights and obligations for the individual. It merely confirms existing rights and obligations already enjoyed by the individual. In this sense, Article 17 (2) (ex Article 8 (2)) may even be seen as having a limiting function, making it clear that Union citizenship has no significance beyond the enjoyment of EC Treaty-conferred rights and subjection to its obligations.

On the other hand, Article 17 (2) (ex Article 8 (2)) could have a more constructive role. This provision could have a positive 'identity-creating' effect. A national of a Member State will enjoy rights, including the exercise of directly effective rights, and be subject to obligations, such as the observance of EC competition rules, not only as an individual, but also as 'citizen' of a larger Community.[78] This dynamic charactertistic of Union citizenship rights may, in turn, influence the interpretation of such rights by the courts, in particular the Court of Justice, to such rights, i.e. by widely interpreting them concerning the possibility of adding of other rights, perhaps fundamental human rights.

3.3.2(b) Article 18 (ex Article 8a) EC: freedom of movement

The free movement of persons is the cornerstone of the Union citizenship provisions, as it has been throughout the evolution of the concept of European citizenship.

According to Article 18 (ex Article 8a), Union citizens enjoy an unconditional right to remain and reside in the territory of a Member State, including the right to re-enter should they leave for any reason. Therefore, the right of freedom of movement and residence, as established by the TEU, is generally considered to be the most perfect one and the one which effectively renders irrelevant the content of a given nationality vis-à-vis citizenship of the Union. In particular, this is because the right is independent and unconditioned by the scope of the

---

78 Handoll (1995), p. 285.

EC Treaty; it cannot be restricted and it does not depend on the pursuance of the economic goals.

However, the nationality bond still has a more important role to play than the concept of citizenship when it comes to certain EU rights. This can been seen in a number of regulating provisions. Firstly, nationality is the connecting criterion mentioned in both Article 43 (ex Article 52) and the old Article 53 (now deleted) EC. The first of these two Articles does away with restrictions to the freedom of establishment of nationals of a Member State. The old Article 53 obstructed the introduction of new restrictions to the right of establishment. It is unclear whether the use of nationality rather than citizenship is due to a inconsistent use of the two concepts, or is completely intentional.[79]

Also, some authors believe that the TEU has not really advanced in detaching these rights from economic activity. Wouters[80] argues that the free movement of persons as provided for by the EC Treaty will, in the first place, remain a privilege for those citizens of the Union who intend to move to and reside in another Member State for economic purposes. Persons who are not, or not yet, economically active or who will never become economically active will, depending on their personal or family situation, enjoy only a conditional right of free movement as provided for by the secondary Community rules which, after the ratification of the Treaty on European Union, remain in force. Also, the limitations to freedom of movement and residence based on considerations of public order, public security and public health[81] are not affected by the generalisation of these rights in Article 18 (ex Article 8a) EC.

Uniform rights of free movement and residence will only be available to the Union citizen simply by virtue of that status when, and if, the Council acts under Article 18 (2) (ex Article 8a (2)).

Community law already covered both the economically active and inactive. The TEU, through its amendment of the EC Treaty, therefore, appears only to reiterate existing Treaty law with regard to economic actors, and secondary legislation as regards certain categories of non-economic actors.[82] The TEU does not appear to have added anything new to the right of free movement and of residence in existing Community law. According to the Commission no further legislation is necessary at this stage. Nevertheless, it is clear that current legislation does not cover the poor or those who are on the margins of society. These persons do not benefit from many of the citizenship rights.[83]

---

79 Closa (1995), p. 496.

80 Wouters, J., 'European Citizenship and the Case-Law of the Court of Justice of the European Communities on the Free Movement of Persons', in Marias, E., (Ed.) *European Citizenship* (European Institute of Public Administration, Maastrcht, 1994), p. 48.

81 See: Chapter 2, paras. 3.2ff.

82 Directives 90/364-366.

83 Kovar, R. and Simon, D., 'La citoyenneté européenne', *Cahiers de droit européen* (CDE), 3-4, 1993, p. 299.

Only if the legislator uses Article 18 (2) (ex Article 8a (2)) as a basis for further legislation will anything new be added to the rights that already existed before the TEU came into force. The fact that qualified majority, rather than unanimous, voting will be available for legislation involving the free movement of economic actors may help in this matter.[84]

3.3.2(c) Article 19 (ex Article 8b) EC: voting rights in EP and local elections

States' retaining of voting rights for their own nationals is based on the bond between nationality and sovereignty. Accordingly, the necessity of strict political neutrality for foreigners is assumed by most constitutional orders.[85]

Article 19 (ex Article 8b) EC affects this reservation in two areas: European Parliamentary and local elections. However, the new provisions introduced still respect the dominance of the nationality bond. Political rights that are directly connected to national sovereignty, such as the right to vote and stand for office in general elections or the right to participate in referendums, are excluded from the workings of the Article. Secondly, the provision of specific derogations as required by a Member State in order to protect its national identity is within the letter and spirit of Article 19 (ex Article 8b).[86]

The right to vote is the ultimate political right. Political participation in society by exercising the right to vote is seen as one of the inherent rights of citizenship; a right that is on the whole exclusively granted to nationals of the state only, certainly where it concerns national elections and referendums. Non-nationals aliens are excluded from this and other forms of political activity.[87] Community law did not at first confer political rights on economic actors. It also barred them from employment in the public service of Member States by including Article 39 (4) (ex Article 48 (4)) and Article 45 (ex Article 55) in the EC Treaty.[88]

The granting of active and passive voting rights in the Member States of residence may have some significant implications. This right dissolves any

---

84 O'Keeffe (1994), p. 94.

85 See: Rath, J., 'Voting Rights', in Layton-Henry, Z. (Ed.), *The Political Rights of Migrant Workers in Western Europe* (Sage, London, 1990).

86 Closa (1995), p. 498.

87 Evans, A., 'The Political Status of Aliens in International, Municipal and European Community Law', 30 *International and Comparative Law Quarterly* (1981), p. 20.

88 O'Keeffe (1994), p. 95.

conception that those being elected are representatives of purely national collectives,[89] that is to say, a separate and distinct representation for each people.

Granting local election rights to resident foreigners is desirable from the point of view of integrating the individual in the society in which he/she resides, works and has built a life. Local authorities normally control issues which directly touch upon the life of the individual, such as housing, health, education, transport and other public services. Even so, local voting rights are a pale substitute for participation in national parliamentary elections, in direct presidential elections where they exist, and in referendums. It is politics at the national level which most directly affects the political life of a Member State.[90]

The Commission's Report on voting rights in local elections for Community nationals in 1986[91] considered that whereas national elections were considered to be a vital aspect of sovereignty, in which migrants should not participate, local elections did not impinge on national sovereignty and should be accessible to foreigners.

However, some Member States reserved this right for nationals in constitutional provisions.[92] As a result the question of granting voting rights in local elections to non-national Community residents has been at the centre of a political and legal dispute as to whether this would conflict with the reservation of the exercise of national sovereignty for nationals.[93] It was clear that the formalisation of these rights in the TEU made constitutional reform necessary in some Member States before ratification was possible. These required constitutional reforms established that local elections cannot be considered a form of expression of national sovereignty, and that therefore the participation of citizens from other Member States may not be interpreted as a dilution of the political privilege of nationality for nationals.[94]

The derogations foreseen in the wording of Article 19 (ex Article 8b) may be interpreted in relation to Article 7 (ex Article F.1) TEU as devices protecting national identity. This philosophy of protection seems to have inspired the implementation of secondary legislation. For instance, EP elections are regulated by a Council Directive on voting rights in European Parliamentary elections.[95]

---

89 Kovar/Simon, p. 307.

90 O'Keeffe (1994), p. 95.

91 Supplement 2/86 - Bull. EC.

92 The right to vote and stand for office is reserved for citizens in a number of Member States, although whether this reservation extends to provincial and local elections is less clear. A similar reservation exists in France (Art. 3.4), Germany (Art. 20.2), Greece, Italy and Luxembourg.

93 See, e.g. the discussion as described in Closa (1992), pp. 1147-1150.

94 Closa (1995), p. 500/501.

95 Council Directive 93/109/EC of 6 December 1993 establishing the modalities for the exercise of the active and passive right in European Parliament elections by citizens of the Union residing in a Member States in which they are not nationals, O.J. 1993, L329/34.

Although the Directive establishes that the enjoyment of active or passive rights in EP elections is an application of the principle of non-discrimination and connected to the rights of free movement and residence, there are two factors that seem to support the dominance of the link with nationality and national identity as the main criterion. Firstly, the right to vote and stand for elections in the Member State of residence is an *optional* right. In other words, the citizens of the Union are free to choose the country in European elections in which they wish to participate (Article 4). As the Commission explained in its proposal, voting rights in the Member State of residence are not considered to be a *substitutive* right but an *alternative* right.[96] The fact that residence is not the only criterion in choosing the place where an individual wishes to participate in EP elections, seems to point to the idea that the nationality link is considered to be a stronger and more persistent one than merely residence.[97] This is not wholly unexpected, because people do change residence from one country to another more easily than their nationality. Also changing nationality is a more emotive issue, than changing residence. Moreover, Article 19 (ex Article 8b) allows certain derogations when governments consider that they have overriding, specific national problems or feel that the public interest is at stake.[98]

The link between national political rights, which in general continue to be exercised on a strict basis of nationality, and EP electoral rights has been broken now that non-nationals can also vote in the EP elections of a Member State other than that of their own nationality.[99]

In December 1994, the Council approved Directive 94/80.[100] In this Directive detailed arrangements were laid down for the exercise of the right to vote and to stand as a candidate in local elections by citizens of the Union residing in a Member State of which they are not nationals. Its specific aim is not to harmonise the electoral systems of the Member States.[101] The aim of Article 19 (1) (ex Article 8b (1)) is only to do away with the nationality requirement for the exercise of local political rights and to ensure that there is no discrimination between nationals of that State and other citizens of the Union when it comes to the right to vote in and stand for local elections.

---

96 COM (93) 0534 final.

97 Closa (1995), p. 499.

98 Article 14 of Direcive 93/109/CE of 6 December 1993 establishes the possibility of reserving active and passive voting rights for Union citizens with a qualifying period of residence in the host Member State for those Member States in which the share of non-national citizens of the Union is larger than 20%, i.e. Luxembourg.

99 Handoll (1995), p. 297.

100 Handoll (1995), p. 290.

101 OJ 1994 L368/38.

Rights under the Directive are not available to all citizens of the Union. They are only available to those citizens who are nationals of another Member State who reside in the Member State in question and satisfy conditions of eligibility on a par with host State nationals.[102] The exclusions that are applicable to the state's own nationals also apply to them of course. For instance, national requirements on minimum periods of residency in the electorial territory of the Member State concerned must be satisfied.

Under Article 19 (1) (ex Article 8b (1)), Union citizens resident in a Member State of which they are not nationals may become local councillors responsible for supervising the functioning of the very service from which they are excluded by Article 39 (4) (ex Article 48 (4)) from becoming employed. Under these circumstances it becomes increasingly difficult to justify the exclusion of Community nationals from the public service when it comes to local authorities. The concept of nationality which is at the heart of Article 39 (4) (ex Article 48 (4)) and Article 45 (ex Article 55) may face ever increasing strain in this area.[103]

Some of these rights require certain Member States to rethink the content of national citizenship. In relation to rights in local and European Parliamentary elections, Member States are no longer able to reserve rights for their own nationals. Certain non-nationals are now part of the local political community. Although such a development has already been accepted by certain Member States for democratic and immigrant policy reasons, other Member States have had to reverse constitutional traditions to accommodate the new 'quasi-citizens'. Such non-nationals are now also part of the 'national' component in elections to the European Parliament. This involves a shift away from any idea that such elections form an extension of national political processes.

3.3.2(d) Article 20 (ex Article 8c) EC: diplomatic and consular protection

According to Article 20 (ex Article 8c), Union citizens in a non-EU state in which their Member State of nationality is not represented, may receive protection from the diplomatic and consular authorities of any other Member State, on the same conditions as the nationals of that state. This is a new feature in Community law.

Article 20 (ex Article 8c) (together with Article 16 (ex Article J.6) TEU) demonstrates the interest of Member States in limiting the nationality requirement in exercising consular and diplomatic assistance. Some authors argue that

[102] Handoll (1995), p. 291.

[103] See: O'Keeffe, D., 'Judicial Interpretation of the Public Service Exception in Article 48, paragraph 4 of the EEC Treaty', in Curtin, D. and O'Keeffe, D. (Eds.), *Constitutional Adjudication in European Community and National Law* (Butterworth (Ireland) Ltd., Dublin, 1992), pp. 89-106.

this right is merely an extension of the normal practice which already existed. Article 6 of the Vienna Convention of 18 April 1961 on Diplomatic Relations foresaw the possibility of shared diplomatic representation.[104] A more optimistic interpretation is brought to the fore by others who claim that this is a new extension of the principle of equal treatment of EU citizens, one which shows an external dimension of EC law and reflects a certain state-like quality of the Community.[105] However, the likelihood of the exercise of this state-like behaviour is rather diminished by that fact that the Union has no international personality of its own and, therefore, lacks the competence to implement this right directly. It is up to the Member States in negotiation with states outside the Union to ensure that these rights can be of practical benefit to EU citizens abroad. Non-EU states will have to be prepared to accept the fact that a EU citizen is represented and assisted by a state other than his own.

A set of 'Guidelines for the protection of unrepresented EC nationals by EC missions in third countries' were laid down even before the entry into force of the TEU. These guidelines set out the basic principles according to which Community missions have to provide assistance in case of distress. These guidelines came into force on 1 July 1993. In 1995 EU citizens' rights to diplomatic and consular protection were laid down in Decision 95/553/EC.[106]

One of the characteristics of diplomatic protection in public international law is that individuals must be nationals of the State that lodges the claim (the claim is a necessary requirement in exercising protection). It is clear, though, that the only visible link between a Union citizen and a Member State of which he/she is not a national is that both of them are subjects of the Union. Accordingly, Article 20 (ex Article 8c) obliges only the exercise of a *lato sensu* protection: through informal channels and previous to any formal claim. Diplomatic protection *stricto sensu* will require treaties with third party countries where they accept to forgo a strict nationality requirement for the exercise of diplomatic protection by another Member State on behalf of an individual who does not have diplomatic representation of his own nationality in that country.

From the point of view of the Union citizens who need to make use of this opportunity, this citizenship right (or preferably rights) could promote a sense of belonging to the Union. In a situation where a person would need to make use of this right, he would have an immediate and very important benefit of being a Union citizen, over and above being a national of one of the Member States. The crossing of nationality barriers in the exercise of the right to diplomatic and

104 Kovar/Simon, p. 313.

105 O'Leary (1992), p. 383.

106 Decision of the Representatives of the Governments of the Member States meeting within the Council of 19 December 1995 regarding protection of citizens of the European Union by diplomatic and consular representation, OJ, L314, p. 73.

consular protection from other Member States points to a shared responsibility of all Member States towards the citizens of the other Member States. According to O'Keeffe '[t]his could be a significant blurring of the differences imposed by the possession of the nationality of a Member State.'[107]

3.3.2(e) Article 21 (ex Article 8d) EC: petition right and the right to appeal to the Ombudsman

Contrary to the other citizenship rights in the EC Treaty, the bond of nationality is not the determining criterion for the enjoyment of the right of petition to the EP and the right to appeal to the Ombudsman.[108] These two rights are not exclusively connected to the condition of Union citizenship. Both rights, as laid down in Article 20 (ex Article 8d) and Articles 195 and 196 (ex Articles 138d and e), have been given to any physical or legal person. This is consistent with Western constitutional traditions as in most Western constitutional doctrines the Ombudsman (or a similar institution) is considered to be an instrument which serves the person (physical or legal). It is not seen as a privilege which should be attached to the status of citizenship only.[109]

The right of petition is traditionally considered to be an instrument for the direct participation of individuals in political life, because it entails applying to a legislative body for a certain measure. As such it is in essence a political right. However, constitutional orders in some Member States have not exclusivly retained this political right as an entitlement for their own nationals.[110] Within the scope of Union activities, the recourse to petition is no longer a privilege linked to the nationality of one of the Member States. Article 21 (ex Article 8d) has granted these rights to non-EU-nationals too, whereas the EP Rules of Procedure had previously reserved those rights to EC nationals only.

Obviously, a right available to all individuals within the EU (whether Union citizens or not) cannot be strictly considered to be a citizenship right in a manner consistent with the exclusivity attached to the concept of citizenship discussed above. The difference, however, is that for nationals from third coun-

---

[107] O'Keeffe (1994), p. 100.

[108] For a study on the European Ombudsman see: Heede, K., *European Ombudsman: Redress and Control at Union Level* (Kluwer Law International, The Hague, 2000).

[109] Closa (1995), p. 503/504.

[110] The countries that do not limit this right to their own nationals refer to all persons. Art. 8 Dutch Constitution; Art. 17 German Basic Law; Art. 21 Belgian Constitution; Art. 10 Greek Constitution; Art. 27 Luxemburg Constitution. The Danish Constitution regulates an indirect right: petitions have to be presented by members of the Folketing. Spain (Art. 29); Italy (Art. 50) and Portugal (Art. 49) reserve the right of petition to their own nationals.

tries this is not an unconditional right. There are extra criteria attached for non-EU nationals: it can be exercised only under certain conditions, particularly with respect to residence within the European Union. That is to say, third-country nationals must be resident (possibly *lawfully* resident) in a Member State, whilst Union citizens resident outside the territory of the Member States may exercise this right without restraint.[111]

As far as the right to apply to the Ombudsman is concerned, it should be mentioned that the Ombudsman is limited to investigating maladministration by Community bodies only and is not competent to deal with situations which involve the institutions of the Union itself and those which fall within the second and third pillars, respectively the Common Foreign and Security Policy and Co-operation in Justice and Home Affairs.[112]

The Ombudsman may act on his own initiative or on complaints from individuals. Unlike the case of a petition to the EP, there is no requirement that the matter complained of must directly affect the complainant. Complaints may be submitted through members of the European Parliament.

3.4 Fundamental rights

Fundamental human rights are not directly part of the citizenship package. However, according to Article 6 (ex Article F) of the Treaty on European Union, the Union is obliged to respect fundamental rights, as guaranteed by the European Convention for the Protection of Human Rights and Fundamental Freedoms signed in Rome on 4 November 1950 and as a result of the constitutional traditions common to the Member States, as general principles of Community law. This is a strangely confusing provision: the Union has to respect these rights as general principles of *Community* law, not of the Union as a whole. Since Article 6 (ex Article F) is in Title I of the TEU, it is outside the competence of the Court of Justice.[113] The question thus arises who will ensure that fundamental rights will be protected.

On top of that, according to Article 2 (ex Article B) of the Treaty on European Union, the Union is obliged to maintain in full the *acquis communautaire* while, according to Article 3 (ex Article C) of the Treaty, the institutions of the Union in the attainment of the Union's objectives are obliged to respect and to build upon the *acquis communautaire*. It is obvious that the case law of the Court of Justice of the European Communities forms an integral part of the *acquis communautaire*. This means that its case law on the protection of fundamental rights within

---

111 Handoll (1995), p. 302.

112 Ibid., p. 303.

113 O'Keeffe (1994), p. 103.

the framework of the Community must be respected by the institutions of the Union in attaining the Union's objectives. Accordingly, respect for fundamental rights on behalf of the Union stems either from the European Convention for the Protection of Human Rights and Fundamental Freedoms, or from the constitutional traditions common to the Member States or from the case law of the Court.

The Union's obligation to respect fundamental rights is not confined to the context of the European Communities but also extends to every Union decision, act or practice pursued either in the field of Common Foreign and Security Policy or in the field of Justice and Home Affairs. Yet the Treaty does not provide for the constitutionalisation of fundamental rights in the framework of the Union. Article 6 (ex Article F) of the Union Treaty provides that the Union shall respect fundamental rights as general principles of Community law. Therefore the fundamental rights of the Union's citizens are guaranteed and protected by the Union, albeit as general principles of Community law.[114]

It is regrettable that the citizenship provisions themselves do not have a human rights component. However, the Charter of Fundamental Rights of the European Union might go some way to remedying this. The Charter was accepted by the leaders of the EU Member States during the informal European Summut in Biarritz on 13 and 14 October. The text was approved by the European Parliament on November 14th 2000. This new Charter is intended to make the importance and relevance of fundamental rights more visible to the Union's citizens.

3.5 Third-country nationals

Third-country nationals resident in the Union do not fall within the personal scope of the Union citizenship provisions. Nevertheless, under other TEU provisions, i.e. Article 21 (ex Article 8d), they are entitled to two of the rights conferred on Union citizens: the right of petition to the European Parliament, and the right to apply to the Ombudsman.

The Union Treaty otherwise offers third-country nationals little or nothing in the way of citizenship rights. It must be admitted with hindsight that if they had been covered by the TEU provisions, the ratification process would probably have foundered in at least one country, if not others, because it would have been considered too great an infringement of national sovereignty.

The position of third-country nationals is nonetheless a Community-wide issue, and needs a Community response.[115] It is hardly acceptable that 8-9

[114] Marias, p. 13.

[115] For a more detailed description of the rights and duties of third-country residents see: Staples, H., *The Legal Status of Third Country Nationals Resident in the European Union* (Kluwer, The Hague, 1999).

million people according to some estimates (13 million according to others), many of whom live on the margins of society, should be excluded from the rights conferred by Community/Union law. Like Member State nationals, their economic activities contribute to the economic success of the Member States. They are and will continue to be a permanent presence in the Community. Their position cannot be ignored forever.

Their integration is hindered by numerous factors, many of them practical, such as differences in cultures and traditions, or language difficulties. However, these factors also include the often restrictive nationality and naturalisation laws. In some cases, naturalisation is not an option due to the consequences it would have in the state of nationality, where it could result in the loss of, for instance, property rights. In any case, it may be questioned whether it is appropriate to make the acquisition of nationality (and possibly the renunciation of previous nationality) a requirement for the enjoyment of rights by third-country nationals, when this is not required on the part of migrants with the nationality of one of the Member States.[116]

The generalisation of political rights at local and European Parliament levels to Community nationals by the TEU shows that sovereignty is not threatened by the enfranchisement of non-nationals at these levels; the example of granting such rights to Community nationals should make it more difficult to justify denying them to third-country nationals.

The Community regulates the lives of third-country nationals resident in the Member States, but they are on the whole excluded from the decision-making procedure, and they are not represented at municipal,[117] national or European levels. Since they are subjects of Community law, they should not be completely excluded from the democratic process in the Community. The old adage is 'no taxation without representation', but should the opposite also not be the case: third-country nationals contribute to the economic welfare of many Member States and they pay their taxes. Should they also not have a say in how the country is run?

As regards the rights to free movement and residence conferred by the TEU on Union citizens, the case for extending these rights to third-country nationals lawfully resident in the Community seems even stronger than in the case of political rights. Third-country nationals legally resident in a Member State have no right to circulate within the Community, unless they are family members of Community nationals, nationals of EFTA States acceding to the European Economic Area, or their family members, or nationals of other States which

---

[116] O'Keeffe (1994), p. 104.

[117] Except in certain Member States where all non-nationals have been given active and passive voting rights in municipal elections after meeting certain residency requirements. However, these rights are based on national law, not on Community law.

have Association Agreements with the Community providing for free movement. Since the right of free circulation is already granted to certain third-country nationals, it is somewhat anomalous to deny it to third-country nationals lawfully resident within the Community who fall outside these categories.[118]

Union citizenship could be conferred on third-country nationals lawfully resident in the Union. It could be made subject to certain criteria, modelled on those required under national law. Such criteria could include lawful entry and residence, age, employment or other economic activity, good character, loyalty to the aims of the Union, assimilation (language proficiency, knowledge of the fundamental principles of the Union, attachment to the Union, etc.). A qualifying period could be attached, in the same way as residence periods are required for the acquisition of the nationality of Member States.

However, the granting of Union citizenship to third-country nationals resident in the Community might create problems in their orginal state of nationality. Whereas Member States have already consented to their nationals acquiring Union citizenship, this would not be the case for third-country nationals. Their states of origin may object to the acquisition of Union citizenship by their own nationals. As Union citizenship has a complementary character, the laws of the country of original nationality must permit the acquisition of Union citizenship. It could be possible that by the acquisition of Union citizenship an individual will have gained rights (albeit within the European Union) which the state of origin does not subscribe to. Third states would wish to satisfy themselves that what was at issue here was not the acquisition of a form of nationality, but rather of a bundle of rights granted by supranational law through citizenship of a supranational organisation. They would have to be sure that the acquisition of this form of citizenship did not have a bearing on the national citizenship rights and duties of the third-country nationals. For third-country nationals to become EU citizens in the future it would be necessary to conduct negotiations between the EU and third countries in order to explore any difficulties that may arise. These negotiations could perhaps in turn lead to a series of international conventions in which the relationships between the citizenship of the country of nationality and the citizenship of the Union are defined.[119]

3.6 The dynamic character of European citizenship

One of the crucial features of citizenship is apparent in the wording of Article 22 (ex Article 8e EC): it is envisaged as a dynamic concept, with the prospect of change being expressly built into the mechanisms for

[118] See European Parliament Resolution on Migrant workers from third countries, OJ 1990, C 175/180.

[119] O'Keeffe (1994), p. 106.

its future review. This can be concluded from the phrase 'the Council acting unanimously on a proposal from the Commission and after consulting the European Parliament, may adopt provisions to *strengthen or add* to the rights laid down in this Part' [JEB: emphasis added]. What also become apparent is that the citizenship rights may not be removed or diminished. There can only be steps to increase citizenship rights, but since there was comparatively little that was actually new in the citizenship provisions that were brought into being with the Maastricht Treaty, this phrasing in Article 21 (ex Article 8e) has less meaning than it might otherwise have had. The position will change if the catalogue of citizenship rights actually increases.[120] Article 22 (ex Article 8e) makes no reference to increasing the duties imposed on Union citizens.

The catalogue of rights conferred by the Union Treaty can thus be seen as an intermediate stage in the conferring of new rights on the European citizen. These rights could include social rights as well as fundamental rights, additional political rights and unlimited rights of free circulation and residence.

In addition to its dynamic character, the other key feature of Union citizenship is the fact that it is additional to the nationality and the citizenship of a Member State. These concepts remain untouched by the TEU citizenship provisions. Strangely enough, the additional character of Union citizenship is not spelled out in the TEU. However, its legislative history does make this clear.[121]

One might say that the dynamic element laid down in Article 22 (ex Article 8e) is a feature of Union citizenship that might allow the inclusion of new rights over time. This dynamic development could develop in connection with a more defined and perceived Union identity. The more EU citizens see the Union as an entity that affords them certain rights, the more they might feel that they are part of it.

For some, Union citizenship might contribute to the creation, among the peoples of the Union, of a feeling of 'belonging to' a real community in the framework of which the peoples of the Union have a common destiny, common beliefs and common values.[122] This, however, has to be carefully balanced against the respect for national identities of Member States that has been established as one of the principles of the Union by Article 6 (3) (ex Article F (3)) of the TEU: this is the principle underlying some of the particular derogations to the rights of Union citizenship foreseen in the TEU provisions such as those regarding voting rights.

---

[120] Ibid., p. 102.

[121] It was suggested in the Spanish Memorandum on citizenship to the IGC (Towards a European Citizenship, Europe Documents, N. 1653, 2 October 1990), endorsed by the Commission in its submission to the IGC (SEC (91) 500; Supplement 2/91 - Bull. EC) and agreed at the European Council Summit held in Rome in October 1990 (Bull. EC 1990/10).

[122] Marias, p. 19.

Social rights are meant to give the formal status of citizens a material foundation.[123] They therefore require a positive formulation as they need an active and even in some sense, one might say, the interventionist state. Therefore, the development of positive social rights acquired by virtue of being a holder of the citizenship of the Union might lead to the development of solidarity among EU citizens regardless of their nationalities. In its turn this solidarity might lead to the acceptance of duties. Up to now citizenship of the Union has only afforded EU nationals rights. Duties are accepted by individuals as a result of their belonging to a community with which they can identify. As long as there is not such identification of citizens with the Union, the possibility of the Community to impose duties directly on the individual, that is without the mediation of the Member State, still seems a long way off, considering the way things now stand.[124]

The importance of the TEU citizenship provisions lies not so much in their current content, but rather in the promise they hold for the future. The concept is designed to be a dynamic one, capable of being added to or strengthened, but not diminished. The rights conferred are part of Community law and, as such, are capable of being enforced by the Court of Justice and the national courts. The Court may fashion constitutional guarantees from the citizenship provisions through its case law, although this does not seem likely to occur in the near future.

4 Conclusions

As we have seen throughout this chapter, citizenship at the national level remains of great importantance, since the individual Member States retain responsibility for, and control over, who possesses citizenship of their state, and thereby indirectly control over who exactly are Union citizens. However, it is necessary to consider the extent to which the transfer of sovereign powers to the Community and the intergovernmental activity under the Maastricht Treaty provisions have resulted in 'national' citizenship becoming less important.[125]

The wording of Article 17 (1) (ex Article 8 (1)) of the EC Treaty and the Declaration on Nationality indicate a desire on the part of the Member State to retain the autonomous power to determine who is to be a Union citizen. However, whilst the definition of nationality remains a matter for the Member

[123] Steenbergen, B. van, 'The Condition of Citizenship: An Introduction', in Steenbergen, B. van (Ed.), *The Condition of Citizenship* (Sage, London, 1994), p. 3.

[124] Closa (1995), pp. 508/509.

[125] Handoll (1995), p. 305/306.

State, the nature of the link between the Union citizen and the Union is a more direct one, working through directly effective rights as laid down in Community legislation. The Commission has also cautiously argued that a direct link has been forged between the citizens of the Member States and the Union through the election of the EP.[126] This right was designed to foster a sense of identity with the Union. One could say that the indirect political link which already existed between the individual and the Community, enjoyed through citizenship of the individual Member State, has been joined by a direct link.[127]

In terms of positive decision-making powers, the frontier between Member State and Community power has not been fixed. Over the years the boundaries have shifted in favour of the Community. This has been the result of the case law of the European Court which involved wide interpretations of express powers with an eye very much towards *effet utile*, the acceptance of a broad theory of implied powers, as well as the acceptance of the doctrine of pre-emption. This dynamic process has been diminished by the introduction of a number of principles into the EC Treaty by the Maastricht Treaty.[128] The most talked about of these is the principle of subsidiarity in areas of shared competence, which is laid down in the second paragraph of Article 5 (ex Article 3b). The first paragraph of that same Article encorporates the principle of limited attribution of powers to the Community. Over and above those more general principles, which are applicable to all areas within Community competence, there are the clearer delineations of Community and national powers in specific policy areas.[129] Last, but not least, Article 6 (1) (ex Article F (1)) of the TEU lays down the principle of the recognition of national identities.

Union citizenship can best be seen as a *sui generis* status entitling a Member State national, being a Union citizen, to enjoy a number of rights and obligations in certain areas covered by the EC Treaty. The citizenship provisions are designed to make the Union more relevant to the individual, by reinforcing existing, and creating new, rights and duties.[130] By giving EU nationals these rights, and hopefully in the future also additional rights, the hope is that more of a sense of belonging to a European Community outside their own national Community will come into being.

---

[126] Commission Report on the Citizenship of the Union, COM(93) 702 fin.

[127] Handoll (1995), pp. 309/310.

[128] Ibid., p. 307.

[129] For instance, in education (Article 149 (ex Article 126) EC): 'while fully respecting the responsibility of the Member States for the content of teaching and the organization of education systems and their cultural and linguistic diversity') and culture (Article 151 (ex Article 128) EC): 'while respecting their national and regional diversity').

[130] See above paragraphs 3.3.2 ff.

As we have seen these citizenship rights go beyond the set of the well-known EC market freedoms. For instance, the voting rights and the right to consular protection possess what can be called a 'communitarian' dimension and go beyond what is necessary to ensure an effective working of the Common Market. These rights point to the existence of a European community beyond merely adding up the peoples of Europe. It is a new community to which every citizen of the Member States belongs and contributes, and by which he has certain rights irrespective of his nationality of any one Member State.[131]

Article 191 (ex Article 138a) of the EC Treaty, which states that political parties at the European level contribute to forming a European awareness and to 'expressing the political will of the citizens of the Union' is the only direct reference to the constitutive nature of Union citizenship. A more implied reference can be found in Article 189 (ex Article 137), which in defining the role of the European Parliament, states that the European Parliament is to 'consist of representatives of *the peoples of the States* brought together in the Community' [JEB: emphasis added]. According to most authors, for instance Handoll, 'Union citizenship will develop a truly constitutive character only if, and when, the Community/Union replaces the Member State as the primary statal unit seen as protecting the essential interests (life, security, property, etc.) of the individual.'[132] At this moment in time it is obvious that this is not the case and a situation as described above is as yet a long way off. There are certain elements in Union citizenship which point to the beginnings of the constitutive elements of citizenship. For example, Union citizens can exercise the right to vote and stand for EP elections on the basis of residence rather than their nationality. However, there is no constitutive Union citizenship on a par with the national citizenship existing in individual Member States.

The continued central importance of national citizenship has been accepted and, indeed, reinforced in the Maastricht and Amsterdam Treaties. What is also clear is that further progress in the area of Union citizenship rights, through Treaty amendment, is dependent on national citizens of the Member States mandating their governments and endorsing changes in this field. The importance of national governments receiving the support of their national electorates was seen clearly in the processes for ratifying the Maastricht Treaty, although the ratification of the Amsterdam Treaty proceeded relatively smoothly. However, this does not seem likely to happen in the near future, since it has become clear that most of the citizens of Europe are not particularly enthusiastic about the European Union as it now stands and most people seem to consider 'everything going on in Brussels' as being far away and not directly related to their own lives. As a result it does not look likely that it will be the nationals of the Member States who will press for greater European unity at this point in time.

---

131 Everson/Preuss, p. 25.

132 Handoll (1995), p. 310.

CHAPTER 4

Article 39(4) (ex Article 48(4)) EC: the Public Service Exception

1 Introduction

In this chapter I will be looking at Article 39 (4) (ex Article 48 (4)) EC and the case law concerning it. However, before we get to the meaning of the public service exception in Community law, I must first deal with the question of why the public service exception was provided for in the first place. Looking at the wording of the Treaty provisions on free movement it can be seen that it is liberal. The other exceptions contained therein, relating to public policy, public security or public health, are the necessary bare minimum. Why then have a public service exception at all?

Article 39 (4) (ex Article 48 (4)) EC essentially allows a nationality requirement for certain posts within the public service of a Member State. In order to understand the public service exception, we need to look at its history.

2 The history of public service exceptions

The development of nation states led to the expansion of the services provided by the State and to an improvement in the status of persons working in the public service. This has had an influence on the importance of nationality, since it is held by many states that only individuals possessing the nationality of the state in question should perform tasks in the public service.

Historically, there are a number of reasons for the imposition of a nationality requirement for employment in the public service.[1] First, there is the loyalty argument. It is assumed that only nationals have a certain bond with their own nation state. This bond is characterised by a sense of loyalty, fluency in the language, knowledge of the culture of the state and also being representative of, and acceptable to, the population. It should be realised that nationality is not just a legal term, but it also has sociological and psychological elements. Within a state the identification with, and a certain amount of loyalty to, that state by members of the community is essential, or the state will disintegrate.

Secondly, there is a fear of foreign interference if non-nationals are allowed into the public service. This argument comes into play when a post has national security aspects (e.g. defence or foreign policy), or when sensitive information is involved.

A third reason which is sometimes mentioned is a more pragmatic one, namely the protection of the national labour market through exclusion from employment in a broadly-defined public sector. By not allowing non-nationals

---

1 Handoll, J., 'Article 48(4) and Non-National Access to Public Employment', 13 *European Law Review* (1988), p. 223.

access to jobs within the public sector, unemployment can be diminished for nationals.

With all this in mind, the reasons for the public service exception in Article 39 (4) (ex Article 48 (4)) are not difficult to understand. Every Member State is concerned, to a greater or lesser degree, that certain activities carried out by or in the name of that state should be performed only by its own nationals. The idea behind this is that its own nationals have a better understanding of what is needed and are more loyal to their own state, or at least they are assumed to be so on the whole. Also, every state has its own concept of the public service, and what is signified by the status of its officials, be it an Irish civil servant, a French *fonctionnaire* or a German *Beamte.*[2]

The use of nationality requirements in certain areas has its basis in international law.[3] For a start, the right of a state to impose conditions on immigrants is well established, although it is subject to a state's international legal obligations.[4] However, there are no such obligations in respect of employment in the public service. This is apparent from looking at both the 1948 Universal Declaration of Human Rights and the 1966 International Covenant on Civil and Political Rights. Both only provide for an individual's right of access to the public service in *his own* country.[5] The 1965 International Convention on the Elimination of all Forms of Racial Discrimination does not cover distinctions made by a state party between citizens and non-citizens,[6] and Conventions made under the auspices of the International Labour Organisation support this view.[7]

---

[2] O'Keeffe, D., 'Judicial Interpretation of the Public Service Exception in Article 48, paragraph 4 of the EEC Treaty', in Curtin, D. and O'Keeffe, D. (Eds.), *Constitutional Adjudication in European Community and National Law* (Butterworth (Ireland) Ltd., Dublin, 1992), p. 90.

[3] Handoll (1988), pp. 223/224.

[4] See: the 1985 Declaration on the Human rights of Individuals who are not Nationals of the Country in which they live. G.A. Res. 40/144, annex, 40 U.N. GAOR Supp. (No. 53) at 252, U.N. Doc. A/40/53 (1985). Article 2 para. 2 states: 'This Declaration shall not prejudice the enjoyment of the rights accorded by domestic law and of the rights which under international law a State is obliged to accord to aliens, even where this Declaration does not recognize such rights or recognizes them to a lesser extent.'

[5] Article 21 para. 2 of the Declaration ('Everyone has the right of equal access to public service in his country') and Article 25 of the Covenant ('Every citizen shall have the right and the opportunity [...] to have access, on general terms of equality, to public service in his country') respectively. As we can see, the International Covenant on Civil and Political Rights expressly refers to the right as that of a citizen.

[6] Article 1 para. 2: 'This Convention shall not apply to distinctions, exclusions, restrictions or preferences made by a State Party to this Convention between citizens and non-citizens.'

[7] See, e.g. Article 14 of the I.L.O. Migrant Workers (Supplementary Provisions) Convention, 1975, No. 143: 'A Member may [...] restrict access to limited categories of employment or functions where this is necessary in the interests of the State.'

At a European level it is the European Convention on Establishment of 1955 which allows a Contracting Party 'to reserve for its own nationals the exercise of public functions or of occupations connected with national security or defence, or make the exercise of these occupations by aliens subject to special conditions.'[8] Beyond this Article the use of nationality requirements in the public service is left to the state: it is for the Contracting Party *itself* to determine the scope of the excluded activity.[9]

The exclusion of non-nationals from employment in the public service therefore seems to have wide acceptence in both the international and European legal traditions. It is a result which flows from the fact that nationality plays a major part in international relations.

Although the principle of exclusion of non-nationals from public service posts is accepted in all Member States, it is applied differently in each. For instance, the Netherlands has a comparatively narrow interpretation of the public service. In France, on the other hand, a far broader exclusion operates, encompassing employment in state schools, local government and the health sector.

Article 39 (4) (ex Article 48 (4)) EC provides that the freedom of movement does not apply to employment in the public service. In other words: whereas it is forbidden to discriminate on the grounds of nationality in other areas of employment (except when any of the other exceptions in Article 39 (ex Article 48) apply, see paragraph 3 of Chapter 2), it is still permitted to discriminate against non-nationals when it comes to employment in the public service.

Article 39 (4) (ex Article 48 (4)), however, does not define the concept of public service. Neither does Article 45 (ex Article 55), which excludes activities connected with the exercise of official authority from the freedom of establishment.

In its case law on the exceptions in Article 39 (3) (ex Article 48 (3)) the Court has struggled to achieve a balance between several factors. Among these are the needs of market integration, the rights of the individual, the uniformity of Community law and the legitimate rights of the Member States.[10] A parallel development can be observed in the less frequently litigated exception for employment in the public service under Article 39 (4) (ex Article 48 (4)) EC.

---

8 Article 13.

9 Section 1 of the Protocol: 'Each Contracting Party shall have the right to judge by national criteria [...] the reasons of *"ordre public,* national security, public health or morality" which may provide grounds for the exclusion from its territory of nationals of other Parties'.

10 Weatherill, S. & Beaumont, P., *EC Law* (Penguin Books, London, 1993), p. 500.

3 The case law of the European Court

The thrust of this analysis is to explore what part of national public service falls within the 'public service' criterion of Article 39 (4) (ex Article 48 (4)). This means that emphasis is to be placed on two sets of questions. First, the opposition of the institutional and functional approaches, and the reasons why the European Court adopted the latter. Secondly, the definition and application of functional criteria.

That civil servants are regarded as employed persons within the scheme of the EC Treaty can be deduced from the fact that the public service exception is laid down in paragraph 4 of Article 39 (ex Article 48) which is the first Article in Chapter 1 entitled 'Workers' under Title III. Article 39 (ex Article 48) itself deals with the freedom of movement of workers. Therefore, it seems obvious that public servants should be seen as workers, i.e. employed persons.

The Community meaning of the term 'worker' is to be defined according to objective criteria. The essential criteria of an employment relationship are that a person performs services for and under the direction of another person, in return for which he receives remuneration.[11] The fact that Article 39 (4) (ex Article 48 (4)) does not distinguish between employment as civil servants and employment as other staff, except when it comes to the public service exception itself, shows that civil servants are considered as employees or salaried workers.[12] Members of the armed forces also fall within this definition of 'worker', in view of the relationship of subordination in the context of which they perform their military duties, in return for which they receive a salary.[13]

The Court has shown that it pursues two aims when dealing with the free movement of workers. The Court's first aim is to derive directly effective rights from the principle of free movement of workers, rights upon which the individual migrant worker can rely against the authorities in proceedings before the courts of the Member State in which he works. Secondly, the Court aims to guarantee the uniform application of Community law, thereby abolishing the many forms of direct and indirect discrimination which can and do exist.

To start with, the European Court recognised that Article 39 (ex Article 48) was directly effective and subsequently said the same of numerous provisions of the directives covering this subject. This bold approach as met with, at least

---

11 Case 66/85, *Lawrie-Blum*, [1986] ECR 2121, para. 17. See paragraph 2.1.2 of Chapter 2.

12 Case C-71/93, *Van Poucke* v. *Rijksinstituut voor de Sociale Verzekeringen der Zelfstandigen and Algemene Sociale Kas voor Zelfstandigen*, [1994] ECR I-1101, para.17.

13 Case C-248/96, *Grahame and Hollanders* v. *Bestuur van de Nieuwe Algemene Bedrijfsvereniging*, [1997] ECR I-6407, para. 29.

initially, with stubborn resistance from certain major national legal systems and also harsh criticism in political circles.[14]

In the next paragraphs the case law of the European Court regarding the public service exception will be examined in detail.

3.1 *Sotgiu* v. *Deutsche Bundespost*, case 152/73[15]

This was the first case dealing with Article 39 (4) (ex Article 48 (4)) EC. The pertinent facts of the case were as follows. An Italian national, Mr Sotgiu, had been employed under private law by the *Deutsche Bundespost* since 1955. His family remained resident in Italy. In accordance with the collective wages agreement which applied to workers in the Federal Post Office, Mr Sotgiu's remuneration included a separation allowance which was paid at a rate of 7.50 DM a day. From 1 April 1963 this allowance was raised by the Federal Ministery of the Interior to 10 DM a day for workers employed away from the family home, provided this home was situated within the territory of the German Federal Republic. In other words, for the workers whose normal residence was situated abroad the daily allowances remained 7.50 DM a day. Mr Sotgiu considered the lower rate applicable to him to be discrimination contrary to Article 39 (ex Article 48) EEC and to Regulation 1612/68 and filed a suit before a German court. He lost the case at first instance and appealed before the *Bundesarbeitsgericht*, which submitted a prelimenary question to the European Court, which was whether Article 39 (4) (ex Article 48 (4)) was to be interpreted as excluding the application of Article 7 (1) and (4) of Regulation 1612/68 to migrant workers employed by the Federal Post Office on the basis of a contract of employment under private law. The problem was thus not one of access to the public service but one of conditions of employment.

The German court considered that only those employees with the Federal administration (of which the postal service was a part according to the German court) who have the status of public officials are in 'employment in the public service' within the meaning of Article 39 (4) (ex Article 48 (4)) of the Treaty. In other words, Post Office workers who were employed under private law should not be affected by the public service exception.

Advocate General Mayras in his Opinion[16] looked into the question of which parts of a state's administration should fall within the public service exception.

---

[14] Mancini, G., 'The Free Movement of Workers in the Case-Law of the European Court of Justice', in Curtin, D. and O'Keeffe, D. (Eds.), *Constitutional Adjudication in European Community and National Law* (Butterworth (Ireland) Ltd., Dublin, 1992), pp. 67/68.

[15] [1974] ECR 153.

[16] [1974] ECR 167.

He made reference to 'the classical idea inherent in the state'.[17] He was of the opinion that included in the public service are: 'the task of the judiciary, the police, defence and also that of assessing and recovering taxes'. He contrasted these state activities with those such as 'the public industrial and commercial services whose task is to perform services for the public, more often than not administered under conditions similar to those of private law'. The latter he considered not to fall within the Article 39 (4) (ex Article 48 (4)) exception, but the Advocate General nevertheless conceeded that there are no clear boundaries as far as the public service exception is concerned.

According to Advocate General Mayras the postal service is an example of an intermediate situation, because 'although in most countries this service is carried out by a state administration, subject to the rules of public management, and although its guiding principle is the secrecy of the mail, it nonetheless conceals within itself certain aspects of a commercial service and in general enjoys a financial autonomy'.[18]

This was also the case in Germany. The *Deutsche Bundespost* employed for the most part officials *(fonctionnaires,* in the original French text of Advocate General Mayras' Opinion), but it also employed, at the level of technical or purely operational tasks, manual workers *(ouvriers)* and office staff *(employés)*. These employees occupy posts which, whilst forming part of a public service, do not involve national interest with a view to which the exception contained in Article 39 (4) (ex Article 48 (4)) was formulated.[19]

According to Advocate General Mayras the public service exception should 'only be applicable if the person possesses a power of discretion with regard to individuals or if his activity involves national interests - in particular those which are concerned with the internal or external security of the state.'[20]

To start with, the Court emphasised that free movement of workers constituted one of the fundamental principles of the Community and that, therefore, any exception to this rule should be strictly interpreted.

Although acknowledging that the definition of public administration is different in each Member State, the Court decided that Article 39 (4) (ex Article 48 (4)) should have a uniform Community content in order to prevent uneven application of Community law between Member States simply based on the scope of the public sector in the different Member States. It is clear that the application of national criteria alone would lead to a lack of uniformity in the application of the free movement of workers' provisions in the Member States. We shall see that it is the desire to expand the employment opportunities for

---

17 Ibid, p. 171.

18 Ibid.

19 Ibid.

20 Ibid., p. 172.

non-nationals in the Member States and the need to reach some measure of uniformity which underlies the case law of the European Court.[21]

According to the Federal Republic of Germany, the activities of the Federal Post Office undoubtedly fell within the public service.[22] It based this conclusion on Article 87 of the *Grundgesetz* according to which the Federal Post Office was part of the administration pertaining to the Federation and this was also in accordance with the generally accepted view that it exercised attributes of sovereignty. Therefore, according to the German Government, employment in the Federal German Post Office constituted employment in the public service within the meaning of Article 39 (4) (ex Article 48 (4)) of the Treaty.

The Court disagreed with this interpretation. It decided that the fact that non-nationals were employed by the Federal Post Office proved that the 'interests which justify the exceptions to the principle of non-discrimination permitted by Article 48 (4) are not at issue.'[23]

The Court also found it of little consquence whether a function is carried out within the framework of a commitment under public law or on the basis of a contract of employment under private law.[24] Although, on the whole, the public service exception is applicable to 'officials' *(fonctionnaires* or *Beamten)* who have a special status because they are usually entrusted with powers involving the exercise of official authority, it is not impossible for contractual employees *(agents contractuels* or *Angestellten)* to be entrusted with such functions. Whereas the legal nature of the relationship might provide valuable evidence in this context, it could not of itself constitue a decisive criterion.

The Court also decided that Article 39 (4) (ex Article 48 (4)) can only be invoked in respect of a refusal to admit someone to an occupation. It cannot, however, 'justify discriminatory measures with regard to remuneration or other conditions of employment against workers once they have been admitted to the public service.'[25]

In the end, the very fact that Mr Sotgiu (a foreigner) was employed by the Federal Post Office meant that Article 39 (4) (ex Article 48 (4)) was not applicable in this case. However, even if Article 39 (4) (ex Article 48 (4)) had been applicable in this case, it could not have justified the lower separation allowance as the public service exception can only justify refusal to employ a non-national in the public service; it can never be the basis for any other form of discrimination once a person is employed.

---

[21] It should be noted that there is absolutely no parallel between the concept of public service in Article 39 (4) (ex Article 48 (4)) EC and the definition of the state for the purposes of establishing the scope of the direct effect of directives. See Chapter 5.

[22] [1974] ECR 153, p. 157.

[23] Ibid., para.4

[24] [1974] ECR 153, para. 5.

[25] Ibid., para. 4.

3.2 *Commission* v. *Belgium*, case 149/79[26]

Two major Article 226 (ex Article 169) EC cases serve to illustrate the Court's support for the Commission's determination to confine the scope of the exception to a narrow core of posts connected with the vital interests of the state. The first of these is *Commission* v. *Belgium*, the second is *Commission* v. *France* which will be discussed in the next paragraph.

In 1973 the *Société Nationale des Chemins de Fer Belges*[27] advertised vacancies for unskilled workers (loaders, plate-layers and shunters) and for trainee locomotive drivers and signalmen. At the same time the *Société Nationale des Chemins de Fer Vicinaux*[28] advertised a vacancy for an assistant at the printing works of the Central Administration in Brussels. Both advertisements stipulated as a condition the possession of Belgian nationality.

Between 1974 and 1977 the City of Brussels and the *Commune* of Auderghem advertised vacancies for hospital nurses and children's nurses in a creche, for architects, general services and park supervisors, night watchmen and permanent posts for garden hands and plumbers. The latter advertised a reserve list for future recruitment for the post of 'semi-skilled worker' and 'skilled worker Grade B' (plumber, carpenter and electrician). Once again, Belgian nationality was a requirement for access to these posts.

In 1974 the Commission informed the Belgian authorities that it regarded the nationality requirement as discriminatory because those posts could not be exempted from the principle of free movement of workers within the Community in view of the restrictive scope which, according to the Court's case law, should be given to the derogations contained in Article 39 (4) (ex Article 48 (4)) and Regulation 1612/68.[29] The Commission took the view that the nature of the duties connected with the posts in question (lacking the exercise of a power of decision over individuals and of any connection with the exercise of official authority) did not allow them to be considered as falling within the scope of Article 39 (4) (ex Article 48 (4)) EC.

The Belgian Government replied by stating that the second paragraph of Article 6 the Belgian Constitution, which states that 'Belgians are equal before the law; only they shall be admitted to civil and military posts save in special cases for which exception may be made by law', prohibited the *communes* under their staff regulations from employing staff who do not have Belgian nationality.

Having received, in its view, an unsatisfactory reply, the Commission adopted a Reasoned Opinion on 2 April 1979 which stated that 'by imposing or allowing

26 [1980] ECR 3881 and [1982] ECR 1845.

27 Belgian National Railway Company.

28 National Local Railway Company.

29 Advocate General Mayras' Opinion in case 149/79, [1980] ECR 3881, p. 3906.

to be imposed the possession of Belgian nationality as a condition for recruitment to posts (in local authorities or public undertakings) not covered by Article 48 (4), the Kingdom of Belgium has failed to fulfil its obligation under Article 48 (4) of the EEC Treaty and under Regulation 1612/68.' On 27 September 1979 the Commission brought the matter before the Court, restating the text of the Reasoned Opinion in its conclusions.

A number of the posts that were originally at issue were no longer in question in the case before the Court. In one or two cases it turned out that the posts in question did not concern unskilled workers after all, or were not dealt with in the Reasoned Opinion. The Commission seemed no longer to question the offer of posts for architects, supervisors of general services and for hospital and children's nurses in the City of Brussels. During the oral procedure the only relevant point brought to the fore concerned the advertisements by the Belgian National Railway and certain posts advertised by the City of Brussels (for nightwatchmen, garden hands and plumbers) and by the *Commune* of Auderghem (for semi-skilled workers and B-qualified workers: plumbers, carpenters, and electricians).[30]

The Court held that it was necessary to examine the duties involved in the posts in question. In other words it opted for a functional test.[31] The Court looked for powers conferred by public law bearing a responsibility for safeguarding the general interests of the State. In this case the Court found a breach of Article 39 (ex Article 48) where Belgians alone could take up posts as, inter alia, shunters, drivers and plate-layers with the Belgian National Railway and as joiners and gardeners with the City of Brussels. However, the Court also made it clear that considerations of state security could justify restrictions attached to elevated administrative posts in the city of Brussels.

In that case the Court stated 'that the exception clause contained in Article 48 (4) of the Treaty covers only posts whose performance involves actual participation in official authority, that is to say, involving a power of decision over individuals or putting in question national interests, especially those which touch upon the internal and external security of the state'.[32]

The sentence that has been quoted ever since is the following:

'that provision removes from the ambit of Article 48 (1) to (3) [JEB: now Article 39 (1) to (3)] a series of posts which involve direct or indirect participation in the exercise of powers conferred by public law and duties designed to safeguard the general interests of the state or of other public authorities.'

---

30 Ibid., p. 3909.

31 More about the functional test as opposed to the institutional test can be found in paragraph 5.1.

32 [1980] ECR 3881, para. 7.

The Court went on to say that 'such posts in fact presume on the part of those occupying them the existence of a special relationship of allegiance to the state and reciprocity of rights and duties which form the foundation of the bond of nationality.'[33]

The Court decided that the information provided as far as the posts in dispute were concerned was not sufficient to make an accurate appraisal of the actual duties involved, so it could not decide whether these posts were covered by Article 39 (4) (ex Article 48 (4)) or not. It ordered the Commission and the Kingdom of Belgium to re-examine the issue between them in the light of the legal considerations contained in its judgment and to report the results before 1 July 1981[34] at which point the Court would deliver a final decision.

The Commission and the Belgian authorities, however, were unable to agree on a single report to be submitted jointly to the Court and submitted two separate reports on 29 and 30 October respectively. Those reports showed that, although the parties did not disagree on the nature of the duties and responsibilities involved as regards each of the posts at issue, they could not agree on whether or not the posts in question fell within the scope of the public service exception. So the task fell to the Court to settle the dispute by examining whether, and to what extent, the posts at issue should be regarded as posts which fall within the ambit of Article 39 (4) (ex Article 48 (4)).

The Commission acknowledged (rightly according to the Court) that some of the posts described in the aforementioned reports could have characteristics which brought them within the scope of the exception. These were the posts of head technical office supervisor, principle supervisor, works supervisor, stock controller and night-watchmen with the Municipality of Brussels and architect with the Municipalities of Brussels and Auderghem. Those posts were, therefore, no longer at issue.

The Court dismissed the arguments put forward by the Belgian Government with regard to certain posts with the Belgian National Railway Company and the National Local Railway Company according to which the question of the admission of foreign staff should be considered above all in terms of the possibility that a situation may arise in which the security of the state is jeopardised and stated that such arguments could not be accepted in the context of Article 39 (4) (ex Article 48 (4)), stating that they were based on a hypothesis which has no connection with the legal context of the public service exception.[35]

The Court concluded that, apart from the aforementioned posts already acknowledged by the Commission to be within the scope of Article 39 (4) (ex

---

33 Ibid., para. 10.

34 This time-limit was later extended.

35 Case 149/79 (II), *Commission* v. *Belgium II*, [1982] ECR 1845, para. 10.

Article 48 (4)), Belgium had failed to fulfil its obligations under the EEC Treaty by insisting on the possession of Belgian nationality for access to the posts.

3.3 *Commission* v. *France*, case 307/84[36]

From the case law so far, we can surmise that the Court seems to rely on a test based on whether the functions and responsibilities were typical of the public service. As we shall see, this test was not satisfied in *Commission* v. *France*.

The case concerned posts as nurses working in public hospitals, for which French nationality was a precondition for permanent employment. Foreign nationals, contrary to their French counterparts, could not become established *fonctionnaires*, but could only enjoy a temporary status. This requirement was based on Article L 809 of the Public Health Code[37] according to which 'no person may be appointed to a post [...] unless that person possesses French nationality'. This again was based on a condition laid down in Article 16 of the General Rules applicable to employment in the public service,[38] which is laid down in Article 5 of Law No. 83-634 of 13 July 1983 on the rights and duties of employees in the public sector.

As in the case against Belgium, the Commission delivered a Reasoned Opinion on the matter, arguing that France had failed to comply with its Treaty obligations. The French Republic did not respond to the Reasoned Opinion. However, by a Decree of 24 February 1984, it abolished the nationality requirement for permanent posts such as dental practitioners in public hospitals, but the nationality requirement was maintained for appointment and establishment in permanent employment as a nurse in public hospitals. As a result, the Commission brought an Article 226 (ex Article 169) action against the French Republic.

France argued that such nursing posts were covered by Article 39 (4) (ex Article 48 (4)) and based its arguments on the 'organic' or 'institutional' interpretation of Article 39 (4) (ex Article 48 (4)). This approach excludes every kind of employment in the public service, regardless of the nature of the activity involved, from the scope of the principle of free movement for workers.[39] The French authorities furthermore claimed that the definition of the concept of public service should be a matter for the Member States in question.

---

36 [1986] ECR 1725.

37 *Code de la Santé Publique.*

38 Order No. 59-244 of 4 February 1959.

39 For a more detailed description of the institutional approach see: paragraph 5.1 of this chapter.

The Court once again made it clear that it could not be up to the individual Member States to define the concept of public service as far as Article 39 (4) (ex Article 48 (4)) was concerned. It should have the same meaning in all the Member States, or else it would be too easy for Member States to ensure that certain posts remained reserved for nationals merely by classifying a post as being within the public service. This was clear from the first case concerning Article 39 (4) (ex Article 48 (4)) in which the Court decided that the concept of public service requires uniform interpretation and application throughout the Community.[40] Therefore, the arguments put forward by the French Government could not be accepted.

Basing itself on its judgments in *Commission* v. *Belgium* the Court stated that it was necessary to consider 'whether or not the posts in question are typical of the specific activities of the public service in so far as the exercise of powers conferred by public law and responsibility for safeguarding the general interests of the State are vested in it'.[41] The Court decided that 'in view of the nature of the functions and responsibilities which they involve, posts of nurses in public hospitals do not constitute employment in the public service within the meaning of Article 48 (4) of the Treaty'.[42]

The French Government additionally claimed that even if the posts did fall within the public service exception, there was still no discrimination of the sort prohibited by Article 39 (2) (ex Article 48 (2)), because non-nationals could be appointed on a contractual basis instead. The Court rejected this argument because the French Government could 'not establish that all posts as nurses offered in public hospitals were equally accessible to the nationals of other Member States and that when such nationals were recruited they enjoyed conditions - with the exception of promotion to posts in the public service which are within the definition of Article 39 (4) (ex Article 48 (4)) of the EC Treaty - advantages and safeguards which were in every respect equivalent to those deriving from the status of members of the established staff, which was reserved to French nationals.'[43]

Therefore, the Court ruled that the French Republic had failed to fulfil its obligations under Article 39 (ex Article 48) of the EEC Treaty.

---

40 Case 152/73, *Sotgiu*, [1974] ECR 153, Opinion of Advocate General Mayras, p. 169.

41 Case 149/79, *Commission* v. *Belgium*, [1980] ECR 3881, para. 12.

42 Case 307/84, [1986] ECR 1725, para. 13.

43 Ibid., para. 16.

3.4 *Lawrie-Blum* v. *Land Baden-Württemburg*, case 66/85[44]

In this case a British national was denied access to a teacher training course, which involved teaching practice in German State schools. The question before the Court was whether, in Germany, a national of another Member State could gain access as a trainee teacher in a State school system[45] on the same conditions as German nationals.

The plaintiff, Mrs Lawrie-Blum, was a British national born in Portugal. She was married to a German national. She attended school in Austria and England and had obtained her first university degree in England. She went on to study at the University of Freiburg where she took the *Gymnasium* (secondary school) teacher's examination. In August 1979 she applied to the *Oberschulamt Stuttgart*[46] in the *Land* of Baden-Württemberg to be admitted to the period of preparatory service for the profession of teacher at a *Gymnasium*. It was her intention to teach at a private *Gymnasium* after completing her training.[47]

The *Oberschulamt* refused her application for admission and based its decision on paragraph 2(1)(1) of the *Verordnung über den Vorbereitungsdienst und die Pädagogische Prüfung für das Lehramt an Gymnasien*[48] of June 1976. It states that only persons who satisfy the requirements for appointment as civil servants may be admitted to prepatory service. According to paragraph 6 (1) (1) of the *Landesbeamtengesetz*[49] only Germans within the meaning of Article 116 of the *Grundgesetz* may be appointed to posts having civil service status.[50] In short, she was refused because she did not have German nationality.

Mrs Lawrie-Blum decided to bring an action before the *Verwaltungsgericht* Freiburg, which dismissed her claim because in its opinion the post of trainee teacher fell within the public service exception as in the Federal Republic of Germany teachers in State school systems were normally civil servants.

The *Bundesverwaltungsgericht* referred a question to the European Court designed to elicit whether such a trainee teacher could be a worker under Article 39 (ex Article 48) and, if so, whether the post was covered by Article 39 (4) (ex Article 48 (4)). The European Court rejected the argument, by the defendant *Land* that public servants could not be treated as 'workers' within the meaning of Article 39 (ex Article 48). The European Court made it plain that the term

---

44 [1986] ECR 2121.

45 *'Zulassung zum Staatlichen Vorbereitungsdienst'.*

46 Secondary Education Office, Stuttgart.

47 Opinion of Advocate General Lenz, [1986] ECR 2121, p. 2122.

48 Order on Preparatory Service and the Examination for the Profession of Teacher at a *Gymnasium*.

49 Law of the *Land* of Baden-Württemberg on the Civil Service.

50 Paragraph 6 (3) of the *Landesbeamtengesetz für Baden-Württemberg* allows the Minister of the Interior to authorise exceptions in the case of imperative requirements relating to the service.

'worker' in Article 39 (ex Article 48) has a Community meaning and that it must be defined in accordance with objective criteria which distinguish the employment relationship by reference to the rights and duties of the persons concerned. In other words, where duties had been performed under the direction of another in return for remuneration, the non-economic nature of the activity involved was irrelevant.[51]

As to whether the post of trainee teacher could be covered by the public service exception, the Court reiterated that the exception to free movement of workers should be strictly interpreted. It once again referred to the criterion laid down in *Commission* v. *Belgium* and concluded that a post as trainee teacher did not involve direct or indirect participation in the exercise of official powers conferred by public law, nor the discharge of functions whose purpose it was to safeguard the general interests of the State or of other public authorities.[52]

3.5 *Commission* v. *Italy*, case 225/85[53]

This case dealt with the position of research workers with the *Consiglio Nazionale delle Ricerche* (CNR). The facts of this case are as follows. On 20 March 1975 the Italian Republic issued Law No. 70 on new rules relating to public corporations and the terms of employment for staff. It was provided among other things in Article 36 (3) and (4) of that law that persons employed under contract by the CNR who have the requisite qualifications and fulfil the prescribed requirements should be given established posts. If that was impossible owing to a lack of posts, the staff concerned should be retained under contract for an indefinite period and receive the remuneration laid down for the corresponding established posts.[54]

Article 5 (3) of Law No. 70 refers to the legal rules in force in the civil service with regard to recruitment requirements. Those rules include the provisions of the Staff Regulations for Civil Servants, Article 2 of which provides that Italian nationality is a requirement for appointment as a civil servant.

According to Order No. 82 of 1 March 1945 the CNR is an autonomous government agency having legal personality and answering to the President of the Council of Ministers. It is responsible, *inter alia*, for the coordination of the activities of the state in the various scientific fields, for drawing up technical standards, compiling bibliographic and documentary material and for conducting research of its own.

---

51 The European Court referred to its judgment in Case 36/74, *Walrave and Koch*, [1974] ECR 1405. See also paragraph 2.1.2 of Chapter 2.

52 [1986] ECR 2121, paras. 27/28.

53 [1987] ECR 2625.

54 Opinion of the Advocate General in case 225/85, [1987] ECR 2625.

Where rendered necessary by particular requirements of scientific research, the CNR may under Article 36 (1) of Law No. 70 of 1975 recruit foreign staff for advanced research under contract. However, the maximum duration of such contracts is five years.

To date, the provisions of Article 36 (3) and (4) of Law No. 70 had not been applied to foreign researchers working for the CNR because in the view of the Italian authorities, such workers, being foreign nationals, were not entitled to established posts. Instead, the researchers in question continued to be employed under contracts of limited duration.

The Commission brought an action under Article 226 (ex Article 169) because in its opinion the Italian Republic discriminated, as regards conditions of work and employment, against nationals of other Member States working for the CNR since they could only be employed under contracts of limited duration and could not occupy an established post.

The fact that researchers who are not Italian nationals were not established had a number of consequences as far as they were concerned. In the first place, their posts were less secure, since the contracts of employment concluded with them were for limited periods only. Secondly, they could not be promoted since participation in the procedures leading to promotion was restricted to Italian nationals only.[55]

In its defence Italy did not formally contest the Commission's claim. It merely pointed out that the researchers concerned had been retained under contracts for a limited period and that their remuneration corresponded to that of researchers occupying established posts. It also claimed that the Italian Goverment was preparing a bill designed to enable researchers who were nationals of other Member States to be given established posts and, specifically, that efforts were were being made to give the researchers in question established posts and that, consequently, the action was unnecessary.

The Court decided that this was a case of prohibited discrimination, since the Italian Republic could not show that the researchers in question were responsible for management duties in the laboratories or for advising the State regarding scientific questions. The Court inferred from the fact that the researchers had already been employed with the CNR for some time that the general interests of the State or exclusive tasks of the public authorities were not involved in this case. Should that have been otherwise, then the posts might have been covered by the public service exception.

The Court also stated once more[56] that even if employment in the public service within the meaning of Article 39 (4) (ex Article 48 (4)) is involved, this can never justify discriminatory measures with regard to remuneration or other

---

55 [1987] ECR 2625, para. 10.

56 It had also done so earlier in case 152/73, *Sotgiu*, [1974] ECR 153.

conditions of employment against workers from other Member States once they have been admitted to the posts in question.

3.6 *Allué & Coonan*, case 33/88[57]

The next case to be considered by the Court was again about teachers. In *Allué & Coonan* the plaintiffs were a Spanish national and a UK national who worked for the *Università Degli Studi di Venezia*[58] as foreign-language assistants from 1980 to 1986. The Italian legislation laid down special rules governing the work of foreign-language assistants imposing a limit on the duration of their contracts, whilst other state employees are generally guaranteed security of tenure. Article 28 of Decree No. 382/1980 of the President of the Republic provides that Italian Universities could engage assistants with a foreign mother tongue under a contract governed by private law. The contracts could not be extended beyond the academic year in which they are concluded and could be renewed annually for a maximum of five years.

Also, the contracts were for the supply of intellectual services, that is to say for self-employed persons, and not contracts of employment. According to the rules applicable to such contracts, it is up to the person concerned to deduct from his/her remuneration the amounts necessary for the payment of social security contributions. By contrast, in the case of employed persons it is the empoyer who is responsible for paying a substantial part of such contributions.

This administrative practice had already been condemned by the Italian courts when this case was brought before the European Court by means of a request for a preliminary ruling from a national court. It asked whether employment as a foreign-language assistant in a university was covered by the public service exception, and, if not, whether the restriction on the duration of the employment relationship and the five-year limit on the entire period of employment should be regarded as discrimination prohibited by Article 39 (2) (ex Article 48 (2)) EC.

Referring specifically to the cases of *Lawrie-Blum*[59] and *Commission* v. *Italy*,[60] the Court came to the conclusion that employment as a teacher, in general, and as a foreign-language assistant, in particular, was not employment in the public service, since it did not require a special relationship of allegiance to the state, nor any rights or duties which form the foundation of the bond of nationality.[61]

---

57 [1989] ECR 1591.

58 University of Venice.

59 Case 66/85, [1986] ECR 2121.

60 Case 225/85, [1987] ECR 2625.

61 [1989] ECR 1591, para. 8.

3.7 *Bleis* v. *Ministère de l'Education Nationale*, case C-4/91[62]

In this case the position of a teacher was once again at issue. The case turned on the question whether employment as a secondary school teacher in French public establishments constituted employment in the public service.

Mrs Bleis, a German national, had applied to be registered for an external competition for the *certificat d'aptitude au professorat de l' enseignement du second degré*[63] in German. Her application was refused by the deputy director for recruitment at the Ministry of Education on the ground of her nationality. Mrs Bleis made an administrative complaint against that decision to the Minister of National Education. Having received no response for over four months, Mrs Bleis began proceedings before the *Tribunal Administratif* (administrative court), Paris, for the annulment of the tacit decision to be inferred from the absence of a response. The *Tribunal Administratif* referred to the European Court for a preliminary ruling.

Whilst these proceedings were pending, a law was enacted in France which, for certain occupational groups, provided an exception (which also applied to secondary school teachers) to the nationality requirements in the case of nationals from other Member States. Since individuals were at that time, however, still unable to rely directly on the law without the necessary implementing measures, the French government and the Commission assumed that from the point of view of both law and fact an interest was still to be served by the decision.

The Court referred to its judgments in the two earlier cases concerning teachers, *Lawrie-Blum*[64] and *Allué & Coonan*,[65] and swiftly concluded that the same criteria applied with regard to employment as a secondary school teacher. It was obvious that this occupation did not involve direct or indirect participation in the exercise of powers conferred by public law, nor was it connected with the discharge of functions whose purpose is to safeguard the general interests of the state or of other public authorities. It also did not require a special relationship of allegiance to the state. Therefore, the post of secondary school teacher was not covered by the public service exception of Article 39 (4) (ex Article 48 (4)) EC.

---

62 [1991] ECR I-5627.

63 Certificate of aptitude as a secondary school teacher.

64 Case 66/85, [1986] ECR 2121.

65 Case 33/88, [1989] ECR 1591.

3.8 *Commission* v. *Luxembourg*, case C-473/93[66]

On 2 July 1996 the Court pronounced judgment in three joined cases on Article 39 (4) (ex Article 48 (4)). All three cases were brought by the Commission under Article 226 (ex Article 169) against, respectively, Luxembourg, Belgium and Greece to evoke compliance with the Court's case law on the public service exception. These three cases will be dealt with in the next three paragraphs.

In the first case, *Commission* v. *Luxembourg*, the Commission sought a declaration that Luxembourg had failed to fulfil its obligations under Article 39 (4) (ex Article 48 (4)) EC and Articles 1 and 7 of Regulation 1612/68, in that only Luxembourg nationals had access to civil service and public service employment in certain public sectors.

Luxembourg imposed a nationality requirement in relation to posts in the areas of research, teaching, health, inland transport, postal services and telecommunications, and the water, gas and electricity distribution. The requirement applied regardless of the duties entailed in, or the hierarchical level of, the posts in question. It was also irrelevant whether the status of the occupant of the post was that of a civil servant or employee. The Commission sent several Reasoned Opinions giving Luxembourg four months to comply with its Community obligations. Luxembourg did not reply within the stipulated period and the Commission started Article 226 (ex Article 169) proceedings.

Luxembourg contended that the action was inadmissable because the period of compliance was insufficient. It also argued that the Court should depart from the strict manner in which it had previously construed Article 39 (4) (ex Article 48 (4)), and regard the exception as covering all posts which constituted public service posts under national law, including those involving purely executory, technical or manual duties if they were performed for the State or for public authorities. In other words, it wanted the Court to apply an institutional, rather than a functional approach.

Alternatively, Luxembourg objected to the fact that, rather than proceeding on a case-by-case basis, the Commission had designed entire areas which were in principle to be excluded from the Article 39 (4) (ex Article 48 (4)) derogation, thereby placing the burden on Luxembourg to prove the contrary in special cases.

As to admissibility, the Court decided that the action was admissible because the compliance period imposed by the Reasoned Opinions was reasonable, since it was twice as long as normal and, secondly, that Luxembourg had long been aware of the Commission's position and that, thirdly, it had not previously manifested any intention of carrying out legislative reforms.

---

[66] Case C-473/93, [1996] ECR I-3207.

The Court referred to its previous case law and once more stated that the public service exception should be interpreted both strictly and in a functional manner, having regard to the tasks and responsibilities which the posts involved, in order to ensure that it was applied uniformly throughout the Community.

As regards Luxembourg's objection that the Commission had designated whole areas which were in principle outside the scope of Article 39 (4) (ex Article 48 (4)), it appeared that Luxembourg conceded that in all of those areas, with the exception of education, posts were generally remote from the specific activities of the public service. As to the area of education, the protection of national identity was a legitimate aim,[67] but it did not justify excluding nationals from all of the posts in that field, and therefore the Court held the Commission's approach to be valid.

3.9 *Commission* v. *Belgium*, case C-173/94[68]

In contrast to Luxembourg, Belgium, in the second of the joined cases, case C-173/94 *Commission* v. *Belgium*, accepted the sectoral approach proposed by the Commission as a logical development of the Court's case law up to that point.

The bodies under scrutiny in this case were the public bodies responsible for the distribution of water, gas and electricity.[69] On 23 April 1991 the Commission sent the Belgian Government a letter informing them that the practice of requiring Belgian nationality for employment with those bodies was not allowed under the derogation to the principle of free movement of workers as laid down in Article 39 (4) (ex Article 48 (4)) EC. The Belgian Government responded with the statement that a recommendation had been addressed by the competent Minister of the Flemish Executive to the persons in charge of the public bodies concerned. The Commission was not satisfied with this reply, and issued a Reasoned Opinion giving the Belgian Government four months to comply with its obligations. When it received no reply to the Reasoned Opinion, the Commission brought proceedings before the Court.

The Belgian Government did not deny that, in principle, it was guilty of the alleged breach of obligations. However, it rejected the Commission's objections concerning Unerg and Sibelgaz, since, according to the Belgian Government, they were private companies over which the public authorities could exercise no authority and there were no national, regional or local rules requiring those private companies to apply a nationality condition when recruiting their staff.

---

67 Laid down in Article 6 (3) (ex Article F (3)) of the TEU.

68 [1996] ECR I-3265.

69 For example, *Compagnie Intercommunale Bruxelloise des Eaux*, *Vlaamse Maatschappij voor Watervoorziening*, Unerg, Sibelgaz, etc.

The Court upheld the Belgian Government's statement as regards Unerg and Sibelgaz and dismissed the Commission's case as far as those two companies were concerned. However, as far as the posts with *public* bodies responsible for the distribution of water, gas and electricity were concerned the Court decided that Belgium had failed to fulfil its obligations under Article 39 (4) (ex Article 48 (4)) and Article 1 of Regulation 1612/68, since no general interests of the State were involved in the activities of these bodies.

3.10 *Commission* v. *Greece*, case C-290/94[70]

In the third of these joined cases, case C-290/94, *Commission* v. *Greece*, the list of bodies that were involved seemed almost endless: public, semi-public or municipal undertakings and companies distributing water, gas and electricity, the public health service, teaching posts in nursery, primary and secondary schools and higher education establishments and universities, transport services, posts for scientific and non-scientific staff in public establishments conducting research for non-military purposes, postal and telecommunications services, radio and television broadcasting services, and even musicians' posts at the Athens Opera and in municipal and local orchestras.

In all those areas Greek nationality was in principle required as a qualification for the relevant posts. This rule was laid down, first, in Article 4 (4) of the Greek Constitition, which provides that all public functions are to be occupied by Greek citizens, save where exceptions are made by special Laws. Secondly, Law No. 1735/87 and Ministerial Decree No. DIPPP/F of 7/8 January 1988 on access to employment in the public sector required Greek nationality for access to all posts in the public sector, which was defined in Article 1 (6) of Law No. 1256/82 and delimited by Article 51 of Law No. 1892/90. Greek nationality was also prescribed by laws and regulations specific to the areas of activity in question.

After having been informed of the Athens Opera's refusal to engage a German musician on the grounds of his nationality, the Commisssion, in the spring of 1991, sent eight letters calling for observations from the Greek Government concerning the areas listed above. In those letters the Commission requested the Greek Government to take the measure needed to abolish the nationality condition which that State applied for access to employment in those areas and to submit its observations within a period of six months.

The Greek Government replied to seven of the eight letters stating that it had decided to incorporate new rules in its administration modernisation pro-

---

70 [1996] ECR I-3285.

gramme, which was soon to be adopted, and in a future legislative programme. By mid-1992 (and in one case even March 1993) the promised plans had still not been implemented and the Commission sent eight Reasoned Opinions[71] to the Greek Government instructing them to take the measures necessary within four months of the first seven Reasoned Opinions, and within two months of the last Opinion.

When it emerged that no national measures had been adopted within the periods laid down in the Reasoned Opinions, the Commission brought proceedings before the Court.

The Court declared that in not restricting the requirement of Greek nationality to access to posts involving direct or indirect participation in the exercise of powers conferred by public law and duties designed to safeguard the general interests of the State or of other public authorities in the sectors involved the Hellenic Republic had failed to fulfil its obligations under Article 39 (4) (ex Article 48 (4)) and Article 1 of Regulation 1612/68.

The three cases of 6 June 1996, described above, did not result in any changes in the European Court's approach to the public service exception as such. It did not change its interpretation. However, the Court's judgments in these three cases did make it clear that the Commission's approach of declaring whole sections of the public service as not being covered by the Article 39 (ex Article 48) exception as valid. The Commission did not have to resort to a post-by-post examination of the public service.[72]

3.11 Additional case law

The cases dealt with in the previous paragraphs are all cases having the public service exception, as laid down in Article 39 (4) (ex Article 48 (4)) EC, as the central provision in dispute. However, there is also additional case law in which, although not dealing directly with Article 39 (4) (ex Article 48 (4)), the Court has something to say about the interpretation of the said Article. In this paragraph I want to briefly mention some of these cases.

The case of *Commission* v. *Spain*[73] dealt mainly with the freedom to provide services and the freedom of establishment. The facts of the case dealt with a nationality condition imposed on private security undertakings. Article 10 of Law No. 23/1992 of 30 July 1992 precluded nationals from other Member States from carrying out permanently private security activities as employed or self-

71 Seven on 13 July 1992 and one on March 1993.

72 Denys, C., 'Grote schoonmaak in de overheidssector', *Nederlands Tijdschrift voor Europees recht*, 1996/10, p. 221.

73 Case C-114/97, [1998] ECR I-6717.

employed persons. The Spanish Government considered the restrictions to the freedom of movement for workers, to the freedom of establishment and to the freedom to provide services to be covered by the derogations provided by the EC Treaty, i.e. Article 39 (3) and (4) (ex Article 48 (3) and (4)), Article 45 (ex Article 55) and Article 55 (ex Article 66) EC. The Court succinctly dealt with the Spanish Government's opinion by stating that private security undertakings do not form part of the public service and stated that Article 39 (4) (ex Article 48 (4)) was not applicable to this case, because 'merely making a contribution to the maintenance of public security, which any individual may be called upon to do, does not constitute exercise of official authority'.[74]

The case of *Vougioukas* v. *Idryma Koinonikon Asfalisseon (IKA)*[75] dealt with the interpretation of the notion of 'civil servant' in Article 4 (4) of Regulation 1408/71. The case was brought by Mr Vougioukas, a doctor, against IKA, a public legal person. IKA, a Greek Social Security Institution, refused to take into account, for the purpose of Mr Vougioukas's pension entitlements, the period that Mr Vougioukas, a Greek national, had worked in public hospitals in Germany. The national court referred a question to the European Court asking whether the term 'civil servant' in Article 4 (4) of Regulation 1408/71[76] refers only to civil servants covered by the derogation provided for in Article 39 (4) (ex Article 48 (4)) EC. The Court stated that those two terms were not linked. According to the Court the subject matter of the two provisions is different. Whereas Article 39 (4) (ex Article 48 (4)) provides merely that Member States may exclude nationals of other Member States from access to certain posts in the public service, Article 4 (4) of Regulation 1408/71 excludes, in more general terms, special schemes for civil servants and persons treated as such from the coordination of social security schemes under that Regulation.[77] The Court went on to say that the objective of both provisions was also different. Article 39 (4) (ex Article 48 (4)), according to the Court, took into account the legitimate interest of Member States in reserving a range of posts connected with the exercise of powers conferred by public law and with the protection of general interests for their own nationals. In contrast, Article 4 (4) of Regulation 1408/71 merely takes account of the special features of schemes for civil servants in the Member States.[78]

A case which dealt with a similar problem is the case of *Schöning-Kougebetopoulou* v. *Freie und Hansestadt Hamburg*.[79] The applicant in this case was

74 Ibid., para. 37.

75 Case C-443/93, [1995] ECR I-4033.

76 Article 4 (4) of Regulation 1408/71 excludes, *inter alia*, special schemes for civil servants from the workings of the Regulation. See also paragraph 2.2.4 of Chapter 2.

77 Case C-443/93, para. 19.

78 Ibid., para. 20.

79 Case C-15/96, [1998] ECR I-0047.

employed as a specialist doctor by the City of Hamburg. She was appointed as an *Angestellte* (a contractual employee) rather than a *Beamte* (civil servant). As a result her employment relationship was governed by the *Bundes-Angestellten-tarifvertrag*[80] (BAT). The BAT did not allow for periods of employment completed in the public service of another Member State to be taken into account for the purposes of promotion and salary grading. The Court decided that such a clause was indirectly discriminatory, since it would work to the detriment of migrant workers. Such a clause is contrary to Article 7 (4) of Regulation 1612/68. The Court also once again stated that the derogation in Article 39 (4) (ex Article 48 (4)) EC concerns only the *access* of nationals of other Member States to certain posts in the civil service. Also, according to the Court, the post of specialist doctor did not involve direct or indirect participation in the exercise of powers conferred by public law and duties designed to safeguard the general interests of the State or of public authorities.[81]

In the joined cases of *Echternach and Moritz* v. *Netherlands Minister for Education and Science*[82] the Court succinctly stated, without examining the nature of the employment in question,[83] that Article 39 (4) (ex Article 48 (4)) provides only that Member States have the possibility to exclude nationals from other Member States from access to certain posts in the public service. It does not, however, give Member States the right to exclude persons, whom it has nonetheless appointed to such posts, from Community treatment. The applicant and members of his family were entitled to the rights and privileges awarded them in the pertinent provision of the EC Treaty and those laid down in Regulation 1612/68.[84]

4 The Commission's approach

In the late 1980s the Commission issued an action plan for the elimination of restrictions on grounds of nationality to access to posts in parts of the public sector. The Commission did not choose to introduce legislation or produce a list of posts to which Article 39 (ex Article 48) applies. Rather, it

80 Federal Collective Wage Agreement for Contractual Employees.

81 [1998] ECR I-0047, para. 13.

82 Joined cases 389 and 390/87, [1989] ECR 723.

83 The employment in question was a post with the European Space Agency, a post which is governed by special statute under international law. According to the Court an employee of such an organisation is nevertheless a worker under the Community definition and as such Article 39 (ex Article 48) EC applies.

84 [1989] ECR 723, para. 14.

chose to pursue compliance through (the threat of) Article 226 (ex Article 169) infringement proceedings against Member States.

In a statement issued in March 1988,[85] the Commission set out a strategy for the elimination of restrictions, on grounds of nationality, to access to public service posts which do not fall within the public service exception. The clear intent of this statement was to ensure the observance of judge-made Community rules without recourse to new Community legislation.[86]

The Commission firstly defined the limits of the exception, on the basis of current rulings by the Court of Justice and 'bearing in mind the present conditions for establishing the single market'. In its statement the Commission stated that the exception covers 'specific functions of the State and similar bodies such as the armed forces, the police and other forces for the maintenance of order, the judiciary, the tax authorities and the diplomatic corps.'

It can be seen that this embraces the classical functions of the State. The implication seems to be that *all* posts in such bodies are covered by the exception. It is uncertain whether this interpretation can be squared with that of the Court.

The Commission secondly referred to a second category of protected posts outside the 'classical' areas. Posts in state ministries, local and regional authorities and other public bodies are also covered 'where duties of the post involve the exercise of State authority, such as the preparation of legal acts, the implementation of such acts, monitoring of their application and supervision of subordinate bodies.'

Here the Commission indicated that a more critical, i.e. case-by-case, examination of the posts in question is warranted. The Commission stated that posts were not covered by the exception where the functions are 'sufficiently remote' from the specific activities of the public service. Action was to be implemented in the following areas, by order of priority: bodies administering commercial services (e.g. public transport, electricity and gas supply, airlines and shipping companies, postal services and telecommunications, radio and television companies); public health care services; teaching in state educational establishments; and research for non-military purposes in public establishments.

Member States were informed of the conclusions of the Commission's review of the sectors chosen and that, if necessary, recourse would be had to the Article 226 (ex Article 169) procedure, where defendant states have the opportunity to

85 'Freedom of movement of workers and access to employment in the public service of the Member States. Commission action in respect of the application of Article 48(4) of the EEC Treaty', OJ 1988 C72/2.

86 The Commission clearly took the view that there was no need to propose new Community legislation given the direct effect of Article 39 (4) (ex Article 48 (4)) EC and the case law of the Court. See, also, the Commission's answer to WPQ No. 42/91, OJ 1991 C177/24.

show that 'contrary to what might be expected, the post is indeed involved with the specific actions of the public service.' The Commission seemed to be using the threat of continued Court proceedings to induce Member States to comply. In addition, the Commission also pointed out that any misuse of the exception under Article 39 (4) (ex Article 48 (4)) could be dealt with in proceedings before national courts, since Article 39 (4) (ex Article 48 (4)) is directly effective.[87]

The Commission used this statement as the basis for action. In 1992 it issued a series of Reasoned Opinions under Article 226 (ex Article 169) of the EC Treaty in relation to areas specified in the statement: education, civilian research, public health and management of commercial services. It also issued Reasoned Opinions in other areas, covering welfare assistants in a French *département*, musicians in public theatres and operas and university teachers. It appears that most of the Member States concerned accepted in principle the need for change, but problems of implementation remained, as can be seen from the three cases brought before the Court by the Commission in 1993/1994, namely C-473/93, *Commission* v. *Luxembourg*, case C-173/94, *Commission* v. *Belgium*, case C-290/94, *Commission* v. *Greece*.[88]

5 The Court's approach

The European Court's approach has been to treat the exception as a derogation from one of the Community's fundamental principles, namely the principle of free movement and equality of treatment for workers. It has progressively operated a more rigorous approach. By *Lawrie-Blum*[89], it was saying that 'very strict' conditions had to be satisfied. In the following paragraphs we will take a closer look at the central points of the Court's approach.

5.1 The institutional versus the functional approach

In essense there are two broad approaches to the question of non-national acces to the public service.

The institutional approach is based on the idea that, as a rule, a state institution, together with its personnel, is whole and indivisible. Accordingly, it is considered impossible to determine, for the purposes of providing non-nationals

---

[87] See the Commission's answers to WPQ No. 2631/92 (OJ 1993 C106/35), in relation to British crown servants and the European Communities (Employment in the Civil Service) Order 1991, and WPQ No. 599/93, OJ 1993 C264/79.

[88] See paras. 3.8, 3.9 and 3.10, respectively.

[89] Case 66/85, [1986] ECR 2121, para. 28.

with access to employment in such institutions,[90] whether a given post within the institution is or is not central to the interests of the state: the question is whether the *institution* as such is of central importance. Member States have invoked the institutional requirements of their public service against the functional approach favoured by the Court and the Commission.[91]

The reasoning behind this approach is not necessarily based directly on the question of non-national access. For instance, on a constitutional level, Germany has argued that the Community was based on the state organisation of the Member States and the EC Treaty did not seek to harmonise national administrative structures. Therefore, it was for the Member States to determine non-national access on the basis of their own administrative structures.[92]

Other arguments for the institutional approach have focused on specific characteristics of the public service in Member States. In the organisation of the public service emphasis may be put on the flexibility of transfer and promotion, according to the overriding needs of the service.[93] France has argued that the link between an institution and a *fonctionnaire* is such that it precludes non-national access to the latter status.[94] There may be a rule of equality in the service, which would make it difficult to restrict employment opportunities of non-nationals once they were in. This would mean that once non-nationals were in, it could prove difficult to keep them out of posts which *do* fall within the public service exception once they are promoted through the ranks. States have pointed to the difficulties which would be faced were a functional test to apply in such cases and have therefore pleaded for an institutional approach instead.[95]

The issue of recruitment to the public service has always been closely linked to the problem of non-nationals employed in a Member State who find themselves disadvantaged by their nationality in their subsequent career when it comes to promotion and other conditions of employment. Although the exception in Article 39 (4) (ex Article 48 (4)) applies only to *access* to posts forming a

---

90 A state supporting the institutional approach will sometimes allow non-national access to a limited number of institutions, but often with an inferior and more precarious status than that enjoyed by a national.

91 Germany in case 152/73, *Sotgiu*, Belgium, France, UK and Germany in case 149/79, *Commission* v. *Belgium*, and France in case 307/84, *Commission* v. *France*.

92 Case 152/73, *Sotgiu*, and case 149/79, *Commission* v. *Belgium*.

93 Handoll (1988), p. 229.

94 Case 152/73, *Sotgiu*, and, especially, case 307/84, *Commission* v. *France*, [1986] ECR 1725, paras. 8 and 9, where France raised a number of arguments for exclusion, such as: good integration of the *fonctionnaire*, need for loyalty, and special characteristics of the *fonction publique*, e.g. principle of unity, statutory situations and establishment.

95 The Belgian and French government's arguments in case 149/79, *Commission* v. *Belgium*, [1980] ECR 3881, para. 20.

part of the public service, and cannot be invoked to justify discriminatory terms and conditions of employment,[96] a Member State is nevertheless free, under Community law, to restrict in-service promotion or transfer to 'protected' posts,[97] i.e. posts that do fall within the public service exception.

Member States have argued for the exclusion of non-nationals from posts which do not at the outset involve any participation in the exercise of powers conferred by public law if a non-national who has been recruited to a post is then eligible for a career which in the higher grades involves duties and responsibilities involving the exercise of powers conferred by public law.[98] Likewise, Member States have maintained that such an exclusion is necessitated by the fact that flexibility in assignment to posts is a characteristic of the public service and the duties and responsibilities of an employee may consequently change, not only on promotion, but also after a transfer within the same branch, or to a different branch at the same level.[99]

Responding to these arguments, the Court has held that Article 39 (4) (ex Article 48 (4)) allows Member States to reserve for their nationals by appropriate rules entry to posts involving the exercise of such powers and such responsibilities. Replying to the argument that any exclusion of nationals of other Member States from promotion or transfer to certain posts in the public service would have the effect of creating discrimination within such a service, the Court observed that this would have the effect of totally debarring those nationals from posts in the public service. This would involve a restriction on the rights of such nationals which goes further than is necessary to ensure the objective of Article 39 (4) (ex Article 48 (4)). It is clear that the Court's ruling on this matter is an application of the principle of proportionality.

The Court's approach is coherent. By allowing the Member States to reserve for their own nationals those posts which do meet the criteria for the application of Article 39 (4) (ex Article 48 (4)), the Court has effectively safeguarded the legitimite interests of the States. At the same time, by ruling that the exclusion of non-nationals from promotion or transfer on this account should not constitute grounds for total exclusion from the public service, the Court has focused on the exceptional nature of Article 39 (4) (ex Article 48 (4)), and has avoided the temptation of allowing specific difficulties to have an influence on, or indeed replace, the general rule.

---

96 See: case 152/73, *Sotgiu* and case 225/85, *Commission* v. *Italy*.

97 See: case 149/79, *Commission* v. *Belgium* and case 225/85, *Commission* v. *Italy*.

98 Arguments of the Belgian and French Governments in case 149/79, *Commission* v. *Belgium* [1980] ECR 3881, para. 20.

99 Arguments of the German and British Governments, ibid.

5.2 What is the functional approach?

As early as during its first case on Article 39 (4) (ex Article 48 (4)), case 152/73, *Sotgiu*, the European Court made it plain that the exception only applied to *certain* activities in what is broadly known as the public service. In case 149/79, *Commission* v. *Belgium*, it noted that, in various states, public authorities had assumed responsibilities of an economic or social nature or were involved in activities which were not typical of the historical concept of the public service. To exclude posts which did not involve any association with tasks belonging to the public service in this more limited sense would exclude a considerable number of posts from the principle of free movement. It would also bring about inequalities between Member States, reflecting differences in the organisation of the state and sectors of economic life. Although Article 39 (4) (ex Article 48 (4)) took account of national public service structures and constitutional provisions, the demarcation of the concept of public service could not be left to the Member States.

Although the principle of a functional approach has been firmly established, its content is still far from clear. What is clear, however, is that the Article 39 (4) (ex Article 48 (4)) exception demands a special relationship of allegiance to the state. It is probable that the higher echelons of the civil service, the police, and the army, navy and air force and judicial appointments can indeed be confined to nationals. However, more mundane tasks do not fall within the notion of the public service simply because the state happens to be the employer.[100]

In order to get an idea of the content of the functional approach, another look at the case law is warranted.

In case 152/73, *Sotgiu*, the Commission argued that the exception covered activities connected, directly or indirectly, with the exercise of public authority. This included activities which involved state secrets or national security. In the same case, Advocate General Mayras argued that it covered the direct exercise of official authority (that is, involving a power of discretion with regard to individuals) *or* posts which had to be reserved for nationals on grounds of internal security or defence.

In its pleadings in case 149/79, *Commission* v. *Belgium*, the Commission argued that the exception should be limited to direct participation in the exercise of official authority.[101] Finally, in his Opinion in that case, Advocate General Mayras referred to posts directly or indirectly connected with the exercise, if only occasionally, of prerogatives or powers conferred by public law.

---

[100] Weatherill & Beaumont, pp. 500/501.

[101] In its reasoned opinion, it appears, however, to have adopted the test of Advocate General Mayras in case 152/73, *Sotgiu*, [1974] ECR 153, p. 167.

Another issue has been how to treat those posts where the actual exercise of public authority is marginal or ancillary to an otherwise non-protected post. This point was brought up with regard to the local authority posts in case 149/79, *Commission* v. *Belgium*,[102] the nurses in case 307/84, who could authorise allowances charged to the budget of the State or local authority,[103] and the trainee teachers in case 66/85, where day-to-day disciplinary measures were not considered to be central to the teacher's task.[104]

The European Court has not specifically dealt with the question, except to state, in case 307/84, *Commission* v. *France*, that the functional criterion had to take account of the nature of the tasks and the responsibilities which are *inherent* in the posts. Both the Commission[105] and Advocate General Lenz[106] invoked the principle of proportionality when dealing with this issue. Advocate General Mancini[107] and the Commission[108] saw the question as one of severability. They stated that if the ancillary functions are indeed to remain 'protected', the solution is to reallocate them.

5.3 Civil servants versus contractual employees

The European Court has held that the description and legal status of the employee is irrelevant.[109] The crucial point, emphasised by the Court in all the cases, is that a state cannot, by treating a given post as covered by public law, defeat the need for a uniform interpretation throughout the Community. What is critical is the activity involved in a given post.

As far as the public service exception is concerned the differentiation between civil servants and contractual employees is significant, as it is difficult to argue that a function is worthy of protection where it can be exercised by a non-national enjoying a contractual status.

One of the arguments used to justify the institutional rather than the functional approach is the consideration that nationals of other Member States can in fact occupy posts in the public administration. However, not as established

[102] By the Commission.

[103] By Advocate General Mancini and the Commission which both saw the question in terms of the principle of proportionality.

[104] Advocate General Lenz, applying the proportionality principle.

[105] In case 307/84, *Commission* v. *France*.

[106] In case 66/85, *Lawrie-Blum*.

[107] In case 307/84, *Commission* v. *France*.

[108] In case 149/79, *Commission* v. *Belgium*.

[109] Case 152/73, *Sotgiu*, and case 307/84, *Commission* v. *France*.

officials or civil servants, but rather as agents under contract, normally governed by public law.

The Court has given its opinion on this issue in a number of cases, including case 152/73, *Sotgiu*, and case 33/88, *Allué & Coonan*, but is was most explicit in case 307/84, *Commission* v. *France*, and 225/85, *Commission* v. *Italy*.

In *Commission* v. *France*,[110] attention should be drawn to the very unusual manner in which the Court proceeded. After having determined that the post of nurses in public hospitals fell outside the scope of Article 39 (4) (ex Article 48 (4)), rather than simply conclude with this finding and refer it back to the national court, the Court proceeded to inquire whether the contested French nationality requirement led to discrimination of the kind prohibited by Article 39 (2) (ex Article 48 (2)) EC. On the face of it, the reason for this was to deal with the French Government's claim that access to employment as a nurse in public hospitals was open to the nationals of other Member States as they could be recruited as employees under contract as opposed to members of the established staff. At the material time, French public hospitals employeed 89,000 nurses of whom 86,000 were established in their posts and 3,000 were employees under contract. Fewer than 5% of the employees under contract were nationals of other Member States.[111]

The Court rejected the argument of the French Government because it had not 'established that all posts as nurses offered in public hospitals were equally accessible to the nationals of other Member States and that when such nationals were recruited they enjoyed conditions - with the exception of the possibility of promotion to posts in the public service within the meaning of the treaty -, advantages and safeguards which were in every respect equivalent to those deriving from the status of members of the established staff, which is reserved to French nationals.'[112]

In the *Lawrie-Blum*[113] case the numbers of teachers employed in *Gymnasien* in the *Land* Baden-Württemberg in the 1984/1985 school year were as follows: 18,248 teachers had civil servant status as opposed to 651 teachers who did not. There were 1269 trainee teachers and 1894 teachers in private schools.[114] As a general rule, only teachers who were civil servants were employed in State schools; teachers who were not civil servants were employed only in special cases. In other *Länder* it was possible for nationals of other Member States to be admitted to preparatory service and they could be allowed to take the teacher's examination.

---

[110] Case 307/84, [1986] ECR 1725.

[111] Ibid., para. 9.

[112] Ibid., para. 16.

[113] Case 66/85, [1986] ECR 2121.

[114] Opinion of Advocate General Lenz in case 66/85, [1986] ECR 2121, p. 2126.

Several authors[115] have suggested that the approach taken by the Court in this case (although benign as regards the result here) is in fact a dangerous one to take for the following reason. Had France indeed been able to show that nationals of other Member States were recruited as nurses under contract and they enjoyed conditions, advantages and safeguards which were in every aspect equivalent to those deriving from the status of members of the established staff, then it is clear that the Court would have found that there had been no discrimination.

This approach in this way differs radically from the Court's earlier case law. In effect this judgment would seem to make it possible for a Member State to exclude nationals of other Member States from employment in what it designated as the public service, but which does not fall within the ambit of the exclusion contained in Article 39 (4) (ex Article 48 (4)) as interpreted by the Court. This would be allowed provided the Member State also created a separate category of posts, giving rise to employment on a different basis, probably governed by private law contracts, for non-nationals.

The question which arises is whether this really matters, because in order for such an arrangement to satisfy the requirements of the Court's judgment in *Commission* v. *France*, the employees working in that second category must enjoy the conditions, advantages and safeguards which are the same as those of 'proper' civil servants.

In my opinion, this does indeed matter. Even if no material difference results from the fact that a post in the public sector is only open to non-nationals on a different basis to that in the case of nationals of the host state at the present time,[116] such a difference may appear in the future. Over and above the possibility of future differences, there is usually an inherent difference between the duration of established posts and contractual ones. Established posts can be filled for life by the same person, whereas contractual posts are usually only filled for a set period, even though there is the possibility of extensions to that first period many times over. But most of all, such an approach destroys the principle that all posts within the Community should be available to any Community national, subject to the exceptions contained in Article 39 (3) and (4) (ex Article 48 (3) and (4)), which must be interpreted strictly. The approach implied by the Court in case 307/84, *Commission* v. *France*, would add another possible exception. Even though the consequences for the individual migrant contractual worker may not be substantially unfavourable when compared to that of a civil servant (though one should bear in mind my earlier comments regarding the finite duration of contractual appointments), it would represent a

---

115 O'Keeffe (1992b), p. 101.

116 For example, the difference between established and contractual posts for nurses in public hospitals as in case 307/84, *Commission* v. *France*.

tetrograde step in the sense that it partitions the labour market and makes it less transparent.[117]

Unfortunately, the Court continued its reasoning used in case 307/84, *Commission* v. *France*, concerning the issue of the different status of contractual employees/non-nationals, in case 225/85, *Commission* v. *Italy*.[118] The case concerned discrimination as regards job security, promotion prospects, pay and pensions in the case of researchers who were nationals of other Member States working for the *Consiglio nazionale delle ricerche* (National Research Council).

The approach which the Court took in this case is as follows. In its case law the Court introduced the notion of discrimination under Article 39 (2) (ex Article 48 (2)), which may be justified by Article 39 (4) (ex Article 48 (4)). Both in case 307/84, *Commission* v. *France* and case 225/85, *Commission* v. *Italy*, employment in the disputed professions was not entirely closed to non-nationals, but they were given a different status compared to the nationals of the host State. As a result the Court enquired whether non-nationals do not in fact enjoy advantages and guarantees equivalent to those deriving from the status of the host State's own nationals. The Court's approach to this problem of different statuses has been summarised as determining that 'any distinction had to be one without a difference'.[119]

On the whole the case law imposes a heavy burden on the Member States. It is up to them to ensure that non-national employees can enter posts which do not meet the conditions for the application of Article 39 (4) (ex Article 48 (4)), but are barred from entering those posts which do, and which Member States can legitimately reserve for their own nationals. As a result, Member States must examine the position of the non-national at each stage of his/her career, whether concerning promotion, transfer or the alteration of the job description, so as to ensure that the non-national is not admitted to a post which the Member State considers unsuitable for non-nationals and which falls within the meaning of Article 39 (4) (ex Article 48 (4)) EC.

Some posts will be very difficult to classify. Indeed, this has always been one of the crucial points, as far as the Member States are concerned, who have shown a preference for the institutional approach, as it is more workable in respect of the possibilities of promotion, transfer, etc. However, according to the Court this is the price to be paid for the public service exception and the effective working of the EC Treaty and one of its fundamental freedoms, namely the free movement and equality of treatment of workers. One could consider it a necessary evil in seeking to balance the legitimate interests of the Member States with the principle of non-discrimination.[120]

---

[117] O'Keeffe (1992b), pp. 101/102.

[118] [1987] ECR 2625.

[119] Handoll (1998) p. 228.

[120] O'Keeffe (1992b), p. 104.

5.4 The cumulative versus alternative approach

As we have seen before in case 149/79, *Commission* v. *Belgium*, the European Court decided that the exception covered 'a series of posts which involve direct or indirect participation in the exercise of powers conferred by public law and duties designed to safeguard the general interests of the state or of other public authorities. Such posts in fact presume on the part of those occupying them the existence of a special relationship of allegiance to the state and reciprocity of rights and duties which form the foundation of the bond of nationality.'[121]

Ever since the Court phrased this now well-known sentence, it has been unclear whether the conditions of 'exercise of powers conferred by public law' and 'duties designed to safeguard the general interests of the State' are alternative or cumulative.

The Commission[122] and Advocates General Mancini[123] and Lenz[124] have all argued for a cumulative interpretation. Advocate General Mancini has gone so far as to suggest that the occupants of protected posts 'must don full battle dress; in non-metaphorical terms, the duties must involve acts of will which affect individuals by requiring their obedience or in the event of disobedience, by compelling them to comply.'[125]

However, with its judgment in case 225/85, *Commission* v. *Italy*, the European Court appeared to opt for the alternative approach and seemed to reject the cumulative view. The Court stated that two types of function could be covered by the exception, namely those of management of a public body and those advising the state on scientific and technical questions. The second category does not appear to involve the direct or indirect exercise of public law powers, but it is likely to be covered by the second criterion of safeguarding the general interests of the State.

As a result of this judgment it was generally thought that the issue had been settled in favour of the alternative approach. However, in the next case the Court seemed to have implicitly returned to the cumulative approach. In case 33/88, *Allué & Coonan*,[126] it once again used 'and' instead of 'or'. In this case the Court refers to case 66/85 *Lawrie-Blum* and repeats that 'a teaching post does not involve direct or indirect participation in the exercise of powers conferred by public law *and* in the discharge of functions whose purpose is to safeguard the

[121] [1980] ECR 3881, para. 10.

[122] In case 307/84, *Commission* v. *France*, case 66/85, *Lawrie-Blum*, and case 225/85, *Commission* v. *Italy*.

[123] In case 307/84, *Commission* v. *France*.

[124] In case 66/85, *Lawrie-Blum*, and case 225/85, *Commission* v. *Italy*.

[125] The Advocate General's Opinion in case 307/84, *Commission* v. *France*, [1986] ECR 1725, para. 5.

[126] [1989] ECR 1591.

general interests of the state or of other public authorities and which therefore require a special relationship of allegiance to the state on the part of persons occupying them and reciprocity of rights and duties which form the foundation of the bond of nationality.'[127]

In case C-4/91, *Bleis*,[128] the Court reiterated its decisions in case 66/85, *Lawrie-Blum*, and case 33/88, *Allué & Coonan*, in which it decided that teachers are not covered by article 48 (4) using the 'and' construction like it had in the two earlier cases.

In three more recent cases, the 'and' construction can be found again and again, but the same is also true for the 'or' construction. However, in my opinion it is significant that the Court only uses 'or' when the sentence is constructed in the negative sense. This is the case in all three judgments, for instance in case C-473/93, *Commission* v. *Luxembourg*:[129] 'The Court observes in this regard that, as the Luxembourg Government itself admits, the generality of posts in the areas of research, health, inland transport, postal services and telecommunications and in the water, gas and electricity supply services are remote from the specific activities of the public service because they do *not* involve direct *or* indirect participation in the exercise of powers conferred by public law or duties designed to safeguard the general interests of the State or of other public authorities' [JEB: emphasis added].

Virtually the same sentence can be found in case C-173/94, *Commission* v. *Belgium*.[130] In the third case in this set, case C-290/94, *Commission* v. *Greece*, the Court also uses 'nor' instead of 'or', which in my opinion confirms the fact that the sentences are worded in the negative and this can be considered to be significant.

The conclusion that can be drawn from the Court's case law on the whole is that it prefers the cumulative to the alternative approach and in that sense case 225/85 *Commission* v. *Italy* can be seen as an abberation. However, I hasten to add that the Court has not made a firm commitment either way and could change its mind again in the future.

---

[127] Ibid., para. 7.

[128] [1991] ECR I-5627.

[129] [1996] ECR I-3207, para. 31.

[130] [1996] ECR I-3265, para. 17.

5.5 Posts included in the exception

In its case law the Court has been more specific concerning posts which are *not* covered, than concerning those which are. However it stated that the following posts fall within the public service exception.

In case 149/79, *Commission* v. *Belgium*, the Commission accepted that local authority posts for architects, supervisors and some night-watchmen were covered by the exception. The Court considered that the Commission was correct in finding as it did as the posts 'may have characteristics which bring them within the scope of the exception.' [131]

The Court did not specify on what basis it excluded these posts. Belgium had argued that architects were involved in the supervision of public buildings. They may also have had access to confidential plans. The supervisors presumably exercised some degree of authority, though to what extent this went beyond a private employment relationship is uncertain. The Commission included those night-watchmen whose 'occupation of watching over buildings or premises needed to be guarded may give them easy access to the secrets of the public authority concerned'.

In case 225/85, *Commission* v. *Italy*, the European Court mentioned the following posts as those which could be covered by the exception: management (of a public body) and advising the state on scientific and technical questions.

5.6 Posts not included in the exception

As stated above, it is far easier to say which posts are *not* covered by the exception. In case 149/79, *Commission* v. *Belgium*, the Court stated that railway workers could not be included in the exception, even though Belgium claimed that in a time of war or mobilisation, there was a need to avoid sabotage and espionage and to ensure regular and effective communication. The Court did not consider this an effective line of reasoning and stated that such a reasoning was based on 'an hypothesis which has no connection with the legal context of that provision'.[132]

In the same case the Court, without giving reasons for its decision, also stated that nurses and other local government employees were not included in the exception, although, according to Belgium, nurses performed administrative tasks and local government workers were generally expected to have a certain loyalty and to exercise a special discretion. Although the Court did not state

[131] Case 149/79 (II), *Commission* v. *Belgium II*, [1982] ECR 1845, para. 8.

[132] Ibid., para 10.

this specifically, it is likely that it followed the Commission's reasoning that any exercise of public law powers was marginal and ancillary to the principal functions of nursing, gardening, painting, and so forth.

Again, in case 307/84, *Commission* v. *France*, the Court decided, based on its arguments in case 149/79, *Commission* v. *Belgium*, that nurses were not covered by Article 39 (4) (ex Article 48 (4)).

In case 66/85, *Lawrie-Blum*, the Court decided that trainee teachers were not covered by the exception, even though in Germany, education occupied an eminent place amongst the missions of public authority.[133] The Court, referring to the 'very strict' conditions for exclusion, stated that the preparatory training for the teaching profession could not be treated as employment in the public service, even if the trainee awarded marks to pupils and participated in the decisions as to whether or not they should move to a higher class.[134]

In case 33/88, *Allué & Coonan*, the Court referred to its arguments in case 66/85, *Lawrie-Blum*. It reiterated that employment as a teacher, in general, and as a foreign-language assistant at a university, in particular, is not employment in the public service, since it does not involve direct or indirect participation in the exercise of powers conferred by public law and duties designed to safeguard the general interests of the state or of other public authorities. The Court came to the same conclusion regarding secondary school teachers in case C-4/91, *Bleis*.

In the three most recent cases brought by the Commission as part of its action plan, case C-473/93, *Commission* v. *Luxembourg*, case C-173/94, *Commission* v. *Belgium*, and case C-290/94, *Commission* v. *Greece*, the Court in all three cases looked at posts in the public bodies responsible for the distribution of water, gas and electricity. In case C-473/93, *Commission* v. *Luxembourg* it also looked at public sectors of research, education, health, inland transport, postal services and telecommunications. In addition, in case 290/94, *Commission* v. *Greece*, the Court included radio and television broadcasting services and musicians' posts at the Athens Opera and in municipal and local orchestras. It was only in the last case that the Court was confronted with an individual case, namely where the Athens Opera refused to engage a German musician on the ground of his nationality. The Court dealt with all these posts in one fell swoop by stating that each of the three Member States were in breach of their obligations under Article 39 (4) (ex Article 48 (4)) by excluding non-nationals from *all* posts in these sectors. Only the posts which were covered by the two

133 See Article 7 (1) of the German Constitution *(Grundgesetz)*.

134 It is a little surprising, in the context of an Article 234 (ex Article 177) procedure, that the European Court felt able to apply the law to the post of trainee teacher. Despite its theoretical position that it has 'no power to apply a rule of Community law to a particular case' (see, e.g. Case 137/84, *Ministère Public* v. *Mutsch* [1985] ECR 2681), it is often prepared to carry out some of the national court's work for it. It did so here, declining to develop the test in a way that could usefully be applied by the national court.

criteria laid down in the case law were allowed to have a nationality requirement. However, it was up to the Member State to prove that this is the case for each individual post in the sectors dealt with in these three cases. This is a clear case of shifting the burden of proof to the Member States.

5.7 The effect of the European Court's interpretation of the public service exception

The effect of falling within the exception is that a nationality requirement can be imposed. As the European Court said in case 149/79, *Commission* v. *Belgium*: 'the posts presume on the part of those occupying them the existence of a special relationship of allegiance to the state and reciprocity of rights and duties which form the foundation of the bond of nationality.'[135]

If the criteria used to interpret Article 39 (4) (ex Article 48 (4)) are to be applied cumulatively, as has been argued above, the Court has created a flexible rule which can be applied more narrowly if and when Community powers develop. This flexibility has its advantages: were the Court to formulate a precise and unambiguous test it could have the effect of holding back the process of integration. It also has drawbacks, however, in that it makes it more difficult to state succinctly which posts do and which do not fall within the exception.

Even though the Court has recognised the difficulty of appraisal and demarcation in specific cases, it has continued to apply the test as laid down in case 149/79, *Commission* v. *Belgium*. This test is whether the posts in question are 'typical' of the specific activities of the public service.

6 Further analysis of the European Court's approach

In its judgment in case 149/79 *Commission* v. *Belgium*[136], the Court laid down broad guidelines for the operation of the public service exception. The Court gave two criteria to define the notion of employment in the public service as set out in Article 39 (4) (ex Article 48 (4)) of the Treaty. According to the Court 'that provision removes from the ambit of Article 48 (1) to (3) a series of posts which involve direct or indirect participation in the exercise of powers conferred by public law and duties designed to safeguard the general interests of the State or of other public authorities'.[137] The Court explained that

---

[135] [1980] ECR 3881, para. 10.

[136] Case 149/79 [1980] ECR 3881.

[137] Ibid., para. 10.

'such posts in fact presume on the part of those occupying them the existence of a special relationship of allegiance to the State and reciprocity of rights and duties which form the foundation of the bond of nationality'.[138]

When deciding on the definition of public service as laid down in Article 39 (4) (ex Article 48 (4)) (i.e. 'posts which involve direct or indirect participation in the exercise of powers conferred by public law') the Court seems to have borrowed the wording of Article 45 (ex Article 55)[139] of the EC Treaty which excludes the application of the provisions on the right of establishment to 'activities which [...] are connected, even occasionally, with the exercise of official authority'. The second criterion, that such posts must involve duties designed to safeguard the general interests of the State or of other public authorities is a new criterion which cannot be found anywhere else in the EC Treaty.[140]

The Court's approach in adopting the two criteria should be noted because it avoids giving an abstract definition or a list of what may constitute posts involving the exercise of public authority. It relies on the very broad guidelines noted above and as a result is a flexible tool for the Court to work with. In practice it boils down to a post-by-post evaluation.

In relation to the first criterion, for example, no definition is given of 'exercise of powers'. Should the exclusion in this respect be limited to powers which have a coercive effect or should it apply more generally and include all powers which in one way or another affect the position of individuals? The Court seems to go beyond the 'martial' approach, so vividly advocated by Advocate General Mancini.[141] It is not just coercive powers which fall within the first criterion. The exception also includes discretionary powers affecting individuals in a financial sense, for example powers which are exercised in the welfare field. For instance, the decision whether or not to award a social security payment is covered when this constitutes a policy decision, rather than the mere application of existing rules and regulations.[142]

The meaning of '*indirect* participation in the exercise of public law powers' is also problematical. One could say that *anybody* working in an institution headed by somebody directly exercising public power could be considered to be indirectly participating in the exercise of official powers. In case 149/79, *Commission* v. *Belgium*, the European Court recognised the dangers of a 'through the back door' introduction of the institutional approach.[143] When studying the Court's case law, one can deduce that a more direct functional link with author-

---

[138] Ibid.

[139] See also paragraph 7.

[140] O'Keeffe (1992b), p. 93.

[141] In case 307/84, *Commission* v. *France*, Opinion of the Advocate General, [1986] ECR 1725, para. 5.

[142] Handoll (1988), pp. 234/235

[143] [1980] ECR 3881, para. 19.

ity is required in order for a post to fall within the public service exception as defined by the Court. On the whole, it is easier to exclude fairly obvious cases like manual workers,[144] than it is to define those who are to be included. According to Handoll, the test could be 'whether the task in question in itself enables or supports the activity of the individual who exercises direct power: this may, for example cover secretaries, personal assistants, clerks and doormen, but not painters, carpenters and cleaners'.[145]

In case 225/85, *Commission* v. *Italy*,[146] the Court indicated that those who advise the State on scientific and technical questions could be covered by the public service exception. The reason why advisory bodies, which do not exercise official powers themselves, can nevertheless be covered by the public service exception is because they may advise public bodies. Such advice could be crucial to the proper exercise of official powers and to the development of public policy in certain (sensitive) sectors. The use of the criterion which includes indirect participation in public law powers enables the key personnel of advisory bodies to be covered. This could explain the acceptance by the Court that the management of a research body advising the government as to key scientific matters could be covered by the exception.

Turning to the second criterion of 'safeguarding the general interests of the state' it should be noted that the Court has given no definition of the term 'general interests'. It seems appropriate to consider the question in the context of state functions. Successive Advocates General have used the notion of 'classical functions' as a starting point:[147] thus activities connected with the internal order (policing and justice), defence and diplomacy, as well as taxation are included.

One can also consider the difference between a state's functions which are laid down by law, and those which are considered to be a public duty and in the general interest of the state, as well as other activities which could just as easily be performed by private companies. The former functions can only be exercised by the state or a state body, but the latter group is not restricted to state bodies only. This distinction is also made, for instance, when considering whether a decentralised government body can be prosecuted for a criminal offence in the Netherlands.[148] The *Hoge Raad* (Dutch Supreme Court) here drew the distinction between decentralised government exercising functions laid down by law and considered to be part of the public duty (in which case, broadly speaking, a criminal prosecution could not be brought) and activities of a more commercial nature. Once again the defining criterion seems be whether the state body is

---

144 Except maybe manual workers in highly sensitive areas, for example in the armed forces.

145 Handoll (1988), p. 235.

146 [1987] ECR 2625, para. 9.

147 See AG Mayras in Case 152/73 *Sotgiu* and AG Mancini in Case 307/84 *Commission* v. *France*.

148 *Pikmeer-II* case, Hoge Raad, 6 January 1998, NJ 1998/367.

working in the general interests of the state or pursuing a more commercial goal.

The 'classical' functions of the state are a useful starting point because they are the hard core of reserved powers and the need for loyalty on the part of the individual towards the state is particularly crucial in these fields. The Court seems to accept that the idea of 'general interests' goes beyond the 'classical' ones of defence, internal order and tax collection so as to include scientific and other more general interests.[149] It remains an open question whether educational and cultural interests can be protected. It must be emphasised, however, that in case 225/85, *Commission* v. *Italy*, the Court limited itself to advisory positions, which involve a link with policy formulation. The position of posts which do not involve this kind of advisory function is less certain. The second criterion is also likely to cover occupations which involve a security risk. Here low-grade jobs could well be covered by the exception.[150]

References to 'general interests of the state' in the case law on Article 39 (4) (ex Article 48 (4)) should not only be seen as a limiting criterion within the public service exception. At the same time, it is also a guarantee to the Member State that functions which are characterised as being essential to national state interests (in relation to the Community) are protected. The exception can therefore be extended to areas recognised as constitutionally central to the existence of Member States.[151] The introduction by the Maastricht Treaty of the Article on the principle of subsidiarity into the EC Treaty (Article 5 (ex Article 3b)), as well as the recognition of the need to retain national indentities (Article 6 (ex Article F) of the Treaty on European Union) are proof of the fact that the national interests of the Member States are respected by the EC institutions. The tendency to delineate more clearly the respective competences of the EU and those retained by the Member States also points to the need to protect their 'national interest' in areas such as education and culture.

It should be remembered that, when it comes to the use of the public service exception, national interests can to a certain extent be protected by insisting on the satisfaction of conditions other than possession of the nationality of the state concerned. Member States are still free to insist on the possession of the necessary occupational and professional qualifications. However, since the entry into force of the Directive on the recognition of higher-education diplomas[152] and

[149] Case 225/85, *Commission* v. *Italy*.

[150] For example, cleaners in military establishments and central government departments; see case 149/79, *Commission* v. *Belgium* [1980 ECR 3881.

[151] Handoll (1995), pp. 237/238.

[152] Council Directive 89/48 on a general system for the recognition of higher-education diplomas awarded on completion of professional education and training of at least three years' duration, OJ 1989 L19/6.

more specific directives on this topic, it has become more and more difficult to exclude applicants on the grounds of not having the necessary national diploma when they have an equivalent foreign diploma.

General knowledge and linguistic requirements can also be imposed to the extent that they are necessary for a given post.[153] However, these requirements must not be so strict as to make it impossible for a non-national to satisfy them. Once again proportionality plays a role here. Whether or not such necessary requirements will continue to form a real barrier to working abroad within the Union will to a certain extent a reflect on whether or not a feeling of community at the European level develops. That is to say, whether or not nationals from another Member State will make the necessary effort to integrate into the host society.[154]

And lastly, the possibilities of derogation under Article 39 (3) (ex Article 48 (3)), which were discussed in Chapter 2[155] should not be forgotten. These can, however, only be used where an individual's personal *conduct* justifies such an exception and thus can never apply to him/her not having the right nationality as such.

7 Comparison with Article 45 (ex Article 55) EC

Article 45 (ex Article 55) of the EC Treaty provides that the Treaty provisions on the right of establishment and the freedom to provide services 'shall not apply, so far as any given Member State is concerned, to activities which in that State are connected, even occasionally, with the exercise of official authority.' As with Article 39 (4) (ex Article 48 (4)), this exception to the fundamental right of free movement has been interpreted strictly.

In case 2/74, *Reyners*,[156] the Court considered the application of Article 45 (1) (ex Article 55 (1)) to the activities of a Belgian *avocat* (lawyer). The Court, noting that Article 45 (1) (ex Article 55 (1)) was an exception to the fundamental right of establishment and the rule of equal treatment with nationals, stated that it could not be given scope which would exceed the objective for which it had been inserted. It considered that the objective of Article 45 (1) (ex Article 55 (1)) was fully satisfied, where the exclusion of non-nationals was limited to those activities which, in themselves, constituted a direct and specific connection with the exercise of official authority.

153 See the proviso to Article 3 para. 1 of Regulation 1612/68 which provides that the non-applicability of national provisions restricting the employment opportunities of non-nationals 'shall not apply to conditions relating to linguistic knowledge required by reason of the nature of the post to be filled.'

154 Handoll (1988), p. 236.

155 Para. 3 of Chapter 2.

156 [1974] ECR 631, paras. 33-55.

In considering whether Article 45 (1) (ex Article 55 (1)) could cover the whole of a given profession, the Court held that this could only be so where the activities were linked within the profession in such a way that the freedom of establishment would result in imposing on the Member State concerned the obligation to allow the exercise by non-nationals of functions appertaining to official authority. This could only be so where, within the framework of an independent profession, activities connected with the exercise of official authority were seperable from the professional activities taken as a whole.

In considering the application of Article 45 (1) (ex Article 55 (1)) to the profession in question, that of *avocat*, the Court stated that, in the absence of a harmonising directive, the practice of the profession continued to be governed by the various national laws. The application of Article 45 (1) (ex Article 55 (1)) had to be considered separately for each Member State having regard to the character of the limits under Article 45 (1) (ex Article 55 (1)) in order to avoid unilateral Member State provisions from defeating the effectiveness of the Treaty.[157]

On this basis, the Court treated the relevant authority as the judicial authority and considered the functions of *avocat* in the context of this authority. It considered that professional activities involving contacts, even regular and organic, with the courts including compulsory co-operation between courts and *avocats* did not constitute, as such, a connection with the exercise of official authority.[158] Applying this general rule to the activities of an *avocat*, it held that the most typical activities of this profession (consultation and legal assistance together with representation and defence in court) could not, even where the intervention or assistance of the *avocat* was compulsory or was a legal monopoly, be considered as connected with the exercise of official authority.[159] The exercise of these activities left the discretion of the judicial authority and the free exercise of judicial powers intact.[160]

In *Commission* v. *Greece*,[161] the Commission brought an action under Article 226 (ex Article 169) for a declaration that the Hellenic Republic had failed to fulfil its obligations under the EEC Treaty (as it then was) by not adopting within the prescribed period the laws, regulations and administrative provisions necessary to comply with Council Directive 82/470/EEC of 29 June 1982 on measures to facilitate the effective exercise of freedom of establishment and freedom to provide services in respect of the activities of self-employed persons in certain services incidental to transport and travel agencies and in storage and warehousing.

---

[157] Ibid., para. 40.

[158] Ibid., para. 52.

[159] Ibid., para. 55.

[160] Handoll (1995), p. 242.

[161] Case C-306/89, [1991] ECR I-5863, mainly paras. 6-7.

Greece claimed that the activity of traffic accident expert formed part of the exercise of official authority within the meaning of Article 45 (ex Article 55) of the EEC Treaty and that, accordingly, it was not required to adopt the measures laid down by the Directive with regard to that activity. However, the experts' reports concerning traffic accidents were not binding on the Greek courts. The reports left the discretion of the judicial authority and the free exercise of judicial power intact. According to the Court, the activities of the experts could therefore not be regarded as participating in the exercise of official authority within the meaning of Article 45 (ex Article 55) of the EEC Treaty.[162]

The condition that activities covered by Article 45 (ex Article 55) should have a 'direct and specific connection with the exercise of official authority' was considered in case C-3/88 *Commission* v. *Italy*.[163] Italian rules provided that only companies in public ownership could develop data-processing systems for the public authorities. The Court held that the activities in question, which concerned the design, programming and operation of data-processing systems, were of a technical nature and thus were unrelated to the exercise of official authority.[164]

In a later case brought by the Commission against Italy, case C-272/91,[165] the distinction between technical operations and elements involving the exercise of official authority was maintained in relation to an invitation to tender, limited to companies in public ownership, for the concession of an automatisation for the Italian State lottery. In that case the Court decided that Article 43 (ex Article 52) EC on freedom of establishment and Article 49 (ex Article 59) EC on freedom to provide services had been infringed because Italy had restricted participation in a contract for the concession of the lottery computerisation system to bodies the majority of whose capital was held by the public sector. The contract related to the premises, supplies, installations, maintenance, operation and transmission of data and everything else that is necessary for operating the lottery. It did not involve any transfer of responsibility to the concessionaire for the various activities inherent in the lottery.[166] The lottery collectors were responsible for accepting bets and the function of the concessionaire's terminal was merely to register, automatically check and transmit the data resulting from the steps taken by the person managing the registration point. As a result the derogation laid down in Article 45 (ex Article 55) regarding activities connected with the exercise of official authority did not apply.

---

[162] Ibid., para. 7 (the Court refers to the *Reyner* case).

[163] Case C-3/88, *Commission* v. *Italy*, [1989] ECR 4035, para. 13.

[164] Handoll (1995), p. 243.

[165] *Commission* v. *Italy*, [1994] ECR I-1409, para 12.

[166] Ibid., para. 24.

In case 147/86, *Commission* v. *Greece*,[167] the Court considered an argument that the operation of private 'cramming schools' and vocational training schools together with the giving of private lessons at home fell under Article 45 (ex Article 55) of the EC Treaty. The Court held that, whilst it was for each Member State to determine the role of, and the responsibilities attaching to, official authority in relation to training, the fact that private individuals set up such schools or provided such teaching was not connected with the exercise of official authority under Article 45 (ex Article 55).[168] These *private* activities were subject to supervision by official authorities which could ensure the protection of the interests entrusted to them without the need to restrict freedom of establishment.[169]

In case C-114/97, *Commission* v. *Spain*[170] the Court dealt with nationality conditions imposed on private security undertakings. The Spanish Government defended the national requirements by stating that the activities of such undertakings were covered by the exception as laid down in Article 45 (ex Article 55) EC, since the purpose of such private security undertakings was to maintain public security. According to the Spanish Government, maintaining public security involved the exercise of official authority within the meaning of Article 45 (ex Article 55) EC.[171] The Court did not agree and stated that since the Spanish legislation made clear distinctions between tasks entrusted to security undertakings and security staff, and those reserved to public security forces, the former being strictly auxiliary in nature, it followed that private security undertakings and private security staff were not directly and specifically involved in the exercise of official authority.[172]

8 Conclusions

It is clear from the Court's case law on Article 39 (4) (ex Article 48 (4)) that primacy is given to the principle of free movement of workers. One explanation for the European Court's approach is that it considers the worker to be more than just a worker; he is an 'embryonic Community citizen'.[173]

Article 39 (4) (ex Article 48 (4)) operates in the context of a Community where the Member States continue to have exclusive competence in many impor-

---

[167] [1988] ECR 1637, paras. 8-10.

[168] Ibid., para. 9.

[169] Ibid., para. 10.

[170] [1998] ECR I-6717; see also above, paragraph 3.11.

[171] Ibid., para. 26.

[172] Ibid., paras. 38 and 39.

[173] Handoll (1988), p. 240.

tant policy areas. At the same time it made clear that Community measures such as the rules of free movement can affect these national policies. The Court has acted in a similar spirit in defining the scope of Article 39 (4) (ex Article 48 (4)). It has, as we have seen, refused to apply the exception in the fields of education, health, scientific research and operational services in local government.

Nevertheless, even with a functional interpretation, the exception presupposes the existence of a nation state and the continued existence of national loyalties and national interests. The 'classical' activities of the State remain largely untouched by Community competence.

CHAPTER 5

The Concept of the State in Two Other Areas of European Law

1 Introduction

As we have seen in the previous chapter, when it comes to the public service exception the concept of public service (in other words, 'the state') is given a very narrow interpretation.

One of the leading cases in the field of Article 39 (4) (ex Article 48 (4)) is case 149/79, *Commission* v. *Belgium*[1]. In this case the European Court of Justice held that the exception must be interpreted restrictively as covering only 'posts involving the exercise of official powers conferred by public law and the conferment of responsibilities for safeguarding the general interests of the State'.[2]

Though it is obvious that the concept of public services for the purposes of Article 39 (4) (ex Article 48 (4)) EC is narrow, it is also obvious that the concept itself is far from clear, in the sense that the boundary of what falls within this definition and what does not is not at all evident. The question which arises is whether this is surprising or whether, when looking at other concepts of 'the state' within Community law, this is more or less to be expected.

As we shall see in this chapter, who or what is considered to be an organ of the state for the purposes of Community law depends to a great extent on the provisions of Community legislation which rule the facts of the case.[3] If it is a case dealing with the direct effect of directives, then the body involved can quite easily fall within the meaning of 'emanation of the state'. When the Court is dealing with an exception to one of the fundamental principles of the common market, namely the principle of free movement of persons, then the interpretation of what a body of the state is will be narrower. In other words, there is not one single interpretation of '(organ of) the state' in Community law, but there are in fact several.

In this chapter I want to look at two different fields of Community law where the concepts of 'the state' or 'emanation/organ of the state' are central to the interpretation of the provisions involved. This is to illustrate the different ways in which the concept of the state is interpreted in Community law and can perhaps help us to decide whether the confusion over the concept of the public service as laid down in Article 39 (4) (ex Article 48 (4)) EC is in any way surprising or unique.

---

1 Case 149/79, [1980] ECR 3881.

2 Ibid., para. 10.

3 See also: Jans, J.(*et al.*), *Inleiding tot het Europees Bestuursrecht* (Ars Aequi Libri, Nijmegen, 1999), pp. 110 ff.

2 Direct effect of directives

The case law concerning emanations of the state when it comes to the direct effect of directives is different from the case law on the public service exception even though both deal with organs of the state. This is because both concepts serve different aims. Whereas, as we have seen, the concept of the state is interpreted narrowly for the public service exception, it is interpreted very broadly for the purposes of the direct effect of directives.

In order to explain the differences in the interpretation of 'the state' we have to look at the history of the European Community. One of the doctrines of Community law as interpreted by the European Court of Justice is that the Community constitutes a 'new legal order' which confers rights on individuals. In the *Van Gend en Loos* case[4] the Court stated that certain provisions of Community law are directly effective in that they create 'individual rights which national courts must protect' without the need for implementing legislation from a Member State.[5] This ruling had far-reaching effects because it meant that Community law overrules national law. It also meant that Member State governments could not negate Community legislation simply by not implementing it. It was now up to national courts to also take into consideration any and all applicable Community law provisions.

This ability for individuals to rely on Community law before their national courts is crucial to the effectiveness and enforceability of Community law. National courts can quickly apply directly effective provisions of Community law and make use of their powers to enforce their orders. Such powers include awards for damages, for example.[6]

This enforceability is something which the Court considers to be important. When making decisions in cases before it, more often than not the Court will strive for the maximum effectiveness of Community law.[7] The search for effectiveness is one of the underlying reasons for the direct effect of directives.

---

4 Case 26/62, [1963] ECR 1.

5 Ibid., para. 5.

6 Weatherill, S. & Beaumont, P., *EC Law* (Penguin Books, London, 1993), p. 289.

7 E.g, in case 106/77, *Amministrazione delle Finanze dello Stato* v. *Simmenthal SpA*, [1978] ECR 629, para. 17, the European Court stated that directly effective provisions of Community law render inapplicable any conflicting provision of national law. In case C-213/89, *R* v. *Secretary of State for Transport, ex parte Factortame*, [1990] ECR I-2433, para. 21, the Court stressed the need for effective remedies at the national level, requiring national systems to provide for remedies of interim relief. In joined cases C-6 and C-9/90 *Francovich and others* v. *Italy*, [1991] ECR I-5357, paras. 33-35, the Court ruled that a Member State is obliged to make good any damages to individuals arising from the non-implementation of a directive.

2.1 Conditions for the direct effect of Community law

Not all provisions laid down in secondary Community legislation are directly effective. There are two main conditions which have to be satisfied in order for a Community law provision to have direct effect. In the *Becker* case the Court explained that the provisions of directives are directly effective wherever they 'appear, as far as their subject-matter is concerned, to be unconditional and sufficiently precise'[8]. From this decision we can distil two conditions. I will briefly discuss these conditions.

Firstly, the provision has to be *unconditional*, which means that the right which it grants is not dependent on the judgment or discretion of a Community institution or a Member State.[9]

The second criterion for direct effectiveness is that the provision must be *sufficiently precise*. The question of sufficient precision seems to point to whether or not the provision in question provides 'workable indications for the national court'.[10]

These two conditions for direct effectiveness apply to all Community legislation, however due to the very nature of directives, namely that they need to be implemented into national law, there are other conditions which must be met before the conditions of the directive being 'unconditional and sufficiently precise' come into play. Firstly, it must be established that the Member State concerned has not implemented the directive at all, or not in time, or that it has done so incorrectly.[11] Secondly, the period for implementation must have expired. It is only after it has been established that the Member State has been unable or unwilling to implement the directive correctly or within the time period provided that there is a need for the direct effect of the directive.

2.2 The reasons for the direct effect of directives

Soon after the case law of the Court of Justice on the direct effect of Treaty provisions started to develop, the question was raised whether directives could have direct effect.

Based on the text of Article 249 (ex Article 189) of the EC Treaty one could be forgiven for concluding that directives cannot have direct effect. Article 249

---

8 Case 8/81, [1982] ECR 53, para. 13.

9 For the definition of the term 'unconditional', see: Prechal, S., *Directives in European Community Law* (Clarendon Press/ Oxford Press, Oxford, 1995), pp. 282-284.

10 Pescatore, P., 'The Doctrine of "Direct Effect": An Infant Disease of Community Law', 8 *European Law Review* (1983), p. 175. For a definition of the term 'sufficiently precise', see also: Prechal, S., ibid., p. 281.

11 Case 8/81, *Becker* v. *Finanzamt Munster-Innenstadt*, [1982] ECR 53, para. 25.

(ex Article 189) states that 'a Directive shall be binding, as to the result to be achieved, upon each Member State to which it is addressed, but shall leave to the national authorities the choice of form and methods.' This means that only Member States are the addressees of a directive.

This brings us to the question of emanations of the state. The problem has surfaced in a few areas of EC law, but nowhere as prominently as in cases concerning the direct effect of directives. This is because the direct effect of directives can only be relied upon against a Member State and not against individuals. Therefore the question of whether or not we are dealing with an emanation of the state becomes a crucial one.

It was in case 41/71, *Van Duyn* v. *Home Office*,[12] that the Court established that directives could have direct effect. Its main reason for this decision was that the useful effect of a directive would be 'weakened if individuals were prevented from relying on it before their national courts'.[13] In the *Ratti* case[14] the Court added another argument. It argued that 'a Member State which has not adopted the implementing measures required by the Directive in the prescribed periods may not rely, as against individuals, on its own failure to perform the obligations which the Directive entails'.[15] This is called the estoppel argument.

In the *Becker* case[16] the Court described the estoppel argument in the following terms: 'Particularly in cases in which the Community authorities have, by means of a directive, placed Member States under a duty to adopt a certain course of action, the effectiveness of such a measure would be diminished if persons were prevented from relying upon it in proceedings before a court and national courts were prevented from taking it into consideration as an element of Community law. Consequently, a Member State which has not adopted the implementing measures required by the directive within the prescribed period may not plead, as against individuals, its own failure to perform the obligations which the directive entails.'[17]

2.3 Case law

In order to get an impression of the concept of the state when it comes to the direct effect of a directive we have to take a look at the case law. In the *Becker*[18] case the body in question was a *Finanzamt* (tax office). There can be

12 [1974] ECR 1337.

13 Ibid., p. 1348.

14 Case 148/78, *Pubblico Ministero* v. *Ratti*, [1979] ECR 1629.

15 Ibid., p. 1642.

16 Case 8/81, [1982] ECR 53.

17 Ibid., paras. 23/24.

18 Case 8/81, [1982] ECR 53.

no doubt about a tax office being a state body. The same holds true for the *Ratti*[19] case which dealt with a claim against the *Pubblico Ministero*.

That public authorities providing health services are emanations of the state was made clear in the *Marshall* case.[20] In that case the UK's Court of Appeal had already stated in the order for reference that the Health Authority in question was a public authority. The European Court decided that there was no need to discuss that point any further.

In the *Marshall* case the following was stated by Advocate General Slynn in his Opinion: 'as a matter of Community law, ... the "state" must be taken broadly, as including all the organs of the state. In matters of employment ... this means all the employees of such organs and not just the central civil service'.[21] Therefore, it seems that when it comes to deciding on direct effect, the concept of emanation of the state is to be interpreted broadly.

That the Chief Constable of Police is also a state body is evident from the *Johnston* case.[22] The Court stated that, as regards Directive 76/207 on Equal Treatment of Men and Women, '[i]ndividuals may claim the application [of the principle of equal treatment], as against a state authority charged with the maintenance of public order and safety acting in its capacity of employer'.[23] In essence the Court said about a Chief Constable that 'such a public authority, charged by the state with the maintenance of public order and safety, does not act as a private individual. It may not take advantage of the failure of the state, of which it is an emanation, to comply with community law'.[24] Once again the estoppel argument was brought to bear in this case.

In the *Costanzo* case[25] the court decided that '[i]t follows that when the conditions under which the court has held that individuals may rely on the provisions of a directive before the national courts are met, all organs of the administration, including decentralized authorities such as municipalities, are obliged to apply those provisions'.[26] Therefore, we can deduce that all local and regional governments are included in the concept of state bodies.

In the *Foster* case[27] the Court said that 'a body, whatever its legal form, which has been made responsible, pursuant to a measure adopted by the state, for providing a public service under the control of the state and has for that purpose

19 Case 148/78, [1979] ECR 1629.

20 Case 152/84, *Marshall* v. *Southampton and South-West Hampshire Health Authority*, [1986] ECR 723.

21 Ibid., p. 735.

22 Case 222/84, *Johnston* v. *Chief Constable of the RUC*, [1986] ECR 1651.

23 Ibid., para. 7.

24 Ibid., para. 56.

25 Case 103/88, *Fratelli Costanzo* v. *Commune di Milano*, [1989] ECR 1839.

26 Ibid., para. 31.

27 Case C-188/89, *Foster*, [1990] ECR I-3133.

special powers beyond those which result from the normal rules applicable in relations between individuals is included in any event among the bodies against which the provisions of a directive capable of having direct effect may be relied upon.'[28] 'Special powers' and 'public service under control of the state' seem to be the deciding factors in this case.

The Court of Justice once again adopted a broad view. For the purposes of direct effect 'the state' includes bodies 'providing a public service under the control of the State'.[29]

This judgment followed Advocate General van Gerven's Opinion. He considered that, in the light of the case law of the Court of Justice, the concept of 'the state' should be interpreted broadly. He referred to 'the criterion of actual control' which he then defined as being a 'dominating influence and the possibility on the part of the authorities to give binding directions, regardless of the manner in which such control is exercised'.[30] This includes all bodies which can exercise authority over individuals pursuant to the constitutional structure of a Member State, as well as bodies other than those endowed with public authority whose conduct can be influenced by the authorities.[31]

The Court of Justice concluded that it has jurisdiction to determine the categories of persons against whom a directive may be invoked, although it is for the national courts to decide whether a certain party falls within those categories.[32]

With previous case law in mind, the *Foster* judgment was not entirely unexpected. The Court of Justice had already shown its preference for a broad interpretation of the concept of 'the state', at least on matters dealing with direct effect. It is seen as important to use this broad meaning of 'the state' in order to preclude a Member State from profiting from its failure to comply with Community law (the estoppel argument) as well as to mitigate the consequences of ruling out 'horizontal' direct effect in the *Marshall* judgment. In that case the Court ruled that a directive cannot of itself impose obligations on an individual, but only on Member States. As a result directives cannot be relied upon against another individual.[33]

In a more recent case dealing with the horizontal direct effect of directives, namely the *Faccini Dori* case,[34] the Court referred to its decision in the *Marshall*

---

28 Ibid., para. 20.

29 Ibid., para. 20.

30 Advocate General's opinion in case C-188/89, para. 16.

31 Grief, N., 'Direct Effect of Directives and Organs of the State', 16 *European Law Review* (1991), p. 140.

32 Case C-188/89, paras. 13-15.

33 Case 152/84, *Marshall* v. *Southampton and South-West Hampshire Health Authority*, [1986] ECR 723, para. 48.

34 Case C-91/92, *Faccini Dori* v. *Recreb Srl.*, [1994] ECR I-3325.

case, reiterating that a directive is binding only in relation to the Member States.[35] The case dealt with the interpretation of Directive 85/577[36] on the protection of consumers in respect of contracts negotiated away from business premises. The purpose of the said Directive was to protect consumers against unfair commercial practices by so-called doorstep sellers. Italy had failed to implement Directive 85/557 even though the deadline for implementation had expired. As a result, Miss Dori could not rely on it against Recreb in order to cancel her contract with them. The question in this case concerned whether or not she could rely on the Directive against Recreb even though it had not been implemented by the Italian Government. Pointing to its decision in the *Marshall* case, the Court said that she could not, because Directives are only addressed to Member States. However, in this case the Court gave another reason for not accepting the horizontal effect of directives, namely that the Community does not have the power to enact obligations for individuals, except through the adoption of regulations. To accept the horizontal direct effect of directives would be to give the Community the power to impose obligations on individuals via other means than the adoption of regulations.[37] Through its judgment in *Faccini Dori* the Court seems to want to emphasise and maintain a clear distinction between regulations and directives.[38]

The fact that the Court has ruled out horizontal direct effect makes its case law on this topic interesting when looking at emanations of the state. If there is no horizontal effect, then directives can only be relied upon against the state in its many forms. Therefore, the question of which bodies fall within the definition of the state once again becomes of the utmost importance. Based on the Court's case law, directly effective provisions of directives may only be relied upon against the state or public authorities. However, to mitigate the absence of horizontal direct effect of directives, the Court has widely interpreted this category of bodies. Also, negative results of the absence of horizontal direct effect are diminished by the possibility of the award of damages to individuals if they have suffered negative effects as a result of non-implementation of a directive by a Member State.[39] Having said this, of course, the matter of damages remains a matter between individuals and Member States.

One could argue that if the European Court had the maximum effect of Community law in mind, then it should accept horizontal effect. Two Advocates General with the European Court subscribe to the opinion that in fact the Court

---

35 Ibid., para. 22.

36 [1985] OJ L372/31.

37 Case C-91/92, para. 24.

38 Betlem, G., 'Medium Hard Law - Still No Horizontal Direct Effect of European Community Directives After *Faccini Dori*', Vol. 1, No. 3 *Columbia Journal of European Law* (1995), p. 479.

39 Joined cases C-6 and C-9/90, *Francovich and others* v. *Italy*, [1991] ECR I-5357, paras. 33-35

should accept horizontal direct effect.[40] However, the Court has chosen not to do so. One could conclude that while the Court wants to give Community provisions the maximum effect, it will not give priority to the principle of *effet utile* in every case. The question is why did the Court decide against maximum effect of Community provisions in the case of horizontal direct effect? Some authors venture the opinion that the reason for this was of a political rather than a legal nature.[41] At the time some Members States, and also national courts, had difficulty in accepting direct effect of directives.[42] Extending horizontal direct effect to directives would have been politically difficult, if not unacceptable.[43]

The main reason for discussing the cases mentioned above was the definition of 'organ of the state'. What is problematic in the case law is that different terms are used to describe emanations of the state. For instance, in the *Marshall* case the words 'emanation of the state', 'public authority', 'state authority' and 'organ of the state' all seem to have been used if not synonymously then at least as overlapping terms. The question then arises: which criteria should a national court apply in order to decide whether the public body in question should be subject to the vertical direct effects of a directive?[44]

Having looked at the case law, it is clear that the concept of 'the state', at least when it comes to direct effect, must be interpreted broadly, and the question remains: how broadly?

In addition to this uncertainty, the Court of Justice is not consistent concerning its own definition of the criteria for determining whether direct effect is possible. In paragraph 18 of the *Foster* judgment[45] it stated: directives could be relied upon against bodies which were 'subject to the authority or control of the

---

40 Advocate General Lenz, in his opinion in the *Faccini Dori* case, C-91/92, [1994] ECR I-3325, argues in favour of the horizontal direct effect of directives as far as future cases are concerned. Advocate General Jacobs also pleaded the case for horizontal direct effect in his opinion in *Vaneetveld* v. *SA Le Foyer*, case C-316/93, [1994] ECR I-763. See also: Betlem, ibid., pp. 484ff; Gerven, W. van, 'Horizontal Effect of Directive Provisions Revisted', in Curtin, D., and Heukels, T. (Eds.), *Institutional Dynamics of European Integration, Essays in Honour of Henry G. Schermers* (Nijhoff, Dordrecht, 1994), Vol. II, p. 343.

41 E.g. Wyatt, D., and Dashwood, A., *European Community Law* (3rd Ed.) (Sweet & Maxwell, London, 1993), p. 74.

42 During the proceedings in the *Faccini Dori* case, representatives of the Danish, German, French, Italian, Dutch and British Governments and the Commission's representatives all pleaded against the direct horizontal effect of directives. See: Bracke, N.,'Horizontale Werking van richtlijnen?', *RegelMaat* (1994/5), p. 206.

43 Weatherill, S. & Beaumont, P., *EC Law* (Penguin Books, London, 1993), p. 263, note 94; Trimidas, T., Horizontal Effect of Directives: a Missed Opportunity?, *European Law Review* (1994), p. 635.

44 Szyszczak, E., 'Case Law: *Foster and Others* v. *British Gas plc.*', 27 *Common Market Law Review* (1990), p. 859.

45 Case C-188/89, [1990] ECR I-3133.

state *or* had special powers beyond those which result from the normal rules applicable to relations between individuals'. However, in paragraphs 20, 22 and the formal judgment it changed that definition to: 'under the control of the state *and* has for that purpose special powers beyond those which result from the normal rules applicable in relations between individuals.' The question is whether the two criteria of control and special powers are alternative or cumulative. This is still unclear.

If the criteria are to be applied alternatively then a greater number of bodies will fall within the category to which direct effect will apply. However, if the criteria are applied cumulatively, then fewer bodies will be covered and direct effect will apply in fewer cases. Looking at the Court's efforts to strive for maximum effectiveness, it is more likely that the criteria are to be applied alternatively.

2.4 Results of the direct effect of directives

The ability of individuals to rely on Community law before their national courts greatly enhances its enforceability. It also brings Community legislation closer to the individuals relying on it. The possibility of legal action through the national courts is a far more accessible means of enforcement than an action against a Member State for the failure to fulfil its obligations under Community law brought by the Commission or another Member State under Article 226 (ex Article 169) or Article 227 (ex Article 170) EC. That is a slow and arduous process. Also until the Maastricht Treaty amendments it lacked any real sanctions. On top of this process being slow, individuals can only benefit from such an action if, as a result, the state changes its internal law to comply with its Community law obligations. This also does not provide a remedy for the wrong suffered by individuals before the changes were made. National courts, on the other hand, can apply directly effective Community law without delay and without the litigants incurring excessive costs. National courts also have numerous powers to enforce the law, including the award of damages.[46]

The Court's clear preference has been to decide each case on an *ad hoc* basis and with the specifics of the case in mind, without giving much attention to the crucial issue of the nature of the legal relationship between the bodies in question and the state.[47]

The estoppel argument, which we see appearing in many of the cases before the Court, does not provide support for directives being invoked against

[46] Weatherill & Beaumont, p. 289.

[47] Curtin, D., 'The Province of Government: Delimiting the Direct Effect of Directives in the Common Law Context', 15 *European Law Review* (1990), p. 198.

individuals, that is, having horizontal direct effect. The Court ruled out the possibility of the horizontal direct effect of directives in the *Marshall* case.[48] In that case, the Court ruled that directives may only give rise to vertical direct effects in the national courts. However, the Court of Justice mitigated this literal interpretation of Article 249 (ex Article 189) EC by ruling that the organs of the state against which a provision of a directive may be enforced must be given a broad interpretation.

3 Public procurement

Apart from the public service exception and the direct effect of directives, there are also other areas of EC law where the concept of the state is of importance. For instance, the provisions which concern the applicability of the competition rules to 'public undertakings' (Article 86 (ex Article 90) EC), state aid (Article 87 (ex Article 92) EC) and public procurement.[49] It is the last of these fields which I want to address in the next paragraphs.

The establishment of the Common Market meant that all obstacles to intra-Community trade should be eliminated. This had to include the public sector markets. In its White Paper of 14 June 1985 on Completing the Internal Market, the Commission stressed the need for the adoption of legislation designed to make sure that the markets of government procurement were opened to Community-wide competition.[50]

The battle to implement the necessary legislation proved to be difficult. The Member States were very reluctant to accept procedures which largely deprived them of the means to pursue a number of policy objectives such as regional and social development, specific economic goals, the development of competitive national industrial bases in 'high-tech' areas (telecommunications, medical equipment, aeronautics) and so on.[51] However, in the end a number of Directives dealing with public procurement came into force.

3.2 Public procurement provisions

There were no explicit provisions on public procurement in the EEC Treaty. However, there was no doubt that the Treaty provisions on non-discrimination and on the prohibition of barriers to interstate trade and the

48 Case 152/84, [1986] ECR 723.

49 See the Public Works Contracts Directive of 26 July 1971 (71/305/EEC).

50 Com. (85) 310 final, paras. 81-87.

51 Winter, J., 'Public Procurement in the EEC', 28 *Common Market Law Review* (1991), p. 742.

free supply of services could be used to counter discriminatory procurement practices in the Member States. The Council adopted General Programmes for the elimination of the existing restrictions.[52]

However, starting in the early 1970s a number of Council Directives imposed greater discipline on governments and other public authorities when it came to compliance with Treaty prohibitions of discrimination against foreign goods or services. These Directives attempted to achieve a limited degree of coordination as regards rules on national tendering procedures and practices and greater transparency in this area.

Nowadays, the directives dealing with public procurement are Directives 93/37/EEC of 14 June 1993[53] (the Works Directive), 9/36/EEC of 14 June 1993[54] (the Supplies Directive) and 92/50/EEC of 18 June 1992[55] (the Services Directive). It is not necessary for the purposes of this Chapter to go into the workings of all these Directives. What concerns us here is their scope: who is considered to be a public authority according to the legislation on public procurement?

3.3 The scope of the public procurement directives

The public sector procurement rules cover, broadly speaking, public bodies of a non-commercial nature. The aim of the legislation is to regulate public authorities likely to be subject to significant pressure to 'buy national', or in other words, to boost local/national industry by granting them the tender for public works.[56]

Such 'public authorities' obviously include central government departments and local authorities, the traditional forms of government authority.[57] However, in view of the diverse organisational forms employed by governments in all Member States, it is necessary to go beyond this, and to formulate a more

---

[52] OJ 1962, p. 32/62 and p. 36/62.

[53] OJ 1993 L 199, p. 54. Directive 93/37 consolidated Council Directive 71/305/EEC (of 26 July 1971) concerning the coordination of procedures for the award of public works contracts (OJ, English Special Edition 1971 (II), p. 682).

[54] OJ 1993 L 199, p. 1. Directive 93/36 consolidated Directive 77/62/EEC (of 21 December 1976) concerning the coordination of procedures for the award of public supply contracts.

[55] Directive 92/50/EEC coordinated the procedures for the awards of public service contracts, OJ 1992 L 209, p. 1.

[56] Arrowsmith, S., *The Law of Public and Utilities Procurement* (Sweet & Maxwell, London, 1996), p. 106.

[57] For more details on (Dutch) public authorities falling within the definition of contracting authorities see also: Nijhof, M.B., *De concessie in Europeesrechtelijk perspectief: een onderzoek naar de plaats van de concessie in het Europese recht en het Nederlandse bestuursrecht* (Dissertation, Universiteit Utrecht, 2000), pp. 31-40.

sophisticated definition of the public sector for the purposes of applying public procurement provisions. The public authorities which are generally covered by the rules on public procurement are referred to in Community legislation as 'contracting authorities'.

In the late 1980s the original Directives dealing with Public Procurement were amended. For instance, the Supplies Directive was amended by Directive 89/440, in which the new concept *'bodies* governed by public law' replaced *'legal persons* governed by public law'. The new concept is defined by reference to a set of criteria that must be cumulatively met.[58]

1 The body must be established for the specific purpose of meeting needs in the general interest not having an industrial or commercial character;
2 it must have legal personality;
3 it must be financed, for the most part, by the State, or regional or local authorities or other bodies governed by public law; or it must be subject to management supervision by those bodies; or have an administrative, managerial or supervisory board, more than half of whose members are appointed by the State, regional or local authorities or other bodies governed by public law.

In order to get an impression of the scope of the Public Procurement Directives, we have look at the relevant case law.

3.4 Case law

In order to give the rules as laid down in the Directives their maximum useful effect, the European Court decided on a wide interpretation of the concept of 'State or regional or local authority'. This follows from the Court's judgment in case 31/87, *Beentjes*,[59] in which it decided that in order to give the rules on public procurement their maximum useful effect, it was important that the concept of a contracting authority be given a wide interpretation. In that case the Court was asked to rule on the question whether the Works Directive applied to the award of public works contracts by a body with no legal personality of its own, but whose functions and composition were governed by legislation and whose members were appointed by a regional authority. Stressing once again the importance of the *effet utile* of Community legislation, the Court found that there was a sufficient degree of involvement of the state with the operations of the body to consider that body as a part of the public administration, even though it was formally separate from the state. Even though the local Land Consolidation

---

58 Article 1 of Directive 93/37.

59 [1988] ECR 4635.

Committee (the body in question) was not part of the state, the Court found that it could be considered as such in *functional* terms.[60]

The concept of 'the state' was interpreted widely in the *Beentjes* case in the context of the Works Directive. It covers at least a body 'whose composition and functions are laid down by legislation and which depends on the authorities for the appointment of its members, the observance of obligations arising out of its measures and the financing of the public works contracts which is its task to award'.[61]

As an aid to interpreting the concept of 'bodies governed by public law', the Directives provide for a list to be drawn up of relevant bodies in each Member State; the list is to be 'as exhaustive as possible', and may be updated. This list can be found in Annex 1 of the Works Directive, but it applies to all three Directives. This list is not intended to be exhaustive; bodies that are not on the list, but are covered by the general definition will still be covered, and, conversely, those on the list but not within the general definition would appear to be not included.[62]

Once again it can be seen that the European Court takes a functional approach, rather than choosing a clear, but rigid interpretation of 'the state'. With regard to the effectiveness of Community law, this is probably a good thing, but it does make the application of the provisions more difficult and ambiguous.

In more recent case law, namely the *Mannesmann* case,[63] it was once again made clear that the three criteria, as set out in the Directives, must be applied cumulatively.[64] However, it is not necessary that the body in question should *only* meet needs in the general interest.

The question before the European Court was whether the *Österreichische Staatsdruckerei* (Austrian State Printing Office; hereinafter referred to as ÖS) should be regarded as a body governed by public law and thus as a contracting authority within the meaning of Article 1 of Directive 93/37. It was clear that the ÖS complied with the first criterion laid down in Article 1 (b) of the said Directive, namely that of being established to meet needs in the general interest, not having an industrial or commercial character, since it was established to produce, for the Austrian State, such official administrative documents as passports, driving licences, etc. The Court concluded that such documents were 'closely linked to public order and the institutional operation of the State'.[65] The

---

60 Case 31/87, para. 11.

61 Ibid., para.12.

62 Arrowsmith, p. 113.

63 Case C-44/96, *Mannesmann Anlagenbau Austria AG and Others* v. *Strohal Rotationsdruck GesmbH*, [1998] ECR I-0073.

64 Ibid., para. 21.

65 Ibid., para. 24.

fact that the ÖS also pursued activities of a commercial nature was immaterial, according to the Court, provided that the body in question continues to attend to the needs for which it was established in the first place.[66] It was clear that the ÖS had legal personality, so the second criterion was covered. The third criterion was also met as the Director-General of the ÖS is appointed by a body consisting mainly of members appointed by the Federal Chancellery and various other ministries. Moreover, the ÖS's finances are under scrutiny by a Court of Auditors and the majority of shares in the ÖS are held by the Austrian State. The Court concluded that the ÖS was indeed a 'contracting authority'.

So, as we can see, it is possible for such a body also to have activities of an industrial or commercial character and still be classified as a body governed by public law for the purposes of the Public Procurement Directives.[67] Once a body can be classified as a contracting authority, then *all* works contracts, whatever their nature, are entered into by that entity and are to be considered public works contracts within the meaning of Article 1 of Directive 93/37.[68]

It is also irrelevant that meeting needs in the general interest in fact constitutes only a small portion of the activities pursued by the entity. This was confirmed in the *BFI* case.[69] This case dealt with the organisation of refuse collection in two Dutch municipalities, namely *gemeente* Arnhem and *gemeente* Rheden (hereinafter 'the municipalities'). These two municipalities decided in 1993 to merge their municipal refuse collection service and entrust them to a new legal entity, a public limited company named ARA. BFI, a private undertaking whose business includes the collection and treatment of household and industrial waste, brought proceedings before the *Arrondissementsrechtbank* (District Court) of Arnhem, claiming that Directive 92/50 applied and that the municipalities should have observed the tendering procedure laid down in the said Directive. The District Court found in favour of BFI. The municipalities appealed and the *Gerechtshof* (Court of Appeal) of Arnhem and it referred to the European Court for a preliminary ruling asking whether the term 'needs in the general interest, not having an industrial or commercial character' excludes needs which are also met by private undertakings.

The European Court referred to its decision in that case and stated that in the *Mannesman* case the Court had not considered whether private undertakings might meet the same needs when it decided that a State printer met needs in the general interest not having an industrial or commercial nature.[70] Also in Article 1 (b) of Directive 92/50 there is no mention of the absence of competition as

66 Ibid., para. 25.

67 Ibid., para. 26.

68 Ibid., para. 35.

69 C-360/96, *Gemeente Arnhem and Gemeente Rheden* v. *BFI Holding BV*, [1998] ECR I-6812.

70 Case C-360/96, para. 46.

a condition for the definition of a body governed by public law.[71] However, the existence of significant competition, especially competition in the marketplace, *may* [JEB: emphasis added] be indicative of an absence of a need in the general interest, not having an industrial or commercial character.[72] At the same time, the lack of availability of goods and services in the market place may be indicative of the needs in question being in the general interest, not having an industrial or commercial character.[73]

However, in the *BFI* case the Court concluded that the removal and treatment of household refuse may be regarded as constituting a need in the general interest, since there were aspects such as public health and environmental proctection which should be taken into account.[74] The Court concluded that, therefore, the term 'needs in the general interest, not having an industrial or commercial character' does not exclude needs which are capable of being satisfied by private undertakings as well.[75]

The Court went on to state that the relative importance of a body's duty to meet the needs in the general interest was immaterial. Such entities are free to carry out other activities.[76] The conclusion was that the status of a body governed by public law is not dependent on the relative importance, within its business as a whole, of meeting the needs in the general interest not having an industrial or commercial character.[77] As long as the three conditions laid down in Article 1 of Directive 92/50 are met, such an entity would be classified as a contracting authority. Therefore, as long as the body in question continues to provide the needs for which it was originally established, whether or not it also carries out other activities is of no consequence.

The conclusion that we can draw from these two cases, *Mannesmann* and *BFI*, is that once a body falls within the three criteria for contracting authorities, the whole range of its activities fall within the scope of a public procurement directive. This means that a whole range of activities, including those of a commercial or industrial character, can be subject to legislation applicable to bodies governed by public law. In other words, the pieces of Community legislation dealing with public procurement spread a wide net to cover all possible situations.

Once again the effectiveness of the legislation is the main aim which the Court has in mind. By widely interpreting the phrase 'contracting authorities', the legislation can be at its most effective.

---

71 Ibid., para. 47.

72 Ibid., para. 49.

73 Ibid., para. 50.

74 Ibid., para. 52.

75 Ibid., para. 53.

76 Ibid., para. 55.

77 Ibid., para. 58.

4 Conclusions

It seems that the European Court of Justice wants to interprete the concept of 'the state' very broadly when it comes to the direct effect of directives. Also when we look at the interpretation of 'the state or regional or local authorities' in the Public Procurement Directives, this concept is interpreted widely. Both methods of interpretation seem to be rooted in the notion of effective EC law.

In contrast, when it comes to interpreting the meaning of the public service exception, the Court seems to be doing the opposite, namely reducing the cases in which the public service exception can be used by interpreting emanations of the state very narrowly. It refers to the true interests of the state, whereas in cases of direct effect and public procurement control by the state or a state body seems to be the major issue. When it comes to the public service exception a narrow approach is chosen, but once again with the aim of achieving effective Community law. It is obvious that when it comes to an exception to one of the main principles of European law, e.g. to the principle of free movement of persons, the provision in question should be interpreted narrowly, as is the public service exception. If such a provision includes a definition of 'the state' then that definition should in turn be interpreted narrowly.

On the other hand, if a provision of Community law is to have maximum effect, e.g. directives and the provisions dealing with public procurement, then it is to be interpreted broadly. If such a provision includes a definition of the state, then this definition is also to be interpreted broadly.

All these interpretations are based on the principle of *effet utile*. Since the public service exception is a deviation from the principle of non-discrimination, it needs to be interpreted restrictively. The provisions in the direct effect and the public procurement legislation need to be interpreted broadly for EC law to have the greatest impact on national law and to avoid shirking on the part of the Member State when it comes to doing what they are supposed to do.

Looking at these three areas of Community law, it is safe to say that the idea of what 'the state' is depends on the topic under discussion. More often than not, the European Court takes a *functional approach* in this respect. It looks at the purpose and ideas behind a certain piece of legislation and interprets it with that in mind. It seems that the intention behind this functional approach is to make Community law effective. It does not make it any more transparent, however.

Looking at other areas of European law as we have done in this Chapter does help to explain why the interpretation of Article 39 (4)'s (ex Article 48 (4)) public service exception is a rather vague one. The Court wants to keep its options open and at the same time it is striving towards making Community law more effective, or at least as effective as possible.

This approach does have its drawbacks, however. It is at times difficult for Member States to apply the provisions correctly. Because the different interpretations are vague and often ambiguous, Member States are not always sure whether they apply in an individual case or not. This can also be an excuse for Member States not to adhere to Community law. They can use this uncertainty as a reason for not complying with Community law. As long as no one (i.e. the Commission or a Community citizen) makes a point of bringing such cases before a court, the Member States can continue with non-compliance for quite some time. This problem is compounded by the fact that it is difficult for individuals to be sure of their rights when, to them, the rules are also totally confusing. Situations like this do *not* help to make Community law more effective in that sense.

The main conclusion that can be drawn from all of the above is that the European Court has its eye on the effectiveness of a specific provision or set of provisions, without much regard for the effectiveness of Community legislation as a whole. Citizens of the Union are often quoted in polls and questionnaires as complaining that they do not understand the goings-on 'in Brussels'. Since one of the aims of the European Union after the coming into force of the Maastricht Treaty was to bring it closer to 'the people', i.e. its citizens, maybe the Court should re-evaluate its decisions and instead of aiming for maximum effectiveness on an *ad hoc* basis, it should concentrate on elucidation and more coherence in the use of important definitions which form the basis of Community law, or at the very least is should clarify that the definitions of such concepts as 'the state' or 'emanations of the state' vary drastically from provision to provision and it should then explain why it has a need for such differing definitions.

CHAPTER 6

Access to Public Service Employment in a Number of EU Member States; a General Study

1 Introduction

This chapter deals with how the public service exception is interpreted in a number of Member States. It will look at such things as the legislative basis of the public service exception in national legislation, the possible changes that occurred in national legislation as a result of Community law, whether there have been any cases brought before national courts dealing with the national public service exeption, distinctions made between civil servants proper and contractual employees and whether there are differences as to access to public service employment between EU citizens and third-country nationals.[1]

2 Legislative basis for the public service exception

When investigating the public service exception it is important to look at its legislative basis. Is the basis for the exclusion of non-nationals laid down in the constitution or organic legislation, for instance? It is also worth looking at the wording of the public service exception and the reasons cited for excluding non-nationals from certain posts. Last but not least, it is also important to look at the system used to incorporate the public service exception into national legislation.

When looking at the way in which the different Member States incorporate a public service exception into their national legislation, one can detect four systems. These four systems I have named after the criteria used to determine access to public service for non-nationals. They are: a general criterion, a negative list, a positive list and a mixed system.

2.1 A general criterion

The first of these systems is one where the Member State in question formulates a criterion which is to be applied when deciding whether

---

1 Even though this Chapter does not claim to be complete in demonstrating access to the public service in all the Member States, it does give an overview of the situation in a number of them. In this Chapter I have made use of information supplied by a number of experts in the different Member States. I would like to thank the following for supplying me with invaluable information: Dr. Friedrich Fröhlich from the *Bundesministerium für Finanzen* of the Republic of Austria; Prof. Olli Mäenpää from the University of Helsinki, Finland; Staffan Ingmanson of the *Rättsvetenskapliga Institutionen* of Umeå University in Sweden; Prof. Dr. Günter Frankenberg from the *Institut für Öffentliches Recht* at the Johann Wolfgang Goethe Universität, Frankfurt am Main, Germany; Dr. Roberto Caranta of the University of Turin, Italy; Pierre Neyes, Director of *l'Administration du Personnel de l'Etat* of Luxembourg; and Prof. Dr. Faustos de Quadros, Ms Carla Sequeira and Mr Luis Reis of the Law Faculty (European Institute) of the University of Lisbon, Portugal.

or not a post is to be reserved for its own nationals in its national legislation, whether in the constitution or in an organic law.

This is the case, for instance, in the Republic of Austria. In this Member State the main rules concerning the nationality of civil servants are laid down in the Civil Service Code *(Beamten-Dienstrechtsgesetz)*.[2] According to Section 4, paragraph 1 of the 1979 Civil Service Code, one of the four general appointment requirements for federal civil servants is:

'- Austrian citizenship; in cases not covered by the exception in Article 39, paragraph 4 of the EC Treaty as interpreted by the European Court of Justice the citizenship of other EEA/EU countries is equivalent.'

As we can see, the Article directly refers to Article 39 (4) (ex Article 48 (4)) EC. The Austrian legislator has chosen to link its own public service exception directly to the exception as laid down in the EC Treaty and as interpreted by the European Court. This is the most effective and direct way to ensure compliance with Community law.

However, a downside of this system is that it offers very little in the way of guidance as to which posts are covered by this exception. In practice, the question whether Austrian nationality is a condition for access to the Austrian public service, or whether citizenship of other EEA/EU countries is considered equivalent, is decided on a case-by-case approach. The decision is based on the duties and responsibilities actually associated with the particular position and takes into account the interpretation of Article 39 (4) (ex Article 48 (4)) EC in the case law of the European Court. The legislation that deals with these issues does not incorporate a list containing positions reserved for Austrian nationals. If Austrian nationality is an appointment requirement for any post, then this is indicated in the public notification of the vacancy. The same legal framework applies to civil servants of the states and local communities according to the public service regulations adopted by the state legislators.

In Germany a similar system is applied. The main public service exception is laid down in the Constitution, but it can also be found in organic law.[3] Article 33 paragraph 2 of the German Constitution *(Grundgesetz; GG)*[4] lays down a nationality requirement for certain posts in the public service (the so-called *Funktionsvorbehalt*). It states that a post in the public service is open to each German national alike, taking into consideration his or her skills, abilities and education. It says:

2 BDG 1979, BGBl. No. 333.

3 See section 4 BRRG *(Beamtenrechtsrahmengesetz)* and section 7 BBG *(Bundesbeamtengesetz)*, for instance.

4 Of 23 May 1949, BGBl. S. 1.

'2. Jeder Deutsche hat nach seiner Eignung, Befähigung and fachlichen Leistung gleichen Zugang zu jedem öffentlichen Amte.'

Paragraph 4 of the same Article then goes on to state that official authority can only be exercised by members of the public service who are in an employment relationship with the State or a public body, i.e. by civil servants. It also talks of a relationship based on loyalty:

'4. Die Ausübung hoheitsrechtlicher Befugnisse ist als ständige Aufgabe in der Regel Angehörigen des öffentlichen Dienstes zu übertragen, die in einem öffentlich-rechtlichen Dienst- und Treueverhältnis stehen.'

Putting paragraphs 2 and 4 together, the conclusion seems to be that only Germans can become civil servants dealing with *hoheitsrechtsliche Befugnisse.* The question which then arises is the following: what are *'hoheitsrechtliche Befugnisse'* and should this term be interpreted widely or narrowly? There is no consensus on either of these questions amongst German experts in this field. Looking at the parliamentary history of Article 33 (4) GG, however, it is clear that the legislator intended the term should be interpreted strictly. In particular, the intention was to avoid employing civil servants with the postal and railway services and with so-called *'Betrieben der (kommunalen) Daseinsvorsage'.*[5] As a result of this debate, the original term, *'Ausübung öffentlicher Gewalt'* (exercise of official power) was replaced by *'Ausübung hoheitsrechtlicher Befugnisse'* (exercise of public authority). The idea behind this change of wording is that the exercise of public authority is a narrower term than the exercise of public power. 'Public authority' seems to imply a certain amount of discretion in the process of decision making, whereas 'public power' can also be bestowed upon a person without it necessarily including powers of discretionary decision-making.

There are two criteria which come into play when deciding whether or not the *Funktionsvorbehalt* should be applied. The first question to be asked is whether or not the State has the monopoly to act in the matter concerned. When the State either cooperates with or delegates competences to private companies, then it is difficult to maintain that only civil servants may be employed. The second question is that of the *'Grundrechtsrelevanz'* of the activities: are fundamental rights (which should be protected by the State) involved? In the end, however, it is up to the legislator to state which posts within the public service have to be filled by German nationals only. The consensus

[5] The term *'kommunale Daseinsvorsorge'* can be translated as 'provisions for municipal living'. As a result of the urbanisation process, municipal authorities were confronted with many new tasks in the areas of municipal technology, hygiene and infrastructure. These new public responsibilities fall within the term *'kommunale Daseinsvorsorge'.*

amongst German experts and with the German administration is that the following areas of the public sector fall within the area covered by the public service exception: the police, the military, the judiciary, the tax authorities, the diplomatic service and certain leadership posts concerning core State functions (top-level civil servants).

We see that the German legislator has incorporated the public service exception into the Constitution. Unlike the Austrian legislator, however, there is no direct link with Article 39 (4) (ex Article 48 (4)). The German legislator has chosen to base the *Funktionvorbehalt* for the most part on the criterion whether or not the post involves the exercise of public authority. Secondly, there is also a link to loyalty. Not only is the exercise of public authority limited to civil servants (i.e. those who have a *öffentlichen-rechtlichen Dienstverhältnis*), but there also has to be a *Treueverhältnis*, that is to say: a relationship which expects loyalty. This could be a reference to the idea that nationals are deemed to have an automatic loyalty to their own state, whereas non-nationals will never have total loyalty to their state of residence, since they also retain a loyalty to their state of origin. It could be argued that, purely based on the idea of loyalty, non-nationals would find it more difficult to be appointed to a post alluded to in paragraph 4 of Article 33 GG, even when they are in fact already employed as civil servants in other areas of the German public service.

The Portuguese legislation includes nationality requirements for the public service in its Constitution of 1976 *(Constituição da República Portuguesa de 1976)*. It establishes in Article 15, under the title 'Foreigners, people without known nationality, European citizens' the following principle:

'1 Foreigners and people without known nationality who reside in Portugal have the same rights and duties as Portuguese citizens.

2 Exceptions to the previous rule are: the possibility to engage in political activities, *to become public servants unless in a mainly technical position,*[6] [JEB: emphasis added] and the rights and duties reserved exclusively to the Portuguese citizens by the Portuguese Constitution and by the law.'

The Portuguese legislator has chosen to use a general criterion with which to decide whether or not a post is open to non-nationals. The criterion used is not one in which one could easily recognise the European Court's interpretation of the public service exception of Article 39 (4) (ex Article 48 (4)) EC. The criterion used states that non-nationals can only become public servants in posts of a mainly technical position. The definition of a mainly technical position becomes crucial in deciding whether or not Portugal is in compliance with Community law on this subject.

[6] The Portuguese text reads: *"das funções públicas que não tenham carácter predominantemente técnico"*.

Over the years two interpretations of the phrase 'mainly technical position' have come to the fore in Portugal. There are those who interpret functions of a mainly technical character as functions depending on highly demanding requirements of preparation and specialisation. In other words: functions which require no discretionary decision-making on the part of the person executing them. Those who propagate this interpretation often also go on to claim that non-Portuguese citizens may only perform such functions when there are no Portuguese citizens with similar abilities available to fill such a post. For quite some time this was the interpretation which the Portuguese public administration subscribed to. This rather broad interpretation of the exception was at the time also confirmed by the General Procurator of the Republic *(Procuradoria-Geral da República)*.[7]

However, over the years the views on the public service exception in Portugal have changed. Nowadays, the public administration subscribes to a different, narrower, interpretation. This new interpretation is in accordance with the new interpretations confirmed by the General Procurator of the Republic,[8] who has changed his position since 1977.

These days, whether or not duties fall within the public service does not depend on the degree of technicality or specialisation, but on whether the level of technicality dominates the level of public authority involved. Thus, according to this opinion, public functions with a mainly technical character are those where the technical factor dominates every other characteristic. The functions which are considered to have more than a mainly technical character involve the execution of material services, auxiliary or administrative, or the application of authority or non-technical leadership. This has been the interpretation supported by the courts[9] and accepted doctrine.[10]

---

7 See, the interpretations nos. 258/77, of 16 February 1978, and 260/77 of 21 December 1977, in Bulletin of the Ministry of Justice *(Boletin do Ministério da Justiça)*, no. 291, pp. 195ff., and no. 281, pp. 35ff., respectively. According to these views this constitutional expression used in paragraph 2 of Article 15 should be interpreted not with regard to the degree of technicality, but instead according to the criterion of the dominance of the components of authority or technicality of the position.

8 See, the interpretations nos. 23/81, of 14 January 1982, not published, and 22/90, of 29 May 1991, in Bulletin of the Ministry of Justice, no. 411, pp. 5ff., according to which this constitutional expression used in paragraph 2 of Article 15 should be interpreted not in the light of its degree of technicality, but instead according to the criteria of the dominance of the components of authority or technicality of the duty.

9 See: the agreements of the Supreme Administrative Tribunal *(Supremo Tribunal Administrativo)* of 23 February 1989, appeal no 23 816, in Bulletin of the Ministry of Justice, no. 384, pp. 463ff., of 5 May 1992, appeal no. 16 505, in *Apêndice ao Diário da República* (Appendix to the Diary of the Republic) of 29 November 1994, and of 18 February 1993, appeal no. 13 511, in *Apêndice ao Diário da República* of 14 August 1993.

10 Exponents of this doctrine are: Professor Jorge Miranda, Professor Vital Moreira and Professor Gomes Canotilho, all eminent Portuguese Constitutionalists.

In accordance with this second interpretation, the expression 'public functions without a mainly technical character' has been interpreted as intending to exclude non-nationals from public functions with public powers, both in the internal and administrative scope (leadership and direction positions)[11] and the execution of powers concerning third parties (authoritative acts)[12].[13]

Besides in the Constitution, nationality requirements for access to public functions can be found in other Acts and Statutes. For instance, the Decree of Law number 498/88, of 30 December,[14] which approved the general recruiting and selection guidelines for public administration staff. Article 22 of the said Decree, which establishes the requirements for admittance to public application,[15] states as a first requirement for the candidate the possession of Portuguese nationality, except for those cases which fall within the scope of special laws or international conventions. So the main principle here is that Portuguese nationality is required except when it is decreed by law (national or international) that it is not.

We see this principle reflected in the norms that establish the requirements of admission to the various careers in the public administration. Thus, for example, only Portuguese citizens may apply for a post in the diplomatic service, no exceptions to this rule being possible for the admittance of non-nationals to the diplomatic service. On the other hand, in the general area of teaching, non-Portuguese citizens are allowed to execute public functions in Portugal, as imposed by norms of the European Community, international convention or special laws.[16]

The conclusion is, therefore, that public functions in general are reserved for Portuguese citizens. However, there are many functions which are open to non-nationals, but these are functions which do not deal with the exercise of public power.

In this organic piece of legislation one can detect an indirect reference to the public service exception as laid down in Article 39 (4) (ex Article 48 (4)) EC. The Decree mentioned above refers to complying with both national and international law when it comes to criteria to be applied when deciding whether or not to allow a non-Portuguese national to have access to the recruitment process for the public service.

---

11 *'Funções de direcção e chefia.'*

12 *'Actos de autoridade.'*

13 Such is the opinion of the constitutionalists Professor Vital Moreira and Professor Gomes Canotilho.

14 Changed by the Decree of Law number 215/96, of 22 August.

15 Since 1982 public application is the normal process of recruiting and selecting staff for the boards of the services and organs of the public administration.

16 See, respectively, Decrees of Law nos. 79/92 of 6 May 1992 and 139-A/90 of 28 April 1990.

As far as the need for a nationality requirement is concerned, according to the Portuguese legislator, the following reasons have come to the fore. First of all, the execution of public functions is related to the exercise of political rights, the idea being that such a right should, in principle, be restricted to Portuguese nationals. There is als the notion that certain posts should be restricted to non-nationals because of the immediate importance to the administrative organisation or the impact of such posts on the organisation of the State. Finally, there is the belief that staff and agents have a duty of loyalty towards the State and it is considered to be more likely for nationals to have such a loyalty, than it is for foreigners, who might at the same time still have loyalty towards their country of origin, which could potentially lead to a conflict of interest.

In accordance with the interpretation of the European Court of Justice, the positions within the public administration that are excepted by Article 39 (4) (ex Article 48 (4)) of the EC Treaty are only those duties or activities whose functional description include direct participation in the exercise of public authority and in functions which safeguard the general interests of the State. As we have seen above, the Portuguese legislator also allows restrictions on the access of non-nationals to positions in the public service, but only to those which are not mainly technical in character, that is to say, those functions where the application of public authority dominates. It seems that the Portuguese legislation is in accordance with Community law on this point.

2.2 A negative list

The second possible system for incorporating the public service exception into the national legislation is where the Government or some other competent authorities draw up a list of posts which can only be filled by nationals of the Member State in question. Since such a list specifically names the posts which cannot be filled by non-nationals, I have decided to use the term 'negative list'. This system can be found in a number of Member States, for example Finland, Italy and Sweden.

In Finland the basic rule on nationality for civil servants is laid down in the Constitution. Section 84 of the Constitution Act of 1919[17] lays down the rules on eligibility for public office in the State administration:

'(1) Only a citizen of Finland may be appointed to the offices of Chancellor of Justice or Assistant Chancellor of Justice of the Council of State, or to the office of a judge, or Commander of the Armed Forces or to the office of a member of the board of governors of the Bank of Finland, or

[17] As amended by the Law of 28 July 1989/724.

may be elected to the office of Parliamentary Ombudsman or Assistant Parliamentary Ombudsman.

(2) The other offices to which only a citizen of Finland may be appointed shall be governed by provisions prescribed by Act of Parliament or by other provisions or stipulations issued under the authorisation of an Act of Parliament.'[18]

The Act of Parliament referred to in paragraph 2 is the Public Officials Act.[19] Section 7 (1) includes a list of offices to which only a Finnish citizen may be appointed. These are mainly top-ranking posts in the ministries, police officers and prison officials, posts with the public prosecutor's office and in the army.

Section 7 (2) provides that the Council of State may designate other offices to which only a Finnish citizen may be appointed. Additional requirements for this designation are that:

1 the office is an office in a ministry which is not mentioned in the first paragraph, or
2 the duties of the office involve a considerable exercise of public powers or processing of matters pertaining to external relations or relations to international organisations, or
3 the duties of the office involve access to information pertaining to the security of the State or to a considerable general or private economic interest.

At a local level the following rules apply: concerning municipal administration, in Section 46 of the Municipal Act[20] it is expressly laid down that a person with non-Finnish nationality may be appointed to a municipal office. In other words, there are no nationality requirements for posts at the local government level.

Contrary to the system described in the previous paragraph, the Finnish legislator has chosen to list a number of positions to which only Finnish nationals may be appointed. Over and above these listed exceptions, the Council of State can designate other posts to which the public service exception can also apply. The Public Officials Act refers to a number of criteria which can lead to a post being covered by the exception. These are the exercise of public power, access to sensitive information pertaining to state security or external relations and information of considerable economic interest. Criteria such as the exercise of public power and access to sensitive information are criteria which can often be found when it comes to the public service exception. This is not the case,

---

18 Translation by Prof. Mäenpää.

19 19 August 1994/750.

20 17 March 1995/365.

however, with the last criteria: access to information of considerable public or private economic interest. It is very doubtful whether this is in accordance with the European Court's interpretation of the public service exception of Article 39 (4) (ex Article 48 (4)) EC.

After the legislative reform of the old system in Italy,[21] the Italian Government chose to use the same method as its Finnish counterpart. Access to the public service in Italy is dealt with in Article 37 of the *Decreto Legislativo*[22] of 18 February 1993, n. 29. *Decreto Legislativo* 29/93 follows on from earlier legislation,[23] which had as its main aim to increase efficiency in the public sector by decreasing the number of public servants. The idea behind this original piece of legislation was to create a leaner and more flexible public service. Many former public sector employees were no longer considered to be public servants. The categories of posts which remain in the *pubblico impiego* (public sector) are the armed and security forces, diplomatic staff and certain top-level civil servants in governmental departments.

Article 37 of *Decreto Legislativo* 29/93 deals with the employment of EU nationals in the public service.[24] It reads as follows:[25]

'1 EU Member States' citizens are free to a take a job with a public interest, provided that the positions in question do not involve direct or indirect participation with the exercise of public powers, nor are concerned with the protection of national interests.

2 Jobs and positions which are to be reserved solely for Italian nationals and jobs and positions which have extra requirements in order for EC nationals to be eligible for them are listed by a decree of the Prime Minister adopted pursuant to Article 17 L. 23 August 1988, n. 400.[26]

3 By default of relevant Community provisions, a decree by the Prime Minister, enacted after the proposal of the Secretary of State having jurisdiction on the matter, is to recognise and make foreign diplomas and professional qualifications to equivalent national academic titles. The same procedure is followed concerning academic and past employment titles which are necessary for admittance to a job selection procedure and eligibility for a post.'

---

[21] See paragraph 2.3

[22] A *Decreto Legislativo* is a legislative decree which has the same rank as a statute voted upon by Parliament, but which is drafted by the Government following the guidelines laid down in a statute conferring to the Government the power to legislate in a specific field.

[23] L. 23 October 1992, n. 421.

[24] *'Acesso dei cittadini degli Stati membri della Comunità Europea'.*

[25] Translation by Dr. Roberto Caranta.

[26] Which deals with the enactment of secondary legislation by the Government.

The first paragraph above is worded in the positive sense: it states that EU citizens are allowed to take posts in the public service, *unless* such a post involves the exercise of public powers, or it involves the safeguarding of a national interest. The second paragraph then goes on to authorise the Prime Minister to compose a list of excepted posts. Such a list was implemented by the Decree of 7 February 1994, n. 174.[27] Article 1 of the Decree lists the posts which are reserved for Italian nationals. These include top management positions in State and public bodies, both at the central and local level; judges and State lawyers; military and certain civil service posts with the Prime Minister's Staff, the Foreign Office, the Home Office, the Justice Department, the Department of Defence and the Finance Department. More generally, the Decree goes on to state that there are other posts which can only be held by Italian nationals. These are positions which deal with the preparation, adoption and implementation of administrative decisions and positions which deal with authorisations and coercive orders, as well as judicial review.

Article 1 of the Decree of 7 February 1994, n. 174 creates the possibility of compiling a list of posts which are to be preserved for Italian nationals only. This list is not the last word on the matter, however. Article 2 states that the Prime Minister, acting on a proposal by the Minister for the Public Service and after having heard the competent public body, may decide on a request made by a EU national to be allowed into a post within the Italian administration. Therefore, deviations from the list are possible in theory. A negative decision concerning such a request must be justified.

Article 3 lays down further conditions that EU nationals must meet in order for them to join the Italian public service. The persons who wish to become public service employees must enjoy full civil and political rights in their State of origin. They also need the same or equivalent (professional) qualifications required of Italian nationals for the post in question. Lastly, they must have an adequate knowledge of the Italian language.

These conditions are practical criteria for fulfilling a function within the public service. These criteria would also apply to Italians, but may not be mentioned so explicitly as they are for non-nationals. Such criteria would also apply in the private sector.

As we have seen in Finland, the Italian legislation has chosen to use the system of compiling a list of posts which require Italian nationality. Over and above this list, once again we see a more general criterion to be applied to posts not on the list. This combines the clarity of a list of posts with the flexibility of a more general criterion. This means that the government in question need not be so vigilant concerning inclusion of any new posts on the list as such posts will be covered by the criterion of the general exception.

---

[27] In: *G.U.R.L.* 15 March 1994, n. 61.

In Sweden, according to the *Regeringsformen*[28] (the Swedish Constitution or 'Instrument of Government') foreign citizens have an equal opportunity to be employed in the public sector as do Swedish citizens. However, an exception from that rule as regards public employment is to be found in Chapter 11, Article 9, paragraph 2. It reads:[29]

'Only a Swedish citizen may hold or exercise the functions of a judicial office, an office directly subordinate to the Government, a post or commission as head of an authority directly subordinate to the *Riksdag* or to the Government, or as a member of such an authority or its board, a post in the Government Chancery immediately subordinate to a Minister or a post as a Swedish envoy. Also in other cases no-one who is not a Swedish citizen may hold an office or carry out a commission, if the holder of such an office or commission is elected by the *Riksdag*. Swedish nationality may otherwise be made a prerequisite of the right to hold or exercise an office or commission under the State or a local authority only if laid down in law or under conditions prescribed by law.'

A few examples of posts for which Swedish nationality is a prerequisite are: Attorney-General, Chief Public Prosecutor, Equal Opportunities Ombudsman, Consumer Ombudsman, Under-Secretary of State and ambassador. Furthermore, from Chapter 6 Article 9 of the *Regeringsformen* it follows that Cabinet Ministers have to be Swedish citizens and, according to the *Riksdag* (Parliament) Act, Chapter 9, Article 2, the same applies to a head of division that assists parliamentary committees.

According to the last sentence in Article 9, paragraph 2 of Chapter 11 of the Swedish Constitution (cited above), Swedish citizenship may also be a condition for employment with a national or a local public authority. In Sweden, citizenship is a condition for access to employment in some occupational groups belonging within the sphere of the State. According to paragraph 5 of the said Article, the condition applies to employment as a police officer or a public prosecutor, as well as to employment in the armed forces. Paragraph 6 determines that the Government may prescribe that only Swedish citizens may hold certain posts which involve the management of matters concerning the relations with other states or with international organisations, or be employed in posts

---

[28] Regeringsformen, lag 1974:152.

[29] This is the official translation of the provision as published by the Cabinet Office.

that might involve knowledge of conditions of importance relating to national security or to other important, public or private economic interests.[30]

Nationality requirements for employees in the public sector in Sweden appear at various legislative levels, including the Constitution itself, as we have seen above. Most restrictions apply to posts within state bodies. Swedish citizenship as a requirement for employment in county council districts and municipalities is called for only as regards certain posts that fall under the Security Protection Act.[31] Swedish citizenship is also a condition for access to a wide range of commissions of trust within the public sector. To give a few examples, this is true for layman representatives in the courts and a wide range of public bodies as well as for elected representatives in Parliament and regional and local authorities.

According to the Security Protection Act, employment in the public sector (as well as in the private sector) may be subject to certain restrictions with reference to the need to protect the security of the state, this includes protection against espionage, sabotage and other crimes that might threaten State security. A certain post could, after being classified by the competent authority as involving activities for which some form of security protection is required, be subject to certain restrictions as regards admission by non-nationals.[32] Only a Swedish citizen may hold a so-called classified post in the State or in county council districts and municipalities. It is the Government (or sometimes the *Riksdag*) which decides on the classifications and who has the power to make exceptions in particular cases.[33] The Government may also delegate the task of classifying a certain activity to authorities acting under Government authority,[34] a possibility which has been widely used. As a result, it is difficult to say how many posts in the public sector are covered by this exception since no central register listing such posts is in existence.

The motives for excluding some posts for non-citizens can be found in the *travaux préparatoires* to the pertinent legislation. In the *travaux préparatoires* to the *Regeringsformen*, the requirements of public security and loyalty to the State

---

30 Although the Swedish Government has made use of this power to prescribe Swedish nationality for certain posts (e.g. law clerks with the district courts and county courts, as well as certain posts with international organisations not already covered by the provision in the *Regeringsformen*) there is no official list containing the posts involved.

31 *Säkerhetsskyddslagen* (1996:627).

32 The competent authorities in question are listed in the Security Protection Ordinance (*förordning* 1996:633). The posts which these authorities decide should only be filled by Swedisch nationals are, however, not listed officially. One reason for this could be that such an 'official list' could in itself present a security problem.

33 Article 29 of the Security Protection Act.

34 Ibid., Article 20.

are stressed. They also express a desire that questions concerning the legal status and protection of civilians ought to be dealt with by Swedish citizens. The same motives lie behind the settlement in the Act of Official Employment. Other examples could be drawn from the *travaux préparatoires* to an Act by which the nationality requirement for chartered accountants and chief guardians were abrogated.[35] Here, the Cabinet Minister gave some examples of acceptable motives – the consideration of national independence, national security and the (sensitive) relationship with other states and international organisations.

As to the character of the restrictions, the conclusion must be that the Swedish regulation mainly relies on the application of a negative list. According to legislation, certain cited jobs are excluded. However, in other cases posts within the public service can be excluded on more general criteria, such as the grounds mentioned in the Security Protection Act, which can be seen as a more general criterion to be applied to posts in the public service. In this sense the Swedish system is not a pure system.

This second system, which makes use of lists which which specifically refer to the excepted posts within the public service, has as an advantage the fact that discovering whether or not a post has a nationality requirement is made easier: one can search the appropriate legislation and when a post is not listed, then one can assume it is open to non-nationals except when covered by a more general criterion. It also has some drawbacks. Working with a list, rather than general criteria is less flexible. When new posts are created, the list may need to be updated. This means more work and vigilance on the part of the Member State's government. As a result, often, as we have seen in Finland, Italy and Sweden, there are also some general criteria, over and above the list, which need to be applied to posts not covered by the list. This negates the main drawback of the use of the list: its lack of flexibility. At the same time, it reintroduces the lack of clarity which was the list's main advantage from the point of view of individuals who may wish to occupy such posts.

2.3 A positive list

The third system also works with a list, but with a list which refers to the posts which are open to non-nationals. I have decided to dub this the 'positive list'. Such a list was used in Italy before they altered their legislation and changed over to the second system (see paragraph 2.2). Rather than there being a list of excepted posts, in the Italian legislation there was the possibility for the Italian Government to compose a list of functions which, despite the general public service exception, could be filled by non-nationals.

[35] Proposition (Government bill) 1985/86:7.

The first encroachment into the system which required Italian nationality as a precondition for employment in the *pubblico impiego* (public sector) was made with the coming into force of the *Decreto Legislativo* of 27 January 1992, n. 115. The *Decreto Legislativo* 115/92 implemented EC Directive 89/48/EEC on recognition of diplomas.[36] While *Decreto Legislativo* 115/92 made it possible for non-nationals to take up jobs in Italy as a result of their foreign diplomas being recognised by the Italian authorities, Article 13 (2) stated that the nationality requirement for employment in the public service was not waived by the recognition of a diploma. This did not imply a total ban on non-nationals in the Italian public service because paragraph 3 of Article 13 offered the possibility for the Italian Government to list those posts within the public service which could be filled by EU citizens on a par with Italian nationals. Article 13 (4) stipulated that such a list had to conform with the public service exception as laid down in Article 39 (4) (ex Article 48 (4)) EC and the European Court's case law on that subject.

Like in the Austrian legislation what we see here is a direct link with Article 39 (4) (ex Article 48 (4)) EC in paragraph 4 of Article 13 of the *Decreto Legislativo* 115/92. This means automatic compliance with Community law.

2.4 A mixed system

In the previous paragraphs we have seen three basic systems of incorporation of the public service exception. As we saw, most countries adhere to one of those systems, even though the system is hardly ever pure: when using a negative or positive list, there is often also a general criterion in use to make sure that posts which Member States consider to be covered by the public service exception are caught even though they are not on the list.

One of the Member States covered by the survey could not be placed in one of those three systems, because it has a truly mixed system. That Member State is Luxembourg.

In Luxembourg the Constitution was revised in 1999. The old version of the public service exception was laid down in Article 11 paragraph 2. It read:

'Les Luxembourgeois sont égaux devant la loi; seuls ils sont admissibles aux emplois civils et militaires, sauf les exceptions qui peuvent être établies par une loi pour des cas particuliers.'

---

[36] OJ 1989, L 19/16.

This old version of the Article stated that in principle only Luxembourg nationals could be employed in the public service. Exceptions had to be laid down by law and could only be made in exceptional cases.

With the revision of 29 April 1999, paragraph 2 of Article 11 was deleted. To take its place Article 10bis was inserted. It states in its first paragraph:

'Les Luxembourgeois sont égaux devant la loi.'

It then goes on to state in paragraph 2:

'Ils sont admissibles à tous les emplois publics, civils et militaires; la loi détermine l'admissibilité des non-Luxembourgeois à ces emplois.'

The new Article 10bis states that Luxembourg nationals can be employed in the public, private and military sector. It goes on to state that the employability of non-nationals in these three sectors will be regulated by law.

The pertinent legislation is the *Loi du 17 mai 1999 concernant l'accèss des resortissants communautaires à la fonction publique luxembourgeoise.*[37] This piece of legislation introduced a number of changes into the *Statut général des fonctionnaires de l'Etat*[38] (Civil Servant Statute). Article 1b of the Law of 17 May 1999 modifies Article 2 paragraph 1 of the *Statut.* Article 2 paragraph 1 (a) of the *Statut* states that the possession of the Luxembourg nationality is a condition for access to the Luxembourg civil service. Paragraph 1 (f) of the said Article then mitigates this requirement by stating that the condition of Luxembourg nationality does not apply to nationals of the EU Member States employed in the following sectors:

- research
- educational affairs
- health
- transport systems
- telecommunications
- water, petrolium and electricity supplies.

However, posts in these sectors which involve the exercise of official authority or safeguarding of the general interests of the state are *not* open to non-nationals. The text states that the exception to the requirement of Luxembourg nationality for the sectors named above does not apply to posts which involve *'une participation, directe ou indirecte, à l'exercice de la puissance publique et aux fonctions qui*

---

37 Act concerning the Access of Community Citizens to the Luxembourg Public Service.

38 *Loi du 16 avril 1979.*

ont pour object la sauvegarde des intérêts généraux de l'Etat ou des autres personnes morales de droit public'.

In the text cited above we recognise the European Court's interpretation of Article 39 (4) (ex Article 48 (4)) EC. The Luxembourg legislator has followed the Court's interpretation word for word. As such, we can conclude that Luxembourg does comply with Community legislation on this point.

As we can see, the Luxembourg legislator has chosen to make use of a combination of two systems. First of all, it states a number of sectors to which the nationality requirement does not apply (a 'positive list'). However, within those sectors it still uses a general criterion which decides whether or not a post is open to non-nationals.

3 Changes in the legislation

It is interesting to look into whether there have been any changes made in national legislation dealing with the public service as a result of the European Court's case law on Article 39 (4) (ex Article 48 (4)) EC. It has been difficult to get a clear picture of this process, however. At the same time it is often plain to see that the legislation is in fact very much based on the wording of the Court's case law. In such cases it is easy to conclude that Community law has had an effect. In other cases the influence is not always evident.

One of the most obvious examples of the impact of Article 39 (4) (ex Article 48 (4)) on national legislation can be found in the Austrian legislation. As we saw above the rules dealing with the nationality of civil servants are laid down in Section 4, paragraph 1 of the *BeamtenDienstrechtsgesetz* (Civil Service Code) which states that one of the four general appointment requirements for federal civil servants is:

> '-Austrian citizenship; in cases not covered by the exception in Article 39, paragraph 4 of the EC Treaty as interpreted by the European Court of Justice the citizenship of other EEA-/EU countries is equivalent.'

As we have seen above, there is no list of reserved posts, making this a very flexible piece of legislation which automatically follows any changes in interpretation by the European Court. Because this Article directly refers to Article 39 (4) (ex Article 48 (4)) it is self-regulating. Questions, of course, may arise in situations which have not been covered by the European Court. In such cases it is up to the Austrian authorities (and ultimately the Austrian courts) to decide, based on the European Court's interpretations so far, whether a post falls within the public service exception. In the last resort there is, of course, the European Court itself.

The European Court's interpretation of Article 39 (4) (ex Article 48 (4)) led to changes in Austria's legislation dealing with the public service. These changes are manifested in the *EWR-Dienstrechtsanpassungsgesetz* (Act amending the 1979 Civil Service Code), the *Vertragsdienstetengesetz* (Act for Contractual Employees 1948), and other laws in order to bring legislation into line with the EEA Agreement. Article 1 paragraph 1 (a) of the *EWR-Dienstrechtsanpassungsgesetz* amends the 1979 Civil Service Code by stating that certain posts within the Austrian civil service can only be filled by Austrian citizens.

It says that it requires Austrian citizenship for certain posts in the public service:

'a. bei Verwendungen gemäß § 42a die österreichische Staatsbürgerschaft,'

It refers to § 42a (which is a new paragraph inserted into the 1979 Civil Service Code) which in turn states:

'Verwendungen, die ein Verhältnis besonderer Verbundenheit zu Österreich voraussetzen, die nur von Personen mit österreichischer Staatsbürgerschaft erwartet werden kann, sind ausschließlich Beamten mit österreichischer Staatsbürgerschaft zuzuweisen. Solche Verwendungen sind insbesondere jene, die

1. *die unmittelbare oder mittelbare Teilnahme and der besorgung hoheitlicher Aufgaben und*
2. *die Wahrnehmung allgemeiner Belange des Staates beinhalten.'*

Once again we recognise the European Court's interpretation of the term 'public service' in Article 39 (4) (ex Article 48 (4)) EC in the wording of this paragraph. The two criteria are direct or indirect participation in the exercise of official authority and the safeguarding of national interests. The wording of this paragraph seems to imply that the two criteria are to be applied cumulatively rather than alternatively. If this is indeed the case, then the Article is in accordance with the interpretation of the European Court, which also favours the cumulative approach.[39]

Article 1 paragraph b of the *EWR-Dienstrechtsanpassungsgesetz* states that posts within the civil service which do not fall within the category as laid down in § 42 are therefore open to EU nationals on a par with Austrian citizens. It says:

'b. bei sonstigen Verwendungen die österreichische Staatsbürgerschaft oder die Staatsangehörigkeit eines Landes, dessen Angehörigen Österreich aufgrund eines

---

[39] See paragraph 4.4 of Chapter 4.

Staatsvertrages im Rahmen der europäischen Integration dieselben Rechte für den Berufszugang zu gewähren hat wie österreichischen Staatsbürgern (Inländern),'

The same amendments as described above for the *BeamtenDienstrechtsgesetz* (Civil Service Code 1979) have been made to the *Vertragsdienstetengesetz* (Act for Contractual Employees 1948) and the other legislation dealing with public service employment.[40]

On a more practical note, non-nationals applying for posts in the Austrian civil service have to have a good working knowledge of the German language. This is laid down in Article 1 (4) (1a) of the *BeamtenDienstrechtsgesetz* (Civil Service Code 1979). This criterion is not absolute: for certain posts a less than complete knowledge of the German language may be sufficient. This can be decided on a case-by-case basis.

The Luxembourg legislator in paragraph b of Article 1 of *Loi du 17 mai 1999 concernant l'accèss des resortissants communautaires à la fonction publique luxembourgeoise* (Act concerning the Access of Community Citizens to the Luxembourg Public Service) has also chosen to word the public service exception in virtually identical terms to those used in the European Court's interpretation of Article 39 (4) (ex Article 48 (4)) EC in cases such as *Commission* v. *Belgium*.[41] It stands to reason that this legislation was undoubtedly influenced by the Court's case law.

In Italy, Article 37 *Decreto Legislativo* of 18 February 1993, n. 29 has clearly been influenced by the case law of the European Court of Justice.[42] Indeed, paragraph 2 of Article 37 closely follows the wording of the Italian version of case 149/79 *Commission* v. *Belgium*.[43] Paragraph 3, which provides a system for the recognition of foreign diplomas and other qualifications, complies with the ruling of the Court in case C-419/92 *Scholz*.[44]

However, despite what has been written above, there are some question marks as to whether the relevant text in the Italian legislation is in line with

---

[40] Besides the *Beamten-Dienstrechtsgesetz 1979* and the *Vertragsbedienstetengesetz 1948* these are: the *Bundes-Personalvertretungsgesetz*, the *Ausschreibungsgesetz 1989*, the *Pensionsgesetz 1965*, the *Bundestheaterpensionsgesetz*, the *Bundesforste-Dienstordnung 1986*, the *Landeslehrer-Dienstrechtsgesetz 1984*, and the *Land- und forstwirtschaftliche LandesLehrere-Dienstrechtsgesetz 1985*.

[41] Case 149/79, [1980] ECR 3881.

[42] See Fiorillo, L., in Carince, F. (ed.), *Il lavoro alle dipendenze della amministrazioni pubbliche* (Giuffré, Milano, 1995) p. 666ff.

[43] [1980] ECR 3881.

[44] [1994] ECR I-0505, this case was in fact referred to the European Court by the *Tribunale amministrativo regionale* of Sardina.

the case law of the Court of Justice on Article 39 (4) (ex Article 48 (4)) EC. It has been suggested that Article 37 (1) of *Decreto Legislativo* 29/93 is inconsistent with Community law because it precludes EU nationals from taking posts which *either* involve direct or indirect participation in the exercise of public powers *or* are designed to safeguard the national interest. From this it could be concluded that the Italian legislator has placed as an alternative two criteria which in the case law of the European Court are interpreted as having to be applied cumulatively.[45] However, it has also been submitted that the drafting of Article 37, though regrettable, cannot in itself lead to inconsistencies, since it is very difficult to imagine positions which are designed to safeguard the national interest which do not also involve, at least indirectly, participation in the exercise of public powers.[46] This, however, seems to be an incorrect approach. One can think of research facilities which perform functions for the State which can be highly sensitive and important to the national interest, without those research facilities exercising official authority, even indirectly.

Questions also arise concerning the implementing Decree of 7 February 1994, n. 174. Whilst the requirement of an adequate knowledge of the Italian language is in line with the European Court's ruling in *Groener* v. *Ministry of Education*,[47] the list of positions laid down in Article 1 is worded too widely because, as it stands, it seems to include virtually every post within many governmental departments, without proper exceptions being made for manual and menial tasks. In all fairness, however, the Decree does allow the admission of non-nationals to those posts which require as a precondition only the completion of compulsory schooling (at present eight years), that is to say, most manual and unskilled jobs. On the other hand, it must be stressed that, according to the Decree, even positions which can today be held a (mostly) private law, i.e. contractual, basis can be reserved for Italian nationals. This seems to add inconsistency to the Italian legislator's interpretation of the Community case law.

Although Finland did not become a member of the EU until 1995, the requirements of EC law were already anticipated in the drafting of legislation prior to this date. The most visible effects of this are the provisions in Section 7 of the Public Officials Act, but even in the drafting of Section 46 of the

[45] Fiorillo, p. 670, see also: paragraph 4.4 of Chapter 4.

[46] Moreover, some ambiguities on this point are also present in the Court's own case law. See *Commission* v. *Italy*, case 225/85, [1987] ECR 2625, where the European Court also used the alternative approach. However, it has not done so since, and has consistently used the cumulative approach in its later judgments. The use of the word 'or' rather than 'and' between the two criteria of 'participation in the exercise of official authority' and 'protecting the general interests of the state' in *Commission* v. *Italy* can, in my opinion, be seen as an abberation. See also: paragraph 3.5 of Chapter 4.

[47] Case C-379/87, [1989] ECR I-3967.

Municipal Act the case law of the European Court was already taken into account. Therefore, it is safe to say that European legislation already had an effect even before Finland joined the EU.

In Sweden the interpretation of Article 39 (4) (ex Article 48 (4)) EC by the European Court has not brought about any changes in the Swedish legislation on the nationality requirements for public servants. In the *travaux préparatoires* work to the Act of Official Employment from 1994, the Law Commission concluded that the current exceptions were in line with the Court's case law and the Commission's Communication from 1988[48] on the interpretation of Article 39 (4) (ex Article 48 (4)).[49] In the *travaux préparatoires* to the Security Protection Act,[50] which in 1998 replaced two previous acts on the subject, the Cabinet Minister made a reference to the said Law Commission and came to the conclusion that the Swedish exceptions were not contrary to Community law.

The Swedish Government entrusted a Commission (henceforth referred to as the Citizen Commission) to conduct a survey of the use of Swedish citizenship in national legislation as a precondition for, among other things, employment in the public service in January 1999.[51] By employment in the public service the Citizen Commission refers to being in the employment of the State and bodies that fall under the State, but also employment in county council districts and in municipalities. One of the tasks before the Citizen Commission is, according to its directives, to come up with suggestions that could lead to an opening up of as many professions in the public service as possible to non-Swedish nationals. The purpose is to increase the integration of this part of the population into Swedish society. For example, within the Citizen Commission, the opening up of posts such as that of judge, a public prosecutor and head of an enforcement district to persons other than Swedish citizens have been discussed.

In France the law of 26 July 1991[52] altered the general statute for civil servants allowing EU citizens and citizens of EEA Member States[53] access to certain posts in the French civil service.[54] This law introduced Article 5bis into the general statute for civil servants of 1983. It states that EU and EEA nationals have

48 [1988] OJ C72/2.

49 SOU 1992:60.

50 Proposition (Government bill) 1995/96:129.

51 Direktiv (directive) 1999:4 (to the Department of Culture).

52 *Loi de 26 juil. 1991-715*.

53 Article 47 of *la loi sur l'emploi dans la functions publique* of 16 December 1996.

54 The law of 13 July 1983, which constituted Title I of a new general statute for civil servants. The laws of 11 January 1984, 26 January 1984 and 9 January 1986 concerning, respectively, central government officials, local government officials and public health service officials were introduced to unify the legal regime of the three services.

access to the French public service except for positions linked to the exercise of 'sovereignty'[55] or the 'prerogatives of the state'[56].[57] Since 1992 a number of decrees have been issued. These have opened up the teaching professions, the health service, the Post Office and the *France Télécom*. Additionally, the Ministry of the Interior opened up some positions in local government service.

Although numerous posts have now been opened up to European Union citizens, the results of this process are relatively limited. For instance, in 1992 there were 800 candidates from other European Union Member States out of the 150,000 who took part in the competitive entry examinations for the teaching profession and in 1993 a little over 1500 non-French EU citizens were employed in the French civil service.[58]

In practice the greatest barrier to entry by non-French nationals into the civil service is the mutual recognition of the equivalence of qualifications required for eligibility. In France there is the added problem of the entry examinations. Should the aptitude of candidates continue to be measured by means of the entry examinations alone, or should the level of academic qualification achieved also be of relevance? This problem has yet to be tackled by the French legislator.

As we have seen above, Portuguese law is on the whole in accordance with Community case law, since the public functions closed to non-nationals seem to be in agreement with the Court's interpretation of Article 39 (4) (ex Article 48 (4)). This conclusion can also be found in a document by the *Procuradoria-Geral da República* (General Procurator of the Republic),[59] according to whom one can observe a remarkable similarity, namely the two components of authority and public power, between the criteria followed by the Portuguese Constitution, in its Article 15, paragraph 2, and the criteria developed by the European Court of Justice in its determination of the meaning of the concept 'employment in the public service' used in Article 39 (4) (ex Article 48 (4)) EC. As a result, there is no conflict between the Constitutional restrictions regarding the access of foreigners to public functions in Portugal and the Communitarian principle of free circulation of workers as laid down in Article 39 (ex Article 48) EC and interpreted by the European Court.

Therefore, there was no need for any changes to the Portuguese legislation establishing nationality requirements for access to the public service based on the European Court's restrictive interpretation of Article 39 (4) (ex Article 48 (4)) EC. It should be added that the Portuguese Constitution was reviewed in

---

55 *'L'exercice de la souveraineté'.*

56 *'Participation directe ou indirecte à l'exercice de prérogatives de puissance publique de l'Etat ou des autres collectivités publiques'.*

57 Trotabas, L. and Isoart, P., *Manuel Droit Publique* (L.G.D.J., Paris, 1996), p. 303.

58 Rouban, L., *The French Civil Service* (La Documentation Française, Paris, 1998), p. 79.

59 Cited in number 22/90, May 29, 1991, of the Bulletin of the Ministry of Justice, no. 411, pp. 5 ff.

1998, but no changes were made to Article 15, paragraph 2. Also the Decree of Law number 498/88 of 30 December (which approved the general recruiting and selection guidelines for public administration staff), was reviewed in 1995 by the Decree of Law number 215/95 of 22 August, but the legislator made no changes with regard to nationality requirements.

4 National court cases dealing with the public service exception

It is difficult to gain an impression of the number of court cases before national courts which deal with the public service exception, but on the whole there appear to have been few. The only two countries which have had cases dealing with the public service exception before their national courts, as far as I have been able to ascertain, are Italy and Portugal.

Two older rulings by the Italian courts, delivered in the mid to late eighties by first instance administrative courts, affirmed the nationality requirements with respect to teaching positions.[60] However, since then the case law in the Italian courts has in many respects anticipated the legislative reform of 1993,[61] bringing Italian law into line with the Court of Justice's case law. As early as 1989 the *Tribunale amministrativo regionale per la Lombardia*, which has been at the forefront of the struggle to bring about Community law enforcement in Italy,[62] held that a French national could not be hindered from taking part in the job selection procedure for a research position with a State research institute.[63]

In 1990 the *Consiglio di Stato* (Council of State), which in Italy performs both consultative and jurisdictional functions, delivered an opinion to the Italian Government stating that a Belgian citizen could not be refused inclusion in a list from which schools must appoint their teachers.[64] Later, again the *Tribunale amministrativo regionale per la Lombardia*, citing the *Lawrie-Blum*[65] ruling by the

---

60 T.A.R. Liguria, 20 May 1986, n. 196, in *Trib. Amm. Reg.* 1986, I, 2295; the Italian court did refer to the European Court's ruling in case 149/79 *Commission* v. *Belgium*, but was of the opinion that it only covered the most menial jobs; T.A.R. Campania, Sez. Salerno, 11 December 1987, n. 424, *in Trib. Amm. Reg.* 1988, I, 596, reached the same conclusion, but since this ruling was not reported in full, the reasoning behind this ruling is unclear.

61 See paragraph 2.2.

62 See, for example, case 103/88, *Fratelli Costanzo* v. *Comune di Milano*, [1989] ECR 1839, which followed from a reference by the T.A.R. Lombardia.

63 See T.A.R. Lombardia, Sez. III, 5 december 1989, n. 2125, in *Trib. Amm. Reg.* 1990, I, 58; this judgment expressly follows the European Court's decision in case 225/85, *Commission* v. *Italy* [1987] ECR 2625.

64 Cons. St., Sez. II, 20 June 1990, n. 234, in *Riv. Ital. Dir. Pubbl. Comunitario* 192.

65 Case 66/85, [1986] ECR 2121.

European Court, overruled a decision by a school authority refusing a British national the opportunity to take up a teaching post.[66]

Besides cases of direct discrimination on the basis of nationality, the Italian courts have also referred cases concerning indirect discrimination to the European Court. Most of these cases concerned non-national lecturers in foreign languages. There was no nationality requirement for such posts, but their employment conditions were less favourable than those of other public servants of comporable status, who were, and still are, mainly Italian. One such case led to the Court's ruling in *Allué & Coonan* v. *Università degli Studi di Venezia.*[67] In its decision the European Court stated that a national law setting rigid time-limits to the tenure of positions mainly held by foreigners were in breach of Community law.[68] These judgments have been consistently followed by the lower courts.

In Portugal there have been a number of court cases dealing with the exclusion of non-nationals from employment in the public service. In three of those cases, foreign citizens appealed against public administration acts that excluded them from applying for teaching positions in basic and secondary education for the simple reason that they did not have Portuguese nationality.

In each of these three cases, the *Supremo Tribunal Amministrativo* (Supreme Administrative Tribunal) upheld the appeal[69], revoking the acts on the basis that they were in violation of Article 15, paragraph 2 of the Constitution, since it had always been considered that teaching positions present themselves as mainly technical in character, because in such posts the exercise of public authority does not dominate the function.

However, in these judgments, no reference is made to the case law of the European Court of Justice. Two of the three cases had no relationship with Community law, as the citizens appealing were not nationals from a EU Member State. In the third case the appellant was a citizen from Luxembourg, but the Supreme Administrative Tribunal based its decision solely on the Portuguese Constitution and legislation, without a single reference to Community case law.

---

[66] T.A.R. Lombardia, 1 October 1991, n. 629.

[67] Case 33/88, [1989] ECR 1591.

[68] In order to avoid reverse discrimination, the new (more favourable) conditions have subsequently been extended to lecturers who are Italian nationals.

[69] Judgments of 23 February 1989, appeal no. 23 816, of 5 May 1992, appeal no. 16 505, and of 18 February 1993, appeal no. 13 511.

5 Distinctions between civil servants proper and contractual employees

The question whether or not there is a distinction being made within the public service between civil servants proper and employees on a contractual basis is an interesting one. This is because nationality requirements for the two groups may differ. As we shall see, all the Member States mentioned in this chapter use some form of distinction between civil servants proper and contractual employees, except Sweden, where such a distinction is not evident.

In Sweden there is no clear distinction between civil servants proper and contractual employees over the whole spectrum of the public service. Only permanent salaried judges, i.e. district court judges and judges of higher rank, enjoy a separate status, namely that of being in 'permanent employment'. That is to say, they cannot be dismissed from their position.[70] In this case the special form of employment coincides with a nationality requirement, but this requirement is not exclusively connected with this form of employment. This privileged status is laid down in the Act for Permanent Employment. This Act, however, did not enter into force until 1994. As a result, based on previous legislation, a number of employees within the public service besides judges still have permanent employment, in bodies such as universities and the Church.

Additionally, in the public sector some groups of employees still fall under the operation of a former regulation called 'warrant of appointment'[71]. This form of employment is similar to 'permanent employment' mentioned above. An organisation in which this form of employment still applies is the Post Office Administration. It must be mentioned that this form of employment is no longer applicable and has not been so for quite some time. Those persons to whom it still applies are approaching retirement age as laid down by law.

There is no general connection between opportunities for promotion and forms of employment. To have 'permanent employment' or a 'warrant of appointment' only means that the employee enjoys a higher degree of security of employment.

The other Member States do make a distinction between civil servants proper and contractual employees within the public service. For instance, in the Austrian legislation a distinction is made between *Beamter* (civil servants proper) and *Vertragsbediensteter* (contractual employees). The regulations concerning the employment of non-Austrian applicants with the nationality of a EU Member State are identical for both groups, however.

On the other hand, nationals of non-EU Member States may not be appointed as *Beamter*. They may only be appointed as *Vertragsbediensteter* and only after

---

70 The Swedish expression used is to be employed with *'fullmakt'*.

71 This form of employment is called *'konstitutorial'* in Swedish.

the recruiting authority grants a waiver of the nationality requirement on the basis of there being a lack of qualified Austrian or EU/EEA applicants for the post in question.

Therefore, in Austria a clear distinction is made between non-nationals that are from another EU or EEA Member State and third-country nationals. The latter cannot be employed as civil servants.[72]

There is also a distinction in the Portuguese Law between civil servants proper and contractual employees. All individuals working for the government are known as *agentos administrativos* (administrative agents). This term includes all those who, under any title, exercise an activity in the service of a public body. However, within this broad definition we can distinguish two categories.

First of all, there are *agentes funcionários* (staff agents) or *agentes profissionais* (professional agents). Staff agents are civil servants proper. This status translates into four characteristics, namely, the permanence of the position occupied, that position belonging to a career regime, the payment computed for the execution of the duty on a full-time basis and the fact that the position is executed voluntarily.

The second category consists of *agentes não funcionários* (non-staff agents) or *agentes não profissionais* (non-professional agents). The difference with the first category is that in spite of possibly being juridically equivalent to the civil servants proper, non-staff agents execute functions without a professional character, that is to say, non-staff agents are employed occasionally, temporarily or transiently. Such agents can be employed in a number of different situations, such as political agents, agents in the commission of a certain service, requested agents, agents in a private right regime (tied to a public body by the common regime of a labour contract or of a contract of service delivery), interim agents, temporary agents and apprentices, occasional agents, and agents contracted for a short-term task.

There are differences in the opportunities for promotion between public servants in the strict sense and contractual employees. The Portuguese legislation on careers in the public service, Decree of Law number 248/85 of 15 July, reserves the execution of public services in the career regime for those public servants in the strict sense. As we have seen above, this represents one of the criteria which distinguishes staff agents from non-staff agents. This means that each employee has a category, that is, a determined position within a career, fixed in accordance with the contents and qualifications of the service executed, and this in turn matches a given salary. The member of staff ascends the career-ladder in accordance with the length of service and the merit shown in professional performance. On the other hand, non-staff agents do not execute their services within a career regime. They do not have the possibility of promotion

[72] See paragraph 5.

or career progression, which is a privilege of the public servants in strict sense. However, the law ensures that they receive a remuneration which is identical to that of the equivalent category within the career structure.[73]

In Germany the *Funktionsvorbehalt* applies to *Beamten* (civil servants) only. Like most other public administrations, the German public service also employs on a contractual basis, and these employees are called *Angestellten*. There is certainly a difference between *Beamten* and *Angestellten* in the sense that when it comes to the contractual employees, nationality requirements seem not to be in evidence at all. As we saw in paragraph 2.1, nationality requirements can apply to civil servant posts. This is a clear difference from what we see in Austria, where nationality requirements apply in the same way to both civil servants and contractual employees. In Germany no nationality requirements are applied to contractual employees at all, only to civil servants.

A similar system to the one used in Germany can be found in Finland. There the legislation also differentiates between civil servants proper and contractual employees, both in legislation and in the legal doctrine. The relationship of 'public *officials*' (civil servants) with their employer is governed under separate laws and the relationship falls within the scope of public law. The status of 'public *employees*' (contractual employees) working within the public service is regulated by a separate law falling under private law. The criteria for employment are different for these two categories in the sense that there is no (national) eligibility legislation concerning the latter group. Nationality requirements only apply to public officials, i.e. civil servants proper, as is the case in Germany, as we have seen above. As far as promotion is concerned civil servants are formally on an equal footing with the public employees. Since the duties tend to be different in these two categories, a meaningful comparison is somewhat difficult, however.

In Luxembourg a distinction is made between civil servants employed on a statutory basis and the civil employees, the so-called *employés de l'Etat*. The latter category consists of agents who are employed on a contractual basis. Both categories of employees have to master the three working languages of the Grand Duchy of Luxembourg, namely French, German and Luxembourgish. Grand-ducal regulations may determine posts for which the knowledge of one of these languages is not required. These exceptions depend on the nature of the post as well as on the level of responsibility. The text of Article 2 paragraph 1 (f) of the *Statut général des fonctionnaires de l'Etat* (Civil Servant Statute) states:[74]

---

73 Article 3, no. 5, of the Decree of Law 248/85.

74 After being modified by the *Loi du 17 mai 1999 concernant l'accèss des resortissants communautaires à la fonction publique luxembourgeoise*.

'avoir fait preuve, avant l'admission au stage, d'une connaisance adéquate de trois langues administratives, telles que définies par la loi du 24 février 1984 sur le régime des langues, sauf pour les emplois, à déterminer par règlement grand-ducal pour lesquels la connaissance de l'une ou de l'autre de ces langues n'est pas reconnue nécessaire en raison de la nature et du niveau de responsabilité de ces emplois.'

Because the Act of 17 May 1999 *concernant l'accèss des resortissants communautaires à la fonction publique luxembourgeoise* only deals with non-national candidates being employed in the public service after 1 July 1999, a ministerial decision dated 8 June 1999 determined that those non-national employees which entered the civil service before that date do not have to fulfil these linguistic conditions.

France also has *agents contractuels* (contractual employees) as well as *agents nommés* (tenured staff, i.e. civil servants proper).[75] Contractual employees are usually employed on a three-year (renewable) contract, based on public law. As far as local government is concerned, for instance, a large number of employees are contractual employees.[76]

In France employment conditions, rights and social security provisions vary between the institutions which employ contractual staff. This creates numerous difficulties and often also injustice. To this complex situation is added the fact that the civil service statutes do not apply to contractual staff, but at the same time they can also not resort to the normal labour law.[77] To the French Government, however, the advantage of using contractual staff is that it affords greater flexibility in management.

6 Distinctions between EU citizens and third-country nationals

The next interesting feature to be dealt with is whether distinctions are made, as far as access to public service employment is concerned, between foreigners who have the nationality of one of the EU Members States and foreigners who are not EU citizens. On the whole what we see is that countries have decided either to open up their public service to all foreigners or, alternatively, they have only opened up their public service to EU nationals. In rare cases there are distinctions between posts which are open to all non-nationals and those who are only open to EU nationals or between classes of

75 Chapus, R., *Droit Administratief Général* (Montchrestien, Paris, 1997), p. 59ff.

76 In 1998 some 32 per cent.

77 Rouban, p. 48/49.

third-country nationals. In the last system, certain third-country nationals have a privileged position over others due to special bonds between the countries concerned, as we shall see.

In Finland, no distinction is made between EU citizens and third-country nationals when it comes to employability in the public service. The only distinction made, pursuant to Section 7 of the Public Officials Act, is between Finnish and non-Finnish applicants. Thus nationals from other EU Member States are classed in the same category as nationals from any other foreign country. EU nationals, therefore, do not have preferential treatment over non-EU nationals when it comes to access to the public service.

In Sweden the legislation also does not on the whole make a distinction between EU nationals and third-country nationals. The provisions in the *Regeringsformen* (Instrument of Government), the Act of Official Employment, the Security Protection Act and the other laws and ordinances on the subject mentioned above, make no such distinction.

One exception to this general rule, however, can be found in the Code of Judicial Procedure. There a difference is made between EU citizens and third-country nationals concerning the right to work as a lawyer in Sweden. That right, according to the principal rule, is reserved for members of the Swedish Bar Association. To become a member, the applicant has to be a citizen of a state within by the EEA. That means that membership of the association is open to EU nationals and to citizens of Norway, Iceland and Lichtenstein, whereas non-EEA nationals are excluded.

In Portugal the rules dealing with access to the public service for non-nationals are more complicated. Article 15 paragraph 3 of the Constitution of the Portuguese Republic states:

'To the citizens of Portuguese language countries can be attributed, given international convention and in reciprocity conditions, rights not given to foreigners, except for the access to positions in the sovereign organs and in the organs of proper government of the autonomic regions, the military service and the diplomatic career.'

This privileged regime for foreigners who are citizens of Portuguese language countries (Brazil and the African countries with Portuguese as an official language) is based upon the 'special relations of friendship and cooperation' between Portugal and the aforementioned countries.

We can conclude that, as far as the access of non-nationals to the public service is concerned, the Portuguese Constitution makes a distinction between the nationals of other Member States of the European Union (placing them alongside other foreigners in Article 15, paragraph 2), and the nationals of countries speaking the Portuguese language, to whom it grats a privileged regime under Article 15, no. 3. It does not, however, make a general distinction between EU and non-EU citizens with regard to access to the public service.

In France the civil service was opened up to EU citizens by the Law of 26 July 1991.[78] This Act opened up part of the civil service to EU citizens, but makes no mention of access for third-country nationals. Therefore, one can conclude that in France a clear distinction is made between EU citizens and third-country nationals.

As we saw earlier, in Austria nationals of non-EU Member States may only be appointed as *Vertragsbedienssteter* (contractual employees) and not as *Beamter* (civil servants). EU nationals, on the other hand, can be appointed as civil servants in certain posts. Therefore, in Austria a distinction is made between non-nationals that are from another EU or EEA Member State and third-country nationals.

7 Conclusions

In this chapter a number of aspects concerning the public service exception have been investigated. Even though not all Member States, besides the three that are investigated in more detail in the following chapters, are discussed, it nevertheless provides an insight into how the different Member States have complied (to a greater or lesser extent) with the obligations which result from Community legislation and the Court's case law dealing with the public service exception as laid down in Article 39 (4) (ex Article 48 (4)) EC.

What we can conclude is that there are different ways of incorporating the public service exception into the national legislation. Four main systems can be found, namely the use of a general criterion, a positive or a negative list or a mixed system making use of a combination of a general criterion and a negative or positive list.

There are few national court cases dealing with the public service. This could be due to the fact that the Court's case law is clear and that the Member States know how to apply the public service exception correctly. This is not, however, the most likely reason in my opinion. It is my feeling that, on the whole, not many non-nationals apply for posts within the public service, the main reason for this being that overall a thorough knowledge and understanding of both the language and culture of a state is required to be able to fill such a post. Not many non-nationals will be up to the standard required, unless they have been raised in the state in question from a very early age. Over and above this rather practical reason, it may be the case that many more court cases would surface if it was not for the burden of proof. It is very difficult to provide the evidence needed in court that a person was not offered a job because of he or she did not possess the required nationality. In discrimination cases it is difficult to prove that the

[78] *Loi de 26 juil. 1991-715.*

person hired was in fact not the best candidate, but was instead appointed because he/she was a national of the Member State in question.

In most Member States we find that there is a distinction between civil servants proper and contractual employees. However, this distinction has different consequences in different Member States as far as nationality requirements are concerned. It cannot be said that posts filled by contractual employees on the whole do not require nationality requirements, whereas civil servant posts do. The situation is more complicated than this, as we have seen in paragraph 5.

The Member States featured in this chapter also differ as far as access for third-country nationals is concerned. Some countries open up their public service to all non-nationals, not just EU citizens. By doing so they go beyond what is required by Community law. Whether they do so is a decision for the Member States in question. This is not a matter for the European Court, nor for Community legislation. The only requirement according to Community law is that the public service is opened up to EU nationals. While some Member States have chosen to go beyond the requirements laid down by Community law, others have chosen to enact that which is required, and no more. It is within their remit to do so.

CHAPTER 7

Access to Public Service Employment in the Netherlands

1 Introduction

This chapter will deal with the public service in the Netherlands. The central question in this chapter is the following: what may be understood as being typical public service functions in the Netherlands? As we have seen in Chapter 4 the Court of Justice has determined that the following are included within this concept: functions which - not necessarily directly - include participation in the exercise of public authority and activities which include the protection of the general interests of the state or of other public bodies.[1]

We can conclude from Chapter 4 that this is a very vague description. It is also still far from clear which functions do and do not fall within this definition. Up until now there have been a few decisions in which it has been determined whether in individual cases a certain function has or has not been covered by the exception contained in Article 39 (4) (ex Article 48 (4)). Some further clarity has thereby emerged, but a crystal-clear definition is long overdue.

As we saw in Chapter 5, in other areas of European law a different definition of government is employed. For the concept of the direct effect of directives, for example, the notion of government is interpreted very broadly. Also in the Directives on Public Procurement there are differing definitions as to what must be understood as falling under the state. With an eye on the effectiveness of this legislation the Court has also here chosen a broad and functional interpretation. The definitions of the state for the purposes of the direct effect of directives and for public procurement are not, as is the case with 'public service' in Article 39 (4) (ex Article 48 (4)), precise definitions.

Also in the case of Dutch law the objectives of the regulations determine, to a high degree, the way in which concepts are interpreted. The concept of the state or the government will therefore be given different interpretations in various legislative provisions. Apart from investigating the nationality requirements as laid down in Dutch legislative provisions, in this chapter I will also look at a number of Dutch regulations in which the concept of the state is of importance.

2 Nationality requirements in the Netherlands

Article 3 of the Dutch Constitution (*Grondwet*; hereinafter also abbreviated as GW) states that all Dutchmen are eligible to be appointed on an equal footing to the public service.[2] The Article only deals with equal access

---

1 *Commission* v. *Belgium*, case 149/79, [1980] ECR 3881.

2 *'Alle Nederlanders zijn op gelijke voet in openbare dienst benoembaar'.*

to the public service as far as Dutch nationals are concerned, it does not say anything about the possibilities for access by non-nationals. This is in contrast with the old Constition of 1887 which did contain, in Article 5 paragraph 2,[3] a provision dealing with the limited possibility for appointing of non-nationals. This Article was drafted in a rather negative tone. It stated that every Dutch national could be appointed into the service of its country.[4] The next sentence stated that no foreigners could be appointed into the service of the country, except in specific cases laid down by law.[5] This provision was scrapped with the redrafting of the Constitution in 1983 because it placed too much emphasis on the exclusion of foreigners from the national public service.[6] Also the term 'service of the country' was seen as being too narrow and was replaced with the wider term 'public service'. This was done in order to avoid confusion concerning whether or not local authorities and public bodies should also be included in the provision.

Therefore, the main rule, as laid down in Article 3 GW, is that all Dutch nationals should have the same opportunities for employment in the public service, taking into account their abilities and education, of course.[7] Foreigners do not have such unlimited access to the public service. There is another Article in the Constitution dealing with access to public service, though not directly. Article 109 of the Constitution requires the drafting of civil service regulations which contain provisions on a wide range of topics relating to recruitment and selection, resignation, working hours, leave, holidays and disciplinary measures.

The Dutch Constitution also contains a general non-discrimination rule, which is laid down in Article 1 GW. It states that all persons in the Netherlands should be treated equally in equal circumstances. It goes on to say that discrimination on the basis of religion, belief, political opinion, race or sex or on any other grounds is not permitted.[8] The General Equal Treatment Act (*Algemene*

---

3 The old Article 6 (2) of the Constitution of 1848.

4 Article 5 GW 1887, first sentence: *'Iedere Nederlander is tot elke landsbediening benoembaar'.*

5 Article 5 GW 1887, second sentence: *'Geen vreemdeling is hiertoe benoembaar, dan volgens de bepaling der wet'.*

6 Kamerstukken II 1975-1976, 13 872, nr. 3, p. 26.

7 For some posts, such as that of Mayor (*burgemeester*), not only requirements such as education and ability apply, but also political requirements play a role. Before a new Burgomaster is appointed to one of the larger cities in the Netherlands it is decided from which political party he or she should be a member. Candidates with a different party political membership need therefore not apply. The process by which the political 'colour' of a Mayor's post is decided is one based on unwritten (and rather unclear) political processes. At the end of the day it is the Cabinet who decides on the appointment.

8 The text states: *'Allen die zich in Nederland bevinden, worden in gelijke gevallen gelijk behandeld. Discriminatie wegens godsdienst, levensovertuiging, politieke gezindheid, ras, geslacht of op welke grond dan ook, is niet toegestaan'.* (All persons in the Netherlands shall be treated equally in equal circumstances. Discrimination on the grounds of religion, belief, political opinion, race or sex or on any other ground whatsoever is not permitted).

Wet Gelijke Behandeling; AWGB), which elaborates on the general rule of Article 1 GW, states that (both direct and indirect) discrimination on grounds of nationality is prohibited.[9] However, this prohibition is not without exception. Article 2 states that the prohibition of discrimination on the basis of nationality does not apply in cases where the difference in treatment is based on a regulation laid down by law or on written or unwritten principles of international law. Therefore, all nationality requirements must have a basis in law.

Since Article 3 GW does not deal with the exclusion of non-nationals from the public service, we must look at other pieces of legislation which lay down which post within the public service are and are not open to non-nationals. Historically, the Act dealing with this subject was the Act of 4 July 1858, regulating the possibility for the appointment of foreigners to the service of the country.[10] It allowed foreigners to be employed in a number of posts, amongst which were the following: consular-general, consul and consular agent, interpreter at a consulate, professor, lecturer or director with a State institution for education, the arts or sciences, to name but a few. This Act was revoked by the Act of 20 April 1988.[11] There were a number of reasons for this.[12] First of all the Act had become antiquated. Most of the posts mentioned in the Act no longer existed. Non-nationals could already be appointed as civil servants with local authorities (*provincies* and *gemeenten*) and other public bodies. It seemed logical to allow non-nationals into comparable posts within the civil service at the national level too.[13] In practice, non-nationals were already being appointed within the national civil service as contractual employees, since they could not be employed as civil servants. This inequality of status was considered unfair, not to mention contradictory to the principle of non-discrimination on the basis of nationality as laid down in Article 39 (ex Article 48) of the EC Treaty.[14] As a final reason for revoking the Act of 1858 reference was made to the integration of minority groups into Dutch society, the idea behind this reasoning being that the removal of unnecessary barriers to the appointment in the public service for members of minority groups, who do not have Dutch nationality, would help to achieve this aim.[15]

The definition of the term public service as used in Article 3 GW is interesting, but since this Article does not say anything about the exclusion of non-

---

9 Article 1 under b.

10 *Wet van 4 juni 1858 regelende de benoembaarheid van vreemdelingen tot landsbedieningen*, Stb. 46.

11 *Wet van 20 April 1988, houdende intrekking van de wet van 4 juni 1858, regelende de benoembaarheid van vreemdelingen tot landsbedieningen*, Stb. 1988, 231.

12 *Memorie van Toelichting*, Kamerstukken II, 1984-1985 19 076, nr. 3, p. 4.

13 Kamerstukken II 1984-1985, 19 076 , nr. 3, p. 4.

14 Case 152/73, *Sotgiu* v. *Deutsche Bundespost*, [1974] ECR 153.

15 *Memorie van Toelichting*, Kamerstukken II, 1984-1985 19 076, nr. 3, p. 6.

nationals from the public service, it is not paramount when it comes to a public service exception. Still, it is worth looking at what the legislator considered as being included in the term 'public service' (*openbare dienst*). At the time of the introduction of this new Article in the redrafting of the Constitution in 1983 the government did not provide a precise definition of the term 'public service'. The government stated that it depends on the circumstances of each case whether or not one can conclude that it falls within the term public service; however, in the Explanatory Statement (*Memorie van Toelichting*) accompanying the Act revoking the Act of 1858 it is stated that the term public service was chosen because it not only covered central government, but also local government and all public bodies, organs and institutions.[16] However, it did go on to say that bodies incorporated under civil law do not become part of the public service merely because they are subsidised by the government.[17] During the discussion on this Article in Parliament the Government always stressed the formal definition of public service, namely: bodies governed by public law.

The posts which are still considered to be open to Dutch nationals only are the following: the judiciary, members of the government, members of both Chambers of Parliament, the military, the police, the foreign service and positions involving confidentiality (*vertrouwensfuncties*).

So-called *vertrouwensfuncties* require Dutch nationality. This is laid down in Article 125e, paragraph 1, of the Civil Servants Act 1929.[18] However, this prohibition is not absolute. Article 125e paragraph 1 second sentence allows for the possibility to appoint non-nationals to confidential posts where there is a real interest for the civil service to do so.[19]

According to the Security Investigations Act (*Wet Veiligheidsonderzoeken*) it is up to the minister responsible for the policy area, in concordance with the Minister for Internal Affairs, to decide which posts are in fact positions involving confidentiality. The criteria are as follows: a post which offers the possibility of damaging the security or another vital interest of the State.[20] *Vertrouwensfuncties* include both posts within the public service and in the commercial sector. The Internal Security Agency (*Binnenlandse veiligheidsdienst; BVD*) and the Military Intelligence Service (*Militaire Inlichtingendienst; MID*) perform the security

16 Ibid., p. 3.

17 Kamerstukken II 1976-1977, 13 872, nr. 7, p. 20.

18 *'Voor de vervulling van den vertrouwensfunctie komt slechts in aanmerking degene die Nederlander is.'*

19 *'Degene die geen Nederlander is, kan niettemin worden aangesteld wanneer het dienstbelang dat bepaaldelijk vordert.'*

20 Article 3, para. 1 of the *Wet Veiligheidsonderzoeken* defines *vertrouwingsfuncties* as: *"functies die de mogelijkheid bieden de veiligheid of andere gewichtige belangen van de Staat te schaden"* (positions which could compromise the security or important interests of the State).

investigations necessary to decide whether a person is suitable to be appointed to a *vertrouwensfunctie*.[21]

Posts which are considered to be a *vertrouwensfunctie* are classified in three categories: a, b and c posts, with a-posts providing access to top-secret information and b and c-posts to sensitive information considered to be of lesser importance.

There are a number of provisions in the Dutch legislation which lay down specific nationality requirements. The offices which require Dutch nationality are the following:

- Member of both Chambers of Parliament;[22]
- Minister Plenipotentiary (*Gevolmachtigd Minister*);[23]
- Member of the Provincial Council (*Provinciale Staten*);[24]
- King's Commissioner (*Commissaris van de Koning*)[25]
- Mayor (*Burgemeester*)[26]
- Members of the Guardianship Council (*Raad van Voogdij*);[27]
- Members of the Council of State (*Raad van State*);[28]
- Members of the Chamber of Audit (*Algemene Rekenkamer*);[29]
- Members of the main judiciary,[30] as well as judges at specialist courts;[31]
- National Ombudsman (*nationale ombudsman*);[32]
- Members of the military;[33]

---

[21] *Memorie van Toelichting*, Kamerstukken II 1999-2000, 26 883, nr. 3, p. 13.

[22] Article 56 GW.

[23] Article 8, para. 1, *Statuut voor het Koninkrijk der Nederlanden*.

[24] Article 10 *Provinciewet* and Article 129, para. 1, GW.

[25] Article 63 *Provinciewet*.

[26] Article 63 *Gemeentewet*; In 1998 a temporary exchange between Dutch and Belgian *burgemeesters* was suggested in a local newspaper. This was, however, deemed impossible by the Minister for Internal Affairs (after parliamentary questions were raised on the matter), because of Dutch *burgemeesters'* public order duties, and responsibilities under the *Vreemdelingenwet* (Alien's Act). Kamerstukken II 1998-1999 *Aanhangsel van de Handelingen*, nr. 667.

[27] Article 4, para. 2, *Wet Voogdij Minderjarige Koning*.

[28] Article 5 *Wet op de Raad van State*.

[29] Article 42, para. 1 *Comptabiliteitswet*.

[30] Article 3, para. 1, *Wet op de Rechterlijke Organisatie*.

[31] For instance: Military Courts (Article 20 *Wet Oorlogsstrafrecht*); *Pachtkamer* (Article 125, para. 4, *Pachtwet*), *Tariefcommissie* (Article 2, para. 1, *Tariefcommissiewet*).

[32] Article 3 *Wet Nationale Ombudsman*; this Article does not stipulate that the national ombudsman must have Dutch nationality, but does state that he or she will be dismissed from the post upon losing Dutch nationality.

[33] Article 5, para. 1, *Algemeen militair ambtenarenreglement*.

- Police officers[34] and voluntary police officers;[35]
- Notaries (*notarissen*).[36]

One group of offices is conspicuously absent from this list: Ministers and State Secretaries (*ministers* and *staatssecretarissen*). Nowhere in the Dutch legislation can it be found that Dutch nationality is required for the post of Minister or State Secretary, whereas when one looks at the posts listed above, it would seem evident that Dutch nationality should be a requirement for the post of Minister. One explanation for the absence of a nationality requirement for this group of public servants is that the legislator thought it too obvious to mention. Another explanation, though less likely, is that is was left to Parliamentary control to deal with situations that might arise, the idea being that Parliament would not allow a non-national to be appointed, and in the unlikely event that it would allow such an appointment, then it would be considered to be democratically sound.

The conclusion that can be drawn when looking at the nationality requirements is that the exclusion of non-nationals from the public service is limited in the Netherlands. On the whole, the civil service is open to non-nationals, both citizens from other EU Member States and third-country nationals. According to the Home Secretary at the time the Act of 1858 was revoked there were no legitimate reasons for distinguishing between these two groups of non-nationals.[37] This reasoning was based on the non-discrimination principles laid down in Article 1 of the Constitution[38] and on Article 26 of the International Covenant on Civil and Political Rights.[39]

Over and above the possibilities for non-nationals to gain access to employment within the Dutch civil service as it stands, the trend is towards still more leniency. The Government is openly considering actively recruiting non-nationals into the civil service due to a scarcity of workers with Dutch nationality in certain sectors of government.[40] Some experts are questioning the requirement for Dutch nationality for judges, for instance. MP Boris Dittrich stated

34 Article 7, para. 1a, *Besluit Algemene Rechtspositie Politie*.

35 Article 4, para. 1a, *Besluit Rechtspositie Vrijwillige Politie*.

36 Article 6, para. 1 *Wet op het notarisambt*.

37 *Memorie van Antwoord*, Kamerstukken II 1985-1986, 19 076, nr. 5, p. 3.

38 For the text of Article 1 GW, see note 8.

39 Article 26 of the ICCPR reads: 'All persons are equal before the law and are entitled without any discrimination to the equal protection of the law. In this respect, the law shall prohibit any discrimination and guarantee to all persons equal and effective protection against discrimination on any ground such as race, colour, sex, language, religion, political or other opinion, national or social origin, property, birth or other status.'

40 Ministerie van Binnenlands Zaken en Koninkrijkrelaties: Arbeidsmarktrapportage Overheid, May 1999, p. 77.

that he cannot see why non-nationals who have lived in the Netherlands all their lives and are familiar with its culture should not be appointed as judges.[41] Also, recently, the Dutch Police Union (*Nederlandse Politiebond; NPB*) suggested that the requirement of Dutch nationality as part of the application criteria be dropped. When questioned by Members of Parliament about his opinion on the matter, the Home Secretary stated that he saw no reason to change the current policy as described above.[42] The same suggestions have been made by the Netherlands Institute for International Relations 'Clingendael'[43] where it concerns the armed forces. As a solution to the lack of military personnel, Clingendael suggested that non-nationals be recruited into the Dutch army.[44] The Institute's reasoning was that since the Dutch army is primarily deployed in such areas as the protection of universal human rights and safeguarding international law and order, rather than the defence of the Netherlands against foreign enemies, Dutch nationality is no longer a necessary requirement. Members of Parliament responded negatively to this suggestion, as did the military unions. The Ministry of Defence refused to comment, but it seems unlikely that such measures will be taken in the near future.[45]

3 The status of public service employees

The public service knows three basic forms of employees, namely office holders, civil servants and contractual employees. The first two catagories are employed with the legal status of civil servant, the last catagory is employed under a labour law contract. Officials (*ambtsdragers*) occupy posts which have a political character. They are the ones who make policy decisions. Civil servants proper (*ambtenaren*) are the ones who execute policy, as do contractual employees (*arbeidscontractanten*).

Civil servants are appointed to their posts. This is a unilateral act: it is the employer (e.g. the State or a public body) who appoints the individual to the post. The individual in essence has no powers to exert influence on his contract of employment, since there is no such contract to be party to. However, over the last few decades the trend has been to diminish the difference in status between civil

41 Mr., September 1998, p.21.

42 Kamerstukken II 1999-2000, *Aanhangsel van de Handelingen*, nr. 1602; NJB, nr. 30, 1 september 2000, p. 1518/1519.

43 The Netherlands Institute for International Relations 'Clingendael' is a research institute which acts in an advisory capacity to the Government, Parliament and social organizations. It has as its objective the promotion of the understanding of international affairs.

44 See: http://www.nrc.nl/W2/Nieuws/2000/01/25/Vp/03.html (October 2000).

45 See: http://www.nrc.nl/W2/Nieuws/2000/01/25/Vp/03.html (October 2000).

servants and ordinary employees. More and more collective bargaining agreements (*Collectieve Arbeidsovereenkomsten*; CAOs) also apply ordinary employment law to civil servants. Also legislation originally only applying to the private sector has been introduced to the public sector, for instance the Works Council Act (*Wet op de Ondernemingsraden*).

The Dutch public service knows two forms of public service employees. First of all, there are the civil servants proper (see paragraph 4). Secondly, there are employees who are employed under a civil law contract of employment. These contractual employees are called *arbeidscontractanten*. However, the contracts of employment are not exactly the same as ordinary contracts of employment. Article 1637z of the Civil Code (*Burgerlijk Wetboek*; BW) states that the normal rules applicable to the employment contract do not apply to employees working for government bodies. Their legal position is ruled by the regulations (*arbeidsovereenkomstenregeling*) laid down by the government institution which employs them. However, in most cases the regulations state that the rules as laid down in the Civil Code apply in the same manner to these contractual employees as they do to normal employees. Also in certain areas they have the same rights as civil servants, such as, for instance, employee participation (*medezeggenschap*) and pensions.[46]

4 Civil servants

Apart from the strict term civil servant (*ambtenaar*), there are many state employees who are referred to by the public at large as *ambtenaren* (civil servants), but who do not have that legal status. The most identifiable amongst these are the *arbeidscontractanten* (contractual employees). All government employees or employees of public bodies are usually called civil servants, though many of them do not have that official status. Broadly speaking, it can be said that all employees who at some level represent the state, as far as the public is concerned at least, are civil servants.

However, according to Article 1 of the Civil Servants Act 1929 (*Ambtenarenwet 1929*), a civil servant is someone who is appointed to work in the public service.[47] Paragraph 2 then goes on to state that the public service entails all services and enterprises which are administered by the State or public bodies.[48] This is a formal criterion. The status of civil servant is dependent on appoint-

46 Peijpe, T. van, and Riphagen, J., *Schets van het Nederlands Ambtenarenrecht* (Kluwer, Deventer, 1994), p. 146.

47 Article 1, para. 1: *'Ambtenaar in de zin van deze wet is degene, die is aangesteld om in openbare dienst werkzaam te zijn'.*

48 *'Tot den openbaren dienst behooren alle diensten en bedrijven door den Staat en de openbare lichamen beheerd'.*

ment by the State or a public body. It is not based on the activities which are performed in that function. However, as we will see, bodies constituted under private law (mainly foundations, (*stichtingen*)) can also be considered as being part of the public service if there is a paramount government influence on the private body's policy making.[49]

Paragraph 3 of the said Article expressly excludes from this definition of civil servant all those workers within the public service who have a contract based on civil law, i.e. contractual employees.[50]

Article 2 of the Civil Servants Act goes on to exclude a number of posts from this definition of civil servant. The list is long and includes many posts with advisory bodies, but also includes state secretaries and ministers, the judiciary, as well as military personnel.

Article 1 of the Civil Servants Act 1929 contains two concepts which are crucial to the definition of a civil servant. The first of these is 'appointment' (*aanstelling*). Appointment alludes to the fact that civil servants are not employed under civil contract law. Their employment relationship is governed by public law.

The second concept is 'public service' (*openbare dienst*). In order to be a civil servant one has to be appointed by a government institution or body (i.e. Central Government, local authorities, etc.) or by an organisation governed by private law over which the Government has a paramount influence as regards the policy of such an organisation.

In the legal literature and also in the decisions of the Central Appeals Court (for the public service and for social security matters) (*Centrale Raad van Beroep*) it emerges that the official service relationship contains a subordinate element.[51] The public servant relationship is also determined by the power of appointment as well as the competence to dismiss, the power to give orders and instructions, and also the competence to issue sanctions.[52]

Even when a public servant has independent decision-making powers (for example, a Director of an employment office with regard to permission to terminate contracts of employment), instructions may still be given as regards the execution of his/her duties. If this could not be the case, then the political responsibility of the administrative authority in question would thereby cease.[53]

---

49 See, e.g., CRvB 8 March 1988, TAR 1988, 103; CRvB 1 July 1993, TAR 1993, 173; more detailed information on the forms this influence can take may be found below.

50 *'Niet is ambtenaar in de zin van deze wet degene, met wie een arbeidsovereenkomst naar burgerlijk recht is gesloten'.*

51 Roest, O. van der, *Ambtenarenprocesrecht in de praktijk* (VUGA, 's Gravenhage, 1986), p. 24.

52 Jeukens, Annotation with KB 14 January 1971, no. 16 AA 1971, p. 357.

53 Van Zutphen, p. 81.

As has already been said, the notion of 'public service' is to be found in the Civil Servants Act. In Article 1 of the Act, included within the definition of public servant is a person who is appointed for employment in the public service. To public bodies belong, alongside those bodies referred to in the Constitution, also bodies whose responsibilities, establishment and powers are determined through or on behalf of the public authority according to the law and whose eventual legal personality is not determined according to the provisions of the Civil Code. Also bodies with legal personality, which have come into being under a joint scheme between two or more public bodies, belong to the public service.[54]

The second part of Article 1 Civil Servants Act further defines the notion of 'public service' in that hereunder those services and companies which are administered by the state and the public bodies are also understood to belong.[55] These may be companies which possess legal personality which is governed by private law.

A service or company which is administrated by the state or a public body, and which is not a body governed by private law, undoubtedly belongs to the public service.[56] Alongside these organisations we can also include within the public service those legal persons governed by private law but upon whose administration the government exercises a paramount influence. In its case law the Central Appeals Court (for the public service and for social security matters) has chosen a substantive approach with regard to this matter.

The question whether a legal person, usually a *stichting*[57] (foundation), belongs to the public service from the perspective of the Civil Servants Act has been laid before the Central Appeals Court (for the public service and for social security matters) on many occasions. The Central Appeals Court has consistently considered as decisive 'the degree of influence which the Government is able to exercise on the Board of the legal person'.[58] This influence must be capable of being exercised *de jure*. Any other actual influence is therefore not sufficient.[59] In other words, the powers of the Government as they relate to the foundation must be legally relevant[60] and laid down in the legal person's articles (*stichtingsstatuten*).[61] Moreover, it is conceivable that these powers are laid down

54 CRvB 26 November 1985, TAR 1986, 31.

55 Van Zutphen, 1991, p. 88.

56 CRvB 4 May 1938, AB 1938, 528; CRvB 28 September 1948, AB 1948, 924 en Ag. 's-Gravenhage 27 September 1954, AB 1955, 604.

57 For more information on *overheidsstichtingen* (public foundations)see: Schroten, K., *De overheidsstichting op het niveau van de centrale overheid* (W.E.J. Tjeenk Willink, Deventer, 2000).

58 CRvB 6 January 1971, AB 1971, 128.

59 Van Zutphen, p. 91.

60 CRvB 6 May 1977, AB 1977, 267 and CRvB 19 May 1987, TAR 1987, 162.

61 CRvB 8 March 1988, TAR 1988, 103.

in a contract to be concluded between the government and the foundation. A precondition for this is that such a contract has been entered into for a long period of time.[62]

The Government must be able to exert its influence not only *de jure*, but it must also actually make use of this power.[63] Finally, this influence must be such that it is paramount (*overwegende invloed*).

In order to determine whether an influence is paramount, certain criteria have emerged from the case law:[64]

1 The Government must have a paramount influence on the composition of the Board and the appointment of Board Members. The Government must have the power to suspend Board Members and eventually to dismiss them from the Board. The Government can then exercise an indirect influence on the management of the foundation.
2 The government must have an important influence on the foundation's finances. This influence can exist in the determination of the remuneration paid to the foundation's employees, the approval of the budget, exerting control over the foundation's administration and rendering account to the Government.
3 The Government must play a role as regards personnel policy. This role can exist in providing its approval for an appointment, suspension or dismissal. The Government can also carry out these actions of its own accord. Moreover, it can play a role in the determination of the legal status and the other terms of employment relating to the personnel.
4 A certain amount of the foundation's decisions must be approved by or on behalf of the Government. Here we see a more intrinsic involvement in the foundation's activities.

If the legal person in question should fulfil all of these criteria, then the public service tribunal (*ambtenarenrechter*) will reach the conclusion that the foundation in question will belong to the public service and that its employees are therefore civil servants.

In addition, a number of other factors contained in the decisions of the Central Appeals Court (for the public service and for social security matters) may be referred to.[65] However, as regards these factors, they have not all been taken from cases in which the Central Appeals Court has determined that a body was to be considered as part of the public service. These were not therefore viewed as being decisive, but functioned as indications. These factors

62 Van Zutphen, p. 92.

63 CRvB 6 April 1966, AB 1966, 722 en CRvB 18 June 1976, 35.

64 Van Zutphen, p. 92.

65 Van Zutphen, p. 93.

are: the Government's power to amend the articles and to dissolve the foundation, the objective for which the foundation has been created, the source of the foundation's financial resources, the obligation to provide the government with certain information, the Board's lack of freedom when taking decisions to depart from directives laid down by the Government, and the power of the Government with regard to making use of a credit balance in the case of liquidation.

5 The impact of European law on the Dutch public service

It is not a simple matter to gain a clear understanding of to what extent European legislation has influenced the Dutch civil service. It seems that over the last few decades the Dutch legislator has been very forthcoming in opening up the public service to non-nationals. In fact, it seems that for the most part the Dutch legislator has been ahead of the European Court.

This is probably due to the changes made to the Dutch Constitution in the 1980s. It was decided to amend the provisions concerning access to the public service at the same time, as some of these provisions are laid down in the Constitution (see paragraph 2). As by that time it was already clear which way the European Court was heading concerning the public service exception as laid down in Article 39 (4) (ex Article 48 (4)) EC, the legislator decided to anticipate the events to come.

As a result, the Netherlands has not experienced any conflicts with Community legislation. Looking at the legislation as it now stands, problems are also not expected in the future.

6 Other categories of public service employees

For categories of workers who do not work for the Central Government it is less likely, though of course not impossible, to fall within the definition of the public service according to Article 39 (4) (ex Article 48 (4)) EC. Although at present there are no nationality requirements other than those mentioned in paragraph 2, there may be areas within the public service which could hypothetically, and legitimately as far as Article 39 (4) (ex Article 48 (4)) EC is concerned, have a nationality requirement attached. Therefore, we will look at their characteristics in the next few paragraphs.

6.1 Decentralised authorities

The Netherlands has two forms of decentralised authorities. At the lowest level there are the municipalities (*gemeenten*). In between Central Government and these municipalities there is a third layer of government: the Provinces (*provincies*). These two layers of government have as their area of administration all public interests within their own sphere which have not been attributed to other (higher) public bodies.[66] As a second task they have to cooperate and co-govern with the higher authorities.[67] Also local authorities have to cooperate in the execution of regulations laid down by the higher authorities.[68]

The Provinces are the so-called middle layer of government in the Netherlands. They have an integrating function between local government (in the form of the municipalities) and Central Government, but also between the municipalities themselves in certain policy areas, such as environmental legislation. Provinces allocate finances to municipalities. Provinces also have a duty to supervise local councils. According to Article 173 of the Provincial Act (*Provinciewet*) the Provinces' Deputised States (*Gedeputeerde Staten)* must alert the Minister of Home Affairs concerning any apparently illegal decision by a local council.

The Provincial Council (*Provinciale Staten)*, which is the Provinces' representative body, also has as its duty to elect the Members of the Upper House (*Eerste Kamer*) of Parliament.[69] As such, it has an indirect influence on the exercise of public authority. Therefore, it is not surprising that Dutch nationality is required for membership of the *Provinciale Staten*[70] as we have seen in paragraph 2.

Municipalities form the layer of government which is closest to the citizens. They regulate matters such as housing, street lighting, etc., matters which lie at the heart of daily life for the citizens in general.

Unlike for the representative body of the provinces, it is possible for non-nationals to be appointed. The criteria for election on to the local council are laid down in Article 10 of the Council Act (*Gemeentewet*; GemW). The main criteria are residency, a minimum age of 18 years and the fact that individuals in question should not have been stripped of their voting rights.[71] There are additional criteria for non-EU citizens. They have to have been legally resident

---

[66] Article 124, para. 1, GW.

[67] Ibid., para. 2.

[68] Kamerstukken II 1975-1976, 13 990 nr. 3, p. 7.

[69] Article Q1 of the *Kieswet*.

[70] Article 129, para. 1, GW and Article 10 *Provinciewet*.

[71] Article 10, para. 1, *Gemeentewet*.

in the Netherlands for a period of at least five consecutive years.[72] There are no additional criteria for EU citizens. They have the same voting rights as Dutch nationals.

6.2 Police officers

The police force has as its duty to maintain public order and to offer assistance to those who need it.[73] They have to perform this task as subordinates to the appropriate authority, i.e. the Mayor.[74]

The Dutch police force consists of 25 regional police forces (*regionale politiekorpsen*), a national police force (*Korps landelijke politiediensten*) and special police officers (*bijzondere ambtenaren van politie*).[75] The regional police forces are governed by the Mayor[76] in his duty as police force controller (*korpsbeheerder*), assisted by the chief of police (*korpschef*) who is in charge of the daily running of the regional police force.[77] The chief of police is the most important civil servant when it comes to the daily running of the regional police force. His appointment is by Royal Decree.[78] The chief prosecutor (*hoofdofficier van justitie*) is responsible for the investigation and prosecution policy in the region[79] and together with the Mayor and chief of police he is the main policy maker when it comes to regional police forces and together the Mayor and chief prosecutor are responsible for managing the regional police force.[80]

The national police force (*Korps Landelijke Politiediensten*; KLPD) have as their duties those police tasks which require special organisation or dealing with matters of a special nature.[81] They also take over from the regional police forces when required by national or international interests, or when the police duties are such tha they encorporate several regions. The police force controller in this

---

72 Ibid., Article 2.

73 Article 2 *Politiewet* 1993.

74 Article 172 *Gemeentewet* and Article 23, para. 1, *Politiewet* 1993.

75 Article 4 Politiewet 1993.

76 If a region contains more than one *gemeentes*, the mayor of the largest *gemeente* will usually be appointed as *korpsbeheerder.*

77 Article 24 *Politiewet* 1993.

78 Ibid. Article 25.

79 Ibid., Article 13.

80 Ibid., Article 27.

81 Ibid. Article 38, para. 1.

case is the Minister of Internal Affairs,[82] who is assisted in this duty by the chief of police.[83]

Besides the national and regional police forces, there is the Royal Military Police Constabulary (*Koninklijke marechaussee*), which is managed by the Minister of Defence. Their special duties are laid down in Article 6 of the *Politiewet* 1993 and include securing the safety of the members of the Royal family, securing the safety at Schiphol and other airports, assistance and cooperation with police forces from other countries.

As we have seen above in paragraph 2 Dutch nationality is required for all police officers. This is laid down in Article 7, paragraph 1a, *Besluit Algemene Rechtspositie Politie*. The same holds true for members of the voluntary police force, see Article 4, paragraph 1a, *Besluit Rechtspositie Vrijwillige Politie*.

6.3 Parliamentary staff

As we saw in paragraph 2, Members of both Chambers of Parliament have to have Dutch nationality. This is laid down in Article 56 of the Constitution. Nationality requirements are not laid down for their staff. However, these posts could be covered by the definition of a *vertrouwensfunctie*.

6.4 The judiciary

Members of the judiciary are called *rechterlijke ambtenaren* (judicial civil servants). They are, however, not civil servants such as those described in paragraph 4. They do not have a subordinate relationship with those who appoint them. This stands to reason as the judicial branch of government is separate from the executive branch. As such, members of the judiciary are never subordinate to the Government. The only authority they have to accept within the execution of their duties is that of the law, and in some cases that of the *Hoge Raad* (High Council). The judiciary has a duty to be independent of the executive and legislative branch so as to be able to settle disputes involving members of the other two branches of government. The Civil Servants Act 1929 for the most part does not apply to *rechterlijke ambtenaren*, as is the case, for example, for ministers, state secretaries and King's Commissioners and many

---

[82] Until January 2000, this duty fell to the Minister of Justice; the Act of 22 December 1999 transferred this responsibility to the Mininster of Internal Affairs, Staatsblad 2000, 27.

[83] Article 38, para. 3, *Politiewet* 1993.

others.[84] The judiciary has its own Act dealing with their position, namely the *Wet rechtspositie rechterlijke ambtenaren.*

In order to preserve their independence, judges are appointed for life[85] by Royal Decree.[86] They can only be dismissed from their post by the *Hoge Raad* (Supreme Court), the highest judicial authority, and only on certain specified grounds.[87] As we saw in paragraph 2, members of the judiciary have to possess Dutch nationality.[88]

6.5 Public bodies

In the next few paragraphs I want to look at how the term 'public body' or 'administrative authority' is defined in the Netherlands. The reason for doing this is that since public bodies sometimes exercise official power, they may fall within the definition of the term 'public service' as laid down in Article 39 (4) (ex Article 48 (4)) EC. Although, as I have previously stated, there are no other nationality requirements laid down in Dutch legislation other than those listed in paragraph 2, that is not to say that in practice some posts might not indeed be open to Dutch nationals only.

6.5.1 Development of government in the Netherlands

During the course of this century and especially after the Second World War the tasks of government have increased both in number and in scale. The restriction to so-called specific tasks of government was no longer observed. Today, many government tasks are no longer distinguished from activities in the private sector. The question whether in individual cases one can still speak of being employed in the public service has thereby not been made any easier. It was previously also not a simple matter due to the fact that legislation made use of a large number of different terms to mean roughly the same thing: legal person governed by public law (*publiekrechtelijk rechtspersoon*), body possessing public law personality (*rechtspersoonlijkheid bezittend publiekrechtelijk lichaam*), public legal person (*publiekrechtelijke instelling*), public body (*openbaar lichaam*), government body (*overheidslichaam*), legal person set

84 Article 2 *Ambtenarenwet.*

85 Article 4 para. 1 *Wet op de Rechterlijke Organisatie.*

86 Article 117 GW.

87 Article 11 *Wet op de Rechterlijke Organisatie.*

88 Ibid., Article 3, para. 1.

up under public law (*rechtspersoon die krachtens publiekrecht is ingesteld*), administrative authority (*bestuurslichaam*).[89]

This problem was magnified in the 1980s by the trend towards privatisation. Many tasks previously carried out by the government were at that time privatised. In some cases in this respect independent enterprises arose. In other cases, however, the government retained to a greater or lesser degree a certain influence on the policy of such an enterprise, for example by means of its shareholding, the possibility of appointing board members, etc. Particularly in the case of the latter, it is often difficult to decide whether we can speak of a public service or not.

In my investigation into the question of when a body or an agency forms part of the public service I would like to begin by looking at the notion of administrative authority under the General Administrative Law Act (*Algemene wet bestuursrecht*); hereinafter referred to under its Dutch abbreviation: Awb) because such administrative authorities in any case form a part of the public service and as such are public bodies.

6.5.2 The notion of administrative authority under the *Algemene wet bestuursrecht* (Awb)

In the Awb (*Algemene wet bestuursrecht*; the General Administrative Law Act) the notion of administrative authority occupies centre stage. It is important to keep in mind the objective of the legislation. The Awb has as its objective greater clarity within the field of administrative law and safeguarding the legal rights of the citizen.

According to paragraph 1 of Article 1:1, under a, an administrative authority is an organ in the form of a legal entity which has been established under public law.[90] (These administrative authorities are hereafter also referred to as 'a-authorities'). Legal persons instituted under public law are those legal persons which have not been established by the execution of a legal act under private law.[91]

---

89 Lange, R. de, 'Openbare lichamen, rechtspersonen en bestuursorganen: kortsluiting in het publiekrecht', in Vucsán, R. (ED.), *De Awb-mens: boeman of underdog* (Nijmegen, Ars Aequi Libri, 1996). See also: Berge, J. ten and Zijlstra, S, *De publiekrechtelijke rechtspersoon in ontwikkeling* (Preadvies NJV 2000) (W.E.J. Tjeek Willink, Deventer, 2000).

90 Article 1:1 paragraph 1 reads: *'Onder bestuursorgaan wordt verstaan: a. een orgaan van een rechtspersoon die krachtens publiekrecht is ingesteld'.*

91 Bense, M. and Zijlstra, S., 'Het begrip bestuursorgaan - Betekenis en strekking van artikel 1:1 eerste lid, Algemene wet bestuursrecht', *Nederlands Tijdschrift voor Bestuursrecht* 1994/9, p. 254.

Bense and Zijlstra provide the following definition: 'One could only speak of an a-authority if the legal person to which the institution belongs has been instituted according to public law and, as an institution, it has itself a public law basis in the form of a public duty'.[92] However, this does not seem to be completely accurate. The public duty criterion will only apply when there is a question of public authority. In other words, in the case of an administrative authority such as under b.

In Article 1:1, paragraph 1, under b, Awb other persons invested with public authority may also be considered as administrative authorities (so-called 'b-authorities').[93] These b-authorities fall outside the main constitutional structure of the government organisation and have not been modelled along public law lines. In practice these will be natural persons and persons or bodies which are an organ of a legal person governed by private law, such as foundations, associations or companies.[94]

B-authorities come into being by means of attribution or delegation of public law competences. In most cases this will occur when, under the law or the (authority's) decision to delegate, the legal person governed by private law and which is vested with public authority is directly designated as such.[95]

All the dealings carried out by a-authorities will fall under the Awb. The text suggests that the b-authorities with all their dealings will also fall under the Awb. But must b-authorities only be considered as administrative authorities *in so far as* they are vested with public authority? In the Awb's Explanatory Memorandum[96] the Government takes as its point of departure that *certain* legal persons governed by private law fall within the bounds of the Awb as far as 'all their dealings' are concerned. That is to say, not *all* b-authorities will fall under the Awb as far as all their dealings are concerned. In the legal literature it is also accepted that b-authorities will only amount to administrative authorities *in so far as* they are invested with public authority.[97]

The question of the presence of public authority is of crucial importance in the definition of the b-authorities. We are here dealing with persons or bodies which do not belong to the category of legal persons established under public law (a-authorities). These are persons or bodies which are an organ of a legal person governed by private law, such as foundations, associations and companies.[98]

---

92 Ibid., p. 260.

93 Article 1:1 reads: *'Onder bestuursorgaan wordt verstaan: b. een ander persoon of college, met enig openbaar gezag bekleed'.*

94 Berge, J. ten, *Besturen door de overheid* (W.E.J. Tjeenk Willink, Deventer, 1996), p. 83.

95 Bense/Zijlstra, p. 264.

96 *Memorie van Toelichting*, Kamerstukken II, 1991/1992, 22 300, nr. 39, pp. 27-28.

97 Konijnenbelt, W. (*et al.*), *Hoofdlijnen van administratief recht*, (LEMMA, Utrecht, 1994), p. 74.; Berge, J. ten, *Besturen door de overheid* (W.E.J. Tjeenk Willink, Deventer, 1996), p. 84.

98 Berge, J. ten, *Besturen door de overheid* (W.E.J. Tjeenk Willink, Deventer, 1996), p. 83.

There are a number of ways in which a body can be vested with public authority. These are:

- 'under or according to the law'; this concerns the obtaining of competence according to public law. This may be obtained in two ways, namely by attribution[99] and by delegation.[100]
- through subsidisation; the legal competence to grant subsidies and the allocation thereof to a body endowes an organ with public authority and thereby renders it an administrative authority in the sense of the Awb.
- through the exercise of 'paramount government influence'; bodies constituted under private law can also be counted as being part of the public service if there is a paramount government influence on the private body's policy making.[101]

Employees of a-authorities are civil servants, unless there are provisions to the contrary are made and individuals are employed under private law (*arbeidscontractanten*). Employees of b-authorities on the whole do not have the status of civil servants, unless the body in question is covered by the definition of the *Centrale Raad van Beroep* (Central Appeals Court (for the public service and for social security matters)).[102]

After the implementation of the Awb, the new definition of 'administrative authority' no longer has paramount government influence as its prime criterion. The central question here is whether or not there is a case of public authority. Paramount government influence is in itself not sufficient to be able to automatically conclude that an administrative authority in the sense of the Awb actually exists, as is the case under the law which pertains to public servants. There must in addition, and according to the legislative history, be public officials in the employ of the legal person governed by private law and/or there must be a case of 'public authority'.

As we saw in paragraph 4, as far as the law pertaining to public servants is concerned, in order to answer the question of whether a service or company belongs to the public service it is not considered of importance whether the service or company is vested with public authority. The Awb, however, *does* impose this condition where it concerns the question of whether an administra-

---

99 Attribution is the establishment of a certain power and the subsequent granting of that power to a certain organ. The establishment of a particular power is only possible through an organ that that power itself has brought about by statutory provisions.

100 Under Article 10:13 Awb delegation is described as the transfer by an administrative authority of its power to make orders to another organ, which then assumes responsibility for the exercise of this power.

101 For the definition of 'paramount government influence', see paragraph 4.1.

102 See paragraph 4.1.

tive authority exists. The question whether a body is vested with public authority is the *formal question* of whether the body has at its disposal a 'public law competence to determine the legal status (the rights and/or the obligations) of other legal subjects'. The notion of 'public service', as it appears in the Civil Servants Act 1929, on the other hand, is more concerned with the *substantive question* of whether the service or company can be considered to belong to the organisation of government. As it would appear, it is here namely of importance to determine in how far the government can exercise an influence on the management of the service or the company.

6.6 Comparison of two public bodies

As we have seen above, according to paragraph 1 of Article 1:1, under a, an administrative authority is an organ in the form of a legal entity which has been established under public law. It is also possible for bodies encorporated under private law to exercise public authority. As such they can be classified as administrative authorities under Article 1:1, paragraph 1, under b of the the Awb.

In the next two subparagraphs I want to compare two public bodies and see the sort of activities they perform. These are the *Stichting Toezicht Effectenverkeer* (STE, Securities Board), a so-called b-authority and the *Gezondheidsraad* (Health Council), an a-authority.

6.6.1 *Stichting Toezicht Effectenverkeer* (STE)

Since its establishment in 1988, the STE has been entrusted on behalf of the Finance Minister with the supervision of the Dutch stock exchanges. The STE reports to the Minister on the supervision it exercises. It has as its mandate to ensure the proper functioning of the securities markets, to protect the position of investors and to increase the transparency of the securities markets.

The *Wet Toezicht Effectenverkeer* (Act on the Supervision of the Securities Trade; Wte), which took effect on 15 June 1992, contains new regulations for the supervision of the securities trade both on and off the exchanges. The aim of the Wte is to promote the proper functioning of the securities markets and to protect the position of the investor. Under the Wte, most of the Minister's responsibilities and powers are delegated to the STE. Nowadays, the STE itself is responsible for exercising its mandate, such as granting licences, reviewing stock exchange regulations and investigating incidences of insider trading.

Since the Minister of Finance bears the political responsibility for the supervisory activities, he has been involved with the STE ever since it was established. The Minister nominates the STE board members and also approves the STE's budget and any amendments to its statutes.

Taking a look at the duties and responsibilities of the STE as well as its enforcement powers with which to accomplish its tasks one could come to the conclusion that this foundation exercises public authority. It also protects one of the general interests of the state, namely that trading in securities occurs in a legal and controlled way. As such it is possible, and even highly probable, that the STE complies with the criteria laid down in the definition of 'public service' in Article 39 (4) (ex Article 48 (4)) EC. Therefore, it would be allowed under Community law to impose nationality requirements for members of the STE. However, at present there is no such restriction in effect.

6.6.2 *Gezondheidsraad*

The *Gezondheidsraad* (Health Council) has as its task to provide the Dutch Government and Parliament with information concerning the current level of knowledge relating to public health issues.[103] The Council does this by publishing reports at the request of the Ministry of Health, Welfare and Sport and of other ministries, in particular the Ministry of Housing, Spatial Planning and the Environment, the Ministry of Social Affairs and Employment, and the Ministry of Agriculture, Nature Management and Fisheries. The reports the *Gezondheidsraad* produces are public documents.

Sometimes reports are submitted to the government or to Parliament at the Council's own initiative. The usual objective of reports in this category is to draw attention at an early stage to scientific developments which may have consequences for Dutch government policy.

The *Gezondheidsraad* is headed by a President and two Vice-Presidents and boasts approximately 170 members, selected from the scientific and health care communities. Members are nominated by the President of the Council on the basis of their personal expertise and are appointed by Royal Decree. The *Gezondheidsraad* is financed entirely by the government. Depending upon its work programme, the Council is granted a budget which is made up of contributions from the Ministry of Health, Welfare and Sport, the Ministry of Housing, Spatial Planning and the Environment, the Ministry of Agriculture, Nature Management and Fisheries and the Ministry of Social Affairs and Employment.

In contrast to the *Stichting Toezicht Effectenbeheer* this body does not exercise public authority. It does not have powers of enforcement. It is an body which

[103] Article 22 of the *Gezondheidswet*.

supplies the Government with objective information and hands out advice on health issues. Therefore, in the case of the *Gezondheidsraad* it would not be allowable to have a nationality requirement as one of the criteria for appointment as one of its members.

7 Conclusions

If we overlook the nationality requirements as laid down in Dutch legislation the main conclusion that can be drawn is that on the whole the Dutch public service is open to non-nationals. The number of posts which require Dutch nationality have been kept to a minimum as we saw in paragraph 2.

As far as the posts which require Dutch nationality are concerned, I think it is safe to say that all of them are covered by the public service exception as laid down in Article 39 (4) (ex Article 48 (4)) EC. Therefore, there it is not very likely that the Dutch legislation would not be in accordance with Community law.

The Dutch legislator has chosen to open up posts which do not require Dutch nationals to all non-nationals. It has not limited public service posts to EU citizens only. It has thereby gone beyond that which was strictly necessary on the basis of Community law.

The definition of what constitutes the public service in the Netherlands is not always clear. There are many semi-public and also private law bodies of which it is not immediately apparent whether they fall within the definition of public service. However, this need not be a major problem as far as the public service exception is concerned. Currently there are no specific nationality requirements which apply to these bodies, nor is it likely that a *vertrouwensfunctie* would form part of such semi-public or private bodies. However, it is not impossible for such bodies to be covered by the definition of public service as far as Article 39 (4) (ex Article 48 (4)) EC is concerned. As such, should nationality requirements for such bodies be introduced in the future, an examination of the activities of the body in question would be necessary in order to decide whether or not such a restriction would be allowable under Community law.

CHAPTER 8

Access to Public Service Employment in Belgium

1 Introduction

The Belgian state can be described as a devolutionary federation. This refers to the fact that the constitutional order redistributes the powers of a unitary state among a number of component entities.[1] These component entities have an autonomous status with regard to their fields of responsibility.

The Belgian State knows three *Gemeenschappen* (Communities).[2] There is the Flemish (Dutch-speaking) Community, the French-speaking Community and the German-speaking Community. The territory of Belgium is divided into three *Gewesten* (Regions)[3]: the Flemish Region, the Brussels Capital Region (French-Dutch bilingual) and the Walloon Region (French-speaking).

The regions and communities are quite separate entities from the federal state. They are not subordinate to the central authority. Within the areas of their jurisdiction they are in fact themselves the central authority and they organise their own administrations.[4] As a result of this state structure, the public service in Belgium is by no means a national unity. One can say that in Belgium the Federal State has the Communities and Regions as its equal partners. Each has jurisdiction over seperate domains. For instance, the Regions have jurisdiction over economic policy, except for the powers given to the Federal State which deal with safeguarding the unity of economic policy and the Belgian currency, the Frank. The Communities have autonomous powers when it concerns education, although the Federal State still sets the minimum requirements for the awarding of diplomas and such matters.

On the territorial level, the Belgian state is divided into 10 provinces[5] and 589 municipalities.[6] Depending on the subject matter, these decentralised authorities exercise their powers autonomously, but under the supervision of the Regions or the Communities, or ultimately the federal authorities.[7]

---

1 Peeters, P., 'The Federal Structure: Kingdom, Regions and Communities', in Craenen G. (Ed.), *The Institutions of Federal Belgium; An Introduction to Belgian Public Law* (Acco, Leuven, 1996), p. 57.

2 Article 2 of the Constitution

3 Article 3 of the Constitution.

4 Boes, M., 'The Central Administration and the Decentralized Agencies', Craenen G. (Ed.), *The Institutions of Federal Belgium; An Introduction to Belgian Public Law* (Acco, Leuven, 1996), p. 138.

5 Article 5 of the Constitution.

6 http://www.koksijde.be/bestuur/verkiezing/info1.htm (October 2000).

7 Craenen, G., 'Belgium: General Background and Legal Charecteristics', in Craenen G. (Ed.), *The Institutions of Federal Belgium; An Introduction to Belgian Public Law* (Acco, Leuven, 1996), p. 25. See also paragraph 6.1 for more detailed information concerning the decentralised authorities.

2 Nationality requirements in Belgium

The main principle regarding nationality requirements is laid down in Article 10 of Title II, entitled 'Belgians and their rights', of the Belgian Constitution (*Grondwet*; hereinafter also: GW). Article 10 reads:

'There are no class distinctions in the State.'

Belgians are equal before the law; they are the only ones eligible for civil and military service, but for exceptions that could be determined by law in special cases.'[8] From the wording of this Article it could be concluded that only Belgian citizens are entitled to equal protection before the law. This is not the case, however. Article 10 should be read in conjunction with Article 191 GW[9] which states:

'All foreigners on Belgian soil benefit from the protection provided to persons and property, save for those exceptions provided by law.'[10]

The exceptions provided by law also have to abide by the rules and regulations laid down in international conventions to which Belgium has acceded, such as the EC Treaty and the Treaty on European Union, but also the European Convention on Human Rights, for instance.

Belgium also has the Act on the Punishment of Certain Actions Prompted by Racism or Xenophobia of 30 July 1981[11] which criminalises most instances of racism under common penal law. In addition to this general legislation there is a special criminal Act which penalises incitement to discrimination, hatred, violence or segregation against a person or a group of persons on the basis of race, colour, birth, nationality or ethnic origin. This Act also criminalises denying persons access to public goods or services on a discriminatory basis.

In the next paragraphs the legislation concerning nationality requirements for access to the public service will be dealt with in more detail.

---

8 In Dutch the text reads: *'Er is in de Staat geen onderscheid van standen. De Belgen zijn gelijk voor de wet; zij alleen zijn tot de burgerlijke en militaire bedieningen benoembaar, behoudens de uitzonderingen die voor bijzondere gevallen voor een wet worden gesteld.'*

9 Tilleman, B., Van Haegendoren, G and Alen, A., 'Legal Position of Aliens', in Alen, A. (ed.), *Treatise on Belgian Constitutional Law* (Kluwer, Deventer, 1992), p. 236.

10 The Dutch text reads: *'Iedere vreemdeling die zich op het grondgebied van België bevindt, geniet de bescherming verleend aan personen en aan goederen, behoudens de bij de wet gestelde uitzonderingen.'*

2.1 History of the nationality requirement

Article 8, section 2 of the Belgian Constitution states that the law determines the conditions for the exercise of political rights, in addition to Belgian nationality.[12] To be appointed to a public service post is considered to be the exercise of a political right and hence requires, in principle, the possession of Belgian nationality. In addition Article 10 (ex Article 6[13]) of the Belgian Constitution (*Grondwet*; GW) lays down the basic rules as regards the access of non-nationals to the public service. It states that only Belgians can be appointed to civil service and military posts, except where legislation provides otherwise.[14] This nationality requirement was first and foremost inspired by the principle that employees working for public bodies should have a loyalty to the Belgian State.

Even at the time of drafting the Constitution in 1831 there were questions concerning the desirability of excluding all non-nationals from the public service. The National Congress discussed the pros of losing valuable non-nationals from the public service sector against the cons of compromising the principle of loyalty. Those who opposed a wider access for non-nationals stated that acquiring Belgian nationality was the best way to prove loyalty to the Belgian State. In the end the rather wide exclusion received the majority of the votes.

The interpretation of this principle of exclusion in Article 6 of the old Constition became an issue quite early on. When the 1842 Act on Primary Education[15] was discussed in Parliament it was stressed that the term *openbare bediening* (public service) was to be interpreted narrowly, in that it only encompassed public service posts which dealt with the exercise of public authority and that, therefore, teachers in primary education did not fall under this nationality requirement.

This narrow, functional interpretation of Article 6 (as it then was, now Article 10) did not coincide with that of the Legislation Commission of the Ministry of Internal Affairs[16] which in 1867 and 1872 advised on allowing non-nationals to be appointed as teachers in the 'official' schools. This Commission

---

11 *B.S.* 8 August 1981; *Wet tot bestraffing van bepaalde door racisme of xenofobie ingegeven daden.* The Dutch text reads: *'De Grondwet en de overige wetten op de politieke rechten bepalen welke de vereisten zijn waaraan men moet voldoen, benevens de staat van Belg, om die rechten te kunnen uitoefenen.'*

12 Peeters, P., 'The Federal Structure: Kingdom, Regions and Communities', in Craenen G. (Ed.), *The Institutions of Federal Belgium; An Introduction to Belgian Public Law* (Acco, Leuven, 1996), p. 57.

13 The new Coordinated Constitution of 17 February 1994 renumbered the Articles and Article 6 is now Article 10.

14 For the text of Article 10, see p. 196 and note 8.

15 *Wet van 23 september 1842 op het lager onderwijs.*

16 *Wetgevingscommissie van het Ministerie van Binnenlandse Zaken.*

chose to interpret Article 6, second sentence, as covering all posts within the public service. This was the start of a swing away from a functional approach and towards an institutional approach. Any post within the public service now had a nationality requirement.

The institutional approach to Article 6 was never really questioned after that, at least not until the matter once again became paramount as a result of Community legislation. The fact that the text of the Constitutional Article did not make any distinction between the different posts within the public service was seen as an implicit choice by the legislator in favour of the institutional approach.

Historically the possession of Belgian nationality was a requirement for employment in all posts within the public service, regardless of whether the post was part of the civil service proper, or whether it was a contractually-based employment relationship. The only criterion was whether the person in question worked within the public service or for a public body or institution.

The question following on from this interpretation of the nationality requirement is which bodies and organs are part of the public service? A fairly simple description of the public service was held to be applicable here: any body or organ that is established by the government in order to serve a public need and that is under the control of the Government.[17] The central criterion is not whether these bodies execute traditional state functions or more commercial functions which could also be executed by private bodies. The main criterion is their establishment as a public body. An institutional approach, therefore.

The Constitutional Article being as broad as it was, there was no real need for separate nationality requirements in any other legislation. Even so, the requirement was placed in a number of other laws, but always with the same broad meaning. The legislation in question includes the *benoemingsvoorwaarden voor het rijkspersoneel*[18], *benoemingsvoorwaarden voor het tijdelijk rijkspersoneel*[19] and *benoemingsvoorwaarden voor het tijdelijk werkliedenpersoneel van het Rijk*[20] (appointment criteria for several categories of central government personnel). There was no differentiation between personnel of different ranks: the nationality requirement was applicable to any and all posts. This legislation worked as a template for other statutes. According to Article 87 paras. 3 and 4 of the *Bijzondere Wet* (Special Act) of 8 August 1980, the same rules were applicable to local government personnel.

---

[17] Mast, A., Alen, A. and Dujardin, J., *Overzicht van het Belgisch Administratief Recht* (Kluwer Rechtswetenschappen, Antwerpen, 1996), p. 71.

[18] Art. 16, para. 1, 1° KB 2 October 1937, coordinated KB 16 March 1964, *B.S.*, 25 March 1964, *B.S.*, 7 July 1964.

[19] Art. 2a R.B. 30 April 1947, *B.S.*, 15 May 1947, err. *B.S.*, 31 May 1947.

[20] Art. 2a KB 10 April 1948, *B.S.*, 19-20 April 1948.

The nationality requirement also applied to teachers, directly to personnel in public schools,[21] also indirectly to teachers in privately-run schools subject to government subsidies as allowances are only given to personnel with Belgian nationality.[22]

2.2 The demise of the institutional approach

The main Constitutional Article has remained unchanged since it was introduced in the first Belgian Constitution of 1831. However, after it became clear, due to the developments in Community Law dealing with Article 39 (4) (ex Article 48 (4)) EC, that it could no longer be maintained as strictly as it had been, a Declaration[23] was issued so as to reinterpret the Article in question.

After the European Court of Justice delivered its ruling in the case *Commission* v. *Belgium*[24] it was clear that the broad interpretation of Article 6 (2),[25] and the other nationality requirements based on that Article, was at odds with Community law.

As we have seen in the previous paragraph, the nationality requirement was at first not designed to have a broad institutional meaning. Originally, when the Constitution was first drafted in 1831, the requirement was only meant to apply to posts within the public service which required loyalty to the Belgian State from the civil servant in question. It was not until later, after the advice of the Legislation Commission of the Ministry of Internal Affairs that the broader institutional interpretation gained ground and became widely accepted.

This broad interpretation was laid down and enacted in the *Ambtenarenstatuut* (Civil Servants Statute)[26] in 1937. It is not a coincidence that this occurred at a time when unemployment was high. At the same time the employment of non-nationals in the private market was also being curtailed and monitored.[27] One can therefore assume that the main reason for laying down this broad interpretation was not so much the necessity for loyalty to the Belgian State as the protection of the Belgian labour market for the benefit of its own nationals.

---

21 Public schools meaning state-organised schools.

22 Art. 28, para. 1, 1° Act of 29 May 1959, *B.S.*, 19 June 1959.

23 *Verklaring* of 8 November 1987, *B.S.*, 9 November 1987.

24 Case 149/79, [1980] ECR, 3881.

25 As it then was, now: Article 10.

26 KB 2 October 1937.

27 KB nr. 285, 2 March 1936.

2.3 Current nationality requirements

The definition of who has Belgian nationality and how this nationality is acquired or lost is governed by the *Wetboek van de Belgische nationaliteit* (Belgian Nationality Code).[28]

As we have seen in the previous paragraphs, the Constitution in Article 10 (ex Article 6) states that only Belgians can be appointed to posts in the public service and the military. The Article does provide for exceptions to be made in special cases which have to be laid down in legislation. A non-national can only be appointed to a post in the public service if there is an Act which specifically provides for this.[29]

However, due to Community legislation in this area, i.e. Article 39 (4) (ex Article 48 (4)) EC, and the Court's interpretation of that provision it is clear that as far as EU citizens are concerned the meaning of *'burgerlijke en militaire bedieningen'* (public and military service) is to be interpreted narrowly, in accordance with what the European Court has defined as public service for the purposes of Article 39 (4) (ex Article 48 (4)) EC.[30] This restriction to the Constitutional Article has been recognised, but has not led to an amendment of the provision itself, even though this has been proposed in the past.

The rules governing the access of non-nationals to the civil service proper are laid down in Article 1, paragraph 3, 1° of the Royal Decree of 22 September 1994.[31] It states that to be eligible for a civil service post, the candidate must have Belgian nationality if the post directly or indirectly involves participation in the exercise of *openbaar gezag* (public authority) and encompasses activities aiming at the protection of the general interests of the Federal State, the Community or the Region. For other functions, it is sufficient to be a citizen of the European Union.[32]

---

28 Of 28 June 1984, as amended by the Law of 17 June 1991 and the Law of 22 December 1998.

29 Article 10 does not apply to ecclesiastical functions.

30 'A series of posts which involve direct or indirect participation in the exercise of powers conferred by public law and duties designed to safeguard the general interests of the state or of other public authorities.' Case 149/79, *Commission* v. *Belgium*, [1980] ECR 3881, para. 10.

31 Royal Decree concerning general principles of the rules governing the federal civil service employees of the Communities and Regions, *B.S.*, 1 October 1994. This Decree replaces the Royal Decree of 21 November 1991 and has retroactive effect as from 7 March 1992.

32 Article 1 (3) reads, in the Dutch text: *'Tot ambtenaar kan enkel worden benoemd wie aan de volgende algemene toelaatbaarheidseisen voldoet:*

1° Belg zijn indien de uit te oefenen betrekking een rechtstreekse of onrechtstreekse deelneming aan de uitoefening van het openbaar gezag inhoudt en werkzaamheden omvat strekkende tot bescherming van de algemene belangen van de Staat, de Gemeenschap of het Gewest ofwel, in de overige gevallen, Belg zijn of burger van de European Unie'.

Nationality requirements for public sector workers employed under contract were for the most part abandoned by the implementation of a Royal Decree[33] in 1991. This decree was modified in 1995[34] and ever since the rule to be applied is the following: Belgian nationality is required when the post involves direct or indirect participation in the exercise of public authority *and* includes activities designed to safeguard the general interests of the state [JEB: emphasis added].[35] As we can see from the wording of this provision, the two criteria have to be applied cumulatively. It follows the European Court's interpretation of the public service exception as laid down in Article 39 (4) (ex Article 48 (4)) EC in *Commission* v. *Belgium*[36] almost word for word.

Not all Belgian legislation seems to be in accordance with the above mentioned general rule. The *Vlaams Personeelsstatuut* (Flemish Personnel Statute), for example, has a slightly differently worded nationality requirement. Article XIV 7, 6° states that employment on a contractual basis in posts which involve *direct* participation in the exercise of public authority *or* include activities designed to safeguard the general interests of the Flemish Community or other public bodies are open to Belgian nationals only [JEB: emphasis added]. The wording of this Article is too broad in one sense to be allowable under Community law, because it sees the two criteria as having to be applied cumulatively rather than alternatively. On the other hand, this Article does not preclude non-Belgian nationals from posts which involve *indirect* participation in the exercise of official authority. In that sense this Article is narrower than even the European Court's interpretation of Article 39 (4) (ex Article 48 (4)) EC.

Other requirements for access to the public service will be judged according to the relevant legislation in the non-national's country of origin. Such requirements are the possession of civil and political rights and compliance with the legislation on compulsory military service.[37]

There are no general rules dealing with the access of non-nationals to local government posts. However, until recently Belgian nationality used to be required for the following posts: Provincial Governor and members of the Provincial Council,[38] Mayor and members of the Municipal Council,[39] secretary to the local council,[40] under-secretary to the local council[41] and local tax collec-

---

[33] KB 18 November 1991 *tot vaststelling van de voorwaarden voor indienstneming bij arbeidsovereenkomst in sommige overheidsdiensten*, *B.S.* 18 January 1992.

[34] KB 13 April 1995, *B.S.* 29 April 1995.

[35] Article 2, para. 1, 2° of KB 18 November 1991, as replaced by Article 1, 1° of KB 13 April 1995.

[36] Case 149/79, [1980] ECR 3881, para. 10.

[37] See Commentary with the *Vlaams Personeelsstatuut*, part XIV, Title 2, Chapter 2.

[38] Article 23, para. 1 of the Provincial Electoral Act (*Provinciekieswet*).

[39] Article 1 of the Municipal Electorial Act (*gemeentekieswet*).

[40] *Gemeentesecretaris.*

[41] *Adjunct-gemeentesecretaris.*

tor,[42] sublieutenants with the local fire service[43] and police officers.[44] In 1999, subject to the influence of the Maastricht Treaty, these nationality requirements were changed, however.[45]

3 The status of public service employees

The public service can be defined as any organism of public law which has as its duty to serve the public interest. There is also a second, broader definition which describes public service as purely serving the public interest, whether or not this is done by a public body. According to the second definition, a private person or company can also have a public service duty.[46] In this Chapter I am mainly concerned with the first definition of public service. It is within those public bodies that the status of civil servants and nationality requirements play a role.

In the previous paragraph the Belgian public service nationality rules have been discussed. The next few paragraphs discuss the characteristics which are deemed to be specific to Belgian public service employees.

3.1 The public service principles

The Belgian public service is governed by a number of principles. First and foremost, the administration as a whole must pursue the public interest. There is a principle of continuity,[47] which means that the public service has to function without interruption even when there is a change of government. On the other hand, there is also is a certain amount of flexibility within the public service as the rules governing the organisation and operation of the public service can at any time be unilaterally modified by the competent authority. For example, the Royal Decree that decides on civil servants' remuneration and the conditions for their employment can be amended at any time.[48] This is the principle of adaptability or flexibility.[49]

---

[42] *Gemeente-ontvanger,* Art. 2, 1° KB 20 July 1979, *B.S.*, 10 August 1976.

[43] *Beroepsonderluitenant van de gemeentelijke brandweerdiensten,* Art. 5, 1° KB 20 July 1972, *B.S.*, 17 August 1972.

[44] Art. 2, 1° KB 2 April 1979, *B.S.*, 19 April 1979.

[45] See paragraph 6.1.

[46] Mast, A (*et al.*), pp. 75/76.

[47] *Beginsel van de continuïteit;* Peeters, P. and Alen, A., 'The Executive', in Alen, A. (Ed.), *Treatise on Belgian Constitutional Law* (Kluwer, Deventer, 1992), p. 93.

[48] Ibid.

[49] *Beginsel van de veranderlijkheid.*

Then there is also the principle of equal access,[50] which at first sight has less to do with the status of public servants themselves, and more with the rights of the public. It entails that every citizen under the same conditions can lay claim to the public service on an equal basis. This principle, however, also extends to access to the civil service which should be equal for all citizens subject to the same conditions.[51]

4 Civil servants

As is the case almost everywhere, under Belgian law there is a legal difference between civil servants and employees in the private sector. The main reason for the differences in their status is that civil servants are supposed to serve the public interest. A civil servant is in effect a servant of the public good and since the government of a state is supposed to embody the public interest, the relationship between a civil servant and his employer is not one of equality. A civil servant is appointed, whereas an employee has a contract of employment.[52] Legally speaking, the employer and employee have contractual equality, though in actual fact an individual employee is often too weak in relation to the employer to speak of true equality. The appointment of a civil servant is an unilateral act.

Civil servants' rights and duties are laid down in a Statute, namely the *Ambtenarenstatuut* (Civil Servants Statute) which can be unilaterally amended by the competent authorities.

Article 107[53] of the Constitution lays down the principle that the King appoints the civil servants in posts at the federal government level as well as foreign posts, although there can be exceptions to this main rule when laid down by law.[54] Other civil servants can be appointed on grounds of a specific statutory provision.[55] These 'other civil servants' include employees with municipalities or provinces. Since these decentralised forms of government have their own recognised autonomy, they have the authority to appoint their own employees.

---

50 *Beginsel van de benuttigingsgelijkheid.*

51 Peeters/Alen, p. 94.

52 The Supreme Court (*Hof van Cassatie*) decided that civil servants do not have a contractual employment relationship with the public authorities that employ them, Cass. 8 December 1932, Pas., 1933, I, 44.

53 Ex Article 66.

54 The Dutch text reads: *'De Koning benoemt [...] de ambtenaren bij het algemeen bestuur en bij de buitenlandse betrekkingen, behoudens de door de wetten gestelde uitzonderingen'.*

55 The Dutch text reads: *'Andere ambtenaren benoemt hij alleen krachtens een uitdrukkelijke wetsbepaling.'*

Most those working in the Belgian public sector are appointed as *statutair ambtenaar* (statutory civil servants, i.e. civil servants proper) by the Government or another public authority. However, there are numerous persons[56] working within the public sector on the basis of a contract of employment. These are called *contractueel ambtenaar* (contractual employee). However, there is a limitation on the reasons for using contracted employees rather than appointed ones. According to Article 4 of the Statute of 22 July 1993 encompassing certain measures dealing with civil servant affairs,[57] contractual employees can only be used in cases of extraordinary and temporary personnel shortages (paragraph 3), the replacement of civil servants (paragraph 4), and extraordinary increases in the workload or special orders (paragraph 5). The same criteria are present in regional legislation, such as in Article XIV 2 of the *Vlaams Personeelsstatuut* (Flemish Personnel Statute).[58]

The main rule for appointment in the public service remains that a person who is so employed has the status of a civil servant. Appointment of contractual workers is still the exception to this rule, even though numerically they are no longer a small minority. Also in regional, provincial and local government, contractual workers can only be appointed in the above mentioned special cases. This state of affairs was confirmed by the *Raad van State* (Council of State) in a number of court cases brought by contractual employees.[59] The *Raad van State* decided that contractual workers did not have the status of civil servants, even when they were permanently employed by public bodies. However, the *Raad van State* also made clear that there is no legislative prohibition on the employment of contractual workers.

Whether or not the employees of public bodies have a statutory or contractual employment relationship depends on the statute or declaration which instituted the public body. This statute or regulation will lay down the relationship between the public body and its employees. If there is no mention of this in the statute or declaration, then the public body has the choice of taking either route.[60]

In order to be appointed as a civil servant proper (*statutair ambtenaar*) an individual has to pass the so-called comparative application examination

---

[56] At the Federal Ministries the percentage of contractual workers was 21% on 1 January 1996; Janvier, R., *Contractanten in overheidsdienst* (Mys en Breesch, Gent, 1997), p. 12. More up to date figures show that, at a local level, contractual employees are actually outnumbering civil servants: local government employed 75,800 civil servants and 86,700 contractual employees in 1999; (according to the *Vereniging van de Vlaamse Steden en Gewesten* (VVSG; Association of Flemish Cities and Regions).

[57] *Wet houdende bepaalde maatregelen inzake ambtenarenzaken, B.S.* 14 August 1993.

[58] Janvier, R., *Contractanten in overheidsdienst*, (Gent, Mys en Breesch, 1997), p. 12/13.

[59] *R.v.St., Jadot*, nr. 15.908, 8 June 1973; *R.v.St., Dupont* nr. 19.012, 24 May 1978; *R.v.St., Hercot*, nr. 21.558, 18 November 1982.

[60] *R.v.St., Solon*, nr. 19745, 13 July 1979.

(*vergelijkend wervingsexamen*). These examitions are set by a body called Selor[61] which is part of the Civil Service Ministry. According to the application requirements, only Belgians and nationals from EU Member States are allowed to sit these examitions. The results of the examinations are comparative. This means that individuals who have scored the highest have the first option of being appointed to a post.

Appointments on a contractual basis do not require having to sit and pass these examinations. In those cases individuals can apply directly to the public body involved. Sometimes an examination is involved in the application procedure, however, they are not comparative.

4.1 The principle of loyalty and continuity

Civil servants in Belgium have a right to strike. This is not an unlimited right, however. This follows from the general principle of continuity of public service, which entails that the public interest overrides the personal interest of any given civil servant. On the whole, civil servants have to exercise their duties to the best of their abilities.

After the Belgian accession to the European Social Charter[62] in 1990, civil servants' right to strike was accepted, but this right is only enforceable when laid down in legislation.[63] There is no one specific Act which deals with this topic for all civil servants, but the right to collective action has been provided for in numerous Acts for certain categories of civil servants.[64] The military and the operational personnel of the *Rijkswacht/Gendarmerie* (the state police) are prohibited from taking strike action.[65]

4.2 Political neutrality

Civil servants, like ordinary citizens, enjoy the constitutional rights of freedom of expression and the freedom of political conviction. However, as civil servants they are subject to the rules of the administrative apparatus of which they are a part. This means that a civil servant has to exercise his office with loyalty and integrity. This also means, according to the principle of

61 *Selectiebureau van de Federale Overheid.*

62 Of 18 October 1961.

63 Art. 6, para. 4 and Annex II of the European Social Charter.

64 For example, civilian personnel employed by the *Rijkswacht/Gendarmerie*.

65 Mast, (*et al.*), pp. 199/200.

equality, that his conduct cannot be discriminatory when it comes to dealing with the public. Civil servants must also avoid any conduct which might lead to a decrease in the public's faith in the public service.[66]

5 The impact of European law on the Belgian public service

The leading case dealing with the public service exception in Article 39 (4) (ex Article 48 (4)) is *Commission* v. *Belgium*.[67] In that case it was made clear that it was not up to the individual Member States to decide upon the scope of the public service exception. In this, the first major case on Article 39 (4) (ex Article 48 (4)) EC, the European Court defined the exception narrowly, namely to include only those 'posts which involve direct or indirect participation in the exercise of powers conferred by public law and duties designed to safeguard the general interests of the state or of other public authorities.'[68] Jobs such as shunters, drivers and plate-layers with the Belgian National Railway and as joiners and gardeners with the City of Brussels were not to be reserved for Belgian nationals.

The Court's decision in this case led to the very direct resulting impact of European law on the Belgian interpretation of its nationality requirements for the civil service.

As we saw above in paragraph 3.3 the rules governing the access of non-nationals to the civil service proper are currently laid down Article 1, paragraph 3, 1° of the Royal Decree of 22 September 1994.[69] It states that to be eligible for a civil service post, the candidate must have Belgian nationality if the post directly or indirectly involves participation in the exercise of public authority (*openbaar gezag*) and encompasses activities aiming at the protection of the general interests of the Federal State, the Community or the Region.

In the wording of this Article we recognise the European Court's interpretation of Article 39 (4) (ex Article 48 (4)) EC. This legislation was directly inspired by the Court's case law. This can also be deduced from the Report to the King (*Verslag aan de Koning*) which accompanies the Royal Decree concerning general principles of the rules governing the federal civil service employees of the Communities and Regions of 22 September 1994.[70] In this report the Minister of Home Affairs and the Civil Service refers to the European Court's ruling

---

66 Arts. 10 and 11, para. 1, KB of 2 October 1937, as amended by KB of 26 September 1994.

67 Case 149/79, [1980] ECR 3881.

68 Ibid., para. 10.

69 Royal Decree concerning general principles of the rules governing the federal civil service employees of the Communities and Regions.

70 *B.S.* 1 October 1994.

against Belgium and states that it would be desirable to avoid any more such cases. It goes on to say that as a result Article 1, paragraph 3 of the Royal Decree will be worded according to the European Court's interpretation of Article 39 (4) (ex Article 48 (4)) EC.[71] Posts which fall within this definition will be open to Belgian nationals only. All other posts are open to Belgians and European Union citizens alike. It is worth noting here that these posts have *not* been opened up to all non-nationals, merely to European Union citizens.

6 Other categories of public service employees

Apart from civil servants there are other government or public body employees who can be classified as public service employees. Although these categories of workers are less likely to fall within the definition of the public service according to Article 39 (4) (ex Article 48 (4)), this it not impossible and they are not by definition precluded from being covered by the public service exception. Therefore, we will look at their characteristics in the next few paragraphs.

6.1 Decentralised authorities

Like most other states, Belgium has both a central authority and decentralised authorities which perform certain tasks. This is a form of territorial decentralisation. Some decentralised authorities have a certain degree of autonomy. This means that in certain respects they are not hierarchically subordinated to the central authority and have powers independent of the consent or approval of the central government in order to execute their tasks.[72] However, *provincies* (provinces) and *gemeenten* (municipalities) should be viewed as subordinate governments, because the delegation of power to local government is limited. If the delegation of power to local government were absolute, then there would no longer be a unified nation state. Provinces and municipalities are provided with authority over 'all matters of a provincial and of a municipal interest'.[73] The determination of whether a matter is in fact of provincial or municipal interest is up to the national legislature.[74]

---

71 Ibid., 24839.

72 Boes, p. 140.

73 Articles 41 and 162, 2° GW.

74 Alen, A., Tillemans. B. and Meersschaut, F., 'Decentralised Authorities', in Alen, A. (Ed.), *Treatise on Belgian Constitutional Law* (Kluwer, Deventer, 1992), p. 161.

Also, the national authority has a form of control over local government through the appointment of representatives at the provincial and municipal authorities. Local government in Belgium has a threefold structure. First, there is a democratically elected body: respectively, the *provincieraad* (Provincial Council) and *gemeenteraad* (Municipal Council). Within this body the Executive, i.e. respectively, the *bestendige deputatie* (Permanent Deputation) and the *college van burgemeester en schepenen* (the Committee of Mayor and Aldermen), is elected by majority vote from amongst its members. However, the head of the local Executive, the *provinciegouveneur* (Provincial Governor) and the *burgemeester* (the Mayor) is appointed by the national executive. As such the national authority has a form of control, albeit a limited one, over local government.[75]

Finally, there is a more direct form of control which the national authority can assert over provincial or municipal governments. Provincial and municipal by-laws[76] are subject to administrative supervision by the higher authority whose approval, authorisation or advice may be required as a form of preventive control. Also, measures can be suspended or annulled in order to prevent the law from being violated or general interests from being harmed.[77]

As we saw in paragraph 2.3 there are no general rules setting out the nationality requirements for local government officials. There were, however, a few posts which until recently, according to the *Provinciekieswet* (Provincial Electoral Act) and the *Gemeentekieswet* (Municipal Electoral Act), required Belgian nationality. These are the Provincial Governor and members of the Provincial Council,[78] the Mayor and members of the municipal council,[79] secretary to the local council,[80] under-secretary to the local council[81] and local tax collector.[82]

The fact that according to these Acts Belgian nationality was required for members of the municipal councils was in violation of EU law. This was confirmed by the European Court in case C-323/97, *Commission* v. *Belgium*.[83] According to Article 19 (ex Article 8b) of the EC Treaty every citizen of the Union has the right not only to vote in municipal elections, but also to stand for election in local government.

In 1999 a number of legislative acts came into force changing the rules concerning the requirement of Belgian nationality for posts with local, i.e.,

---

75 Ibid.

76 *Besluiten.*

77 Article 162, 6° GW.

78 Article 23, para. 1 of the Provincial Electoral Act (*Provinciekieswet*).

79 Article 13 of the Municipal Act (*gemeentewet*).

80 *Gemeentesecretaris.*

81 *Adjunct-gemeentesecretaris.*

82 *Gemeente-ontvanger,* Article 2, 1° KB 20 July 1979, *B.S.*, 10 August 1976.

83 [1998] ECR I-4281.

municipal government. The first of these was the Act of 27 January 1999[84] which introduced the passive and active voting rights in municipal elections for non-Belgian EU citizens in Article 1 bis of the *Gemeentekieswet*. This means that EU citizens can now take part in and stand for election at the municipal level. However, although they can be part of the municipal council they cannot be put forward as a candidate for the post of mayor and it naturaly follows that they cannot be appointed as Mayor. The changes to be made by the municipalities and the model applications by non-Belgians seeking access to local elections and the model decisions on such applications were set out in a *omzendbrief* (circular letter),[85] *koninklijk besluit* (Royal Decree)[86] and *ministerieel besluit* (ministerial decision)[87], all dated 25 May 1999.

6.2 Police officers

The *commissaris van politie* (Commissioner of police) is a local council civil servant. Police commissioners are appointed by the King.[88] All police officers must possess Belgian nationality.[89] The publications advertising posts with the police force in the *Belgisch Staatsblad* all mention being a Belgian national as the first requirement.

6.3 Parliamentary staff

Members of Federal Chambers, consisting of the *Kamer van volksvertegenwoordigers* (Chamber of Representatives) and the *Senaat* (Senate),

84 *B.S.* 30 January 1999; *Wet tot wijziging van de wet van 19 oktober 1921 tot regeling van de provincieraadverkiezingen, van de nieuwe gemeentewet en van de gemeentekieswet, en tot uitvoering van de richtlijn van de raad van de Europese Unie nr. 94/80/EG van 19 december 1994*.

85 *B.S.* 3 June 1999; *Omzendbrief betreffende de inschrijving van de niet-Belgische burgers van de Europese Unie als kiezers voor de gewone vernieuwing van de gemeenteraden.*

86 *B.S.* 3 June 1999; *Koninklijk besluit tot bepaling van de wijze waarop de erkenning van de aanvraag die de niet-Belgische burgers van de Europese Unie ingediend hebben bij de gemeente van hun hoofdverblijfplaats om ingeschreven te worden op de kiezerslijst die opgesteld wordt voor de verkiezingen van het Europees Parlement of voor de gemeenteraadsverkiezingen, ingeschreven wordt in de bevolkingsregisters.*

87 *B.S.* 3 June 1999; *Ministerieel besluit tot vaststelling van het model van de aanvraag die de niet-Belgische burgers van de Europese Unie die in België gevestigd zijn, moeten indienen bij de gemeente van hun hoofdverblijfplaats als zij wensen ingeschreven te worden op de kiezerslijst die opgesteld wordt voor de gemeenteraadsverkiezingen, evenals de modellen van de beslissing waarbij het college van burgemeester en schepenen deze aanvraag ofwel erkent, ofwel verwerpt.*

88 Article 191 *Nieuwe Gemeente Wet* (New Municipal Act).

89 For instance with the *Rijkswacht*, see: Royal Decree of 24 May 1999, *B.S.* 24 June 1994.

have to have Belgian nationality. This is laid down in Articles 64 and 69 of the Constitution. Also, according to Article 97 of the Constitution, only Belgian nationals can become ministers.[90]

6.4 The judiciary

One of the fundamental principles of the separation of powers in a modern nation state is the independence of the judicial branch of government. This principle is laid down in Article 151 of the Constitution. The judiciary is by definition not a servant of the state in that sense of the word.

There are a number of safeguards as to the independence of the judiciary.[91] First and foremost, there is Article 152 of the Constitution. It states that appointments within the judiciary are for life. They cannot be relieved of their function by the legislative branch of government, nor by the executive branch. They can only be suspended or removed from office by members of the judiciary themselves.[92] Judges' salaries are laid down by law[93] and judges are barred from engaging in other forms of paid employment or activities which are considered to be incompatible with the office of a judge.[94]

Judges are appointed by the King. However, only the judges in the lower courts are appointed directly. For the judges in the higher (appellate) courts appointments by the King take place after nomination by, on the one hand, the *hoven* (courts of appeal) and, on the other, either the *Provincieraden* (Councils of the Provinces) or the *Senaat* (Senate).

Article 151 of the Constitution introduces a *Hoge Raad voor de Justitie* (High Council for Justice). This council deals with all kinds of aspects concerning the appointment of judges and other posts within the Belgian judiciary. The Council should ensure objective appointments and stimulate better management and quality within the Justice department.

The conditions for appointment as a judge are laid down in Title VI of the *Gerechtelijk Wetboek* (Judicial Code).[95] The conditions mentioned for the different judicial posts include age requirements, a law degree and the need to have passed the examination proving professional competence, but the need to possess Belgian nationality is not mentioned (at least not in the Judicial Code

---

90 The text reads: *'Alleen Belgen kunnen minister zijn'.*

91 Alen, A., *Algemene beginselen en grondrechten van het Belgisch Publiek Recht; Boek 1 De Instellingen* (Story-Scientia, Brussel, 1988), pp. 192/193.

92 See Articles 404-413 of the *Gerechtelijke Wetboek* (Judiciary Code).

93 Article 154 of the Constitution (GW).

94 Article 155 GW.

95 *B.S.*, 31 October 1967.

or the Constitution) is the need for possession of Belgian nationality. Article 259bis-1[96] of the Judicial Code states, however, that the High Council for Justice consists of forty-four members, all of whom have to be Belgian nationals.

6.5 Public bodies

Apart from territorially defined decentralised authorities there are also specially created agencies, which are entrusted with the execution of specific duties. The first agencies were created in the late 19th century and nowadays there are numerous autonomous agencies.[97]

Under Belgian law an agency can only be a functionally defined decentralised authority if it has legal personality, which can only be bestowed on a public agency by or by virtue of a legislative decision. Although decentralised authorities are in some sense autonomous, they are still under the control of the central authority, although this is only a limited form of control. This is essentially a negative form of control. On the whole they cannot compel an agency to do anything, but they can forbid certain activities.[98] The degree of autonomy varies greatly between institutions. Often the national executive has a right to appoint key positions in the institutions, as well as having a form of control through administrative oversight and financial control.[99]

There are two main forms of functionally defined decentralised institutions. First, there are the public institutions, which are set up by a unilateral government decision. Secondly, there are public associations which are set up through an association of public bodies or through the association of public bodies and private persons.[100]

6.5.1 *Openbare centra voor maatschappelijk welzijn* (O.C.M.W.s)

O.C.M.W.s (*openbare centra voor maatschappelijk welzijn*; public centres for social welfare) are public institutions with legal personality. By law[101] they have as their duty to provide social services in order to ensure everyone's

96 *B.S.*, 2 February 1999.

97 Boes, p. 141.

98 Ibid., p. 142.

99 Alen (*et al.*), pp. 170/171.

100 Ibid., p. 172.

101 *B.S.*, 5 August 1976; *Organieke wet van 8 juli 1976 betreffende de openbare centra voor maatschappelijk welzijn.*

human dignity (Article 1). O.C.M.W.s are organised at the municipal level. However, the social services that they provide are not part of the municipal powers of authority. Nevertheless, the members of the O.C.M.W.s are appointed by the municipal council,[102] and a certain part of their activities are supervised by the local authorities.[103]

More specifically, the O.C.M.W.s' duties are to offer assistance or services of a social, socio-medical or medical nature to anyone who needs such services. The services provided do not limit themselves to material help to individuals, but also extend to providing information, providing advice, supplying help with official paperwork, offering educational help, and taking part in child protection services. Also, they play a preventative role in individual cases, as well as on a more collective level[104].[105] The service provided by the O.C.M.W.'s are to be extended to all persons who reside within the municipality.

As mentioned above, the members of the O.C.W.M.s' council are appointed by the municipal council. Until recently, in order to become a member of the O.C.W.M's council one had to possess Belgian nationality.[106] This situation was changed by the Decree of 18 May 1999.[107] The requirement of Belgian nationality was replaced by the requirement of being registered as a voter in municipal elections, thereby making membership of the O.C.M.W.s' council available to EU citizens.[108]

7 Conclusions

The conclusion that can be drawn from this chapter is that it has taken Belgium quite some time to comply with the Community legislation on the public service exception as laid down in Article 39 (4) (ex Article 48 (4)) EC.

Twice the Commission had to bring infringement proceedings against Belgium, namely in 1979[109] and again in 1994.[110] Not until the 1990s did the

[102] Article 14 of the Act of 8 July 1976.

[103] Ibid., Articles 109 and 111.

[104] Ibid., Articles 1, 57, 58 and 63-68.

[105] Mast (*et al.*), p. 509.

[106] Article 7 (old) of the Act of 8 July 1976.

[107] *B.S.*, 30 June 1999; *Decreet houdende wijziging van de organieke wet van 8 juli 1976 betreffende de openbare centra voor maatschappelijk welzijn.*

[108] See also the circular letter of 8 June 1999, *B.S.*, 30 June 1999; *Omzendbrief betreffende het overzicht van de diverse wijzigingen die bij de decreten van 18 mei 1999 aangebracht werden in de organieke wet van 8 juli 1976 betreffende de openbare centra voor maatschappelijk welzijn.*

[109] Case 149/79, [1980] ECR 3881.

[110] Case C-173/94, [1996] ECR I-3265.

Belgian legislator make any real changes to the nationality requirements laid down in various legislative acts. The legislator chose not to change the main rule dealing with nationality requirements for the public service, which is laid down in Article 10 of the Constitution.

Nowadays it is clear that as far as EU citizens are concerned the meaning of 'public and military service' in Article 10 of the Constitution is to be considered narrowly, in accordance with the European Court's definition of public service for the purposes of Article 39 (4) (ex Article 48 (4)). This restriction to the Constitutional Article has been recognised by the Belgian Government, but has not led to any amendment of the Constitution provision itself. Instead the Government chose to introduce changes by issuing two Royal Decrees. Nationality requirements for public sector workers employed under contract were for the most part abandoned with the implementation of the Royal Decree of 18 November 1991. The new rules governing access for non-nationals to the civil service proper are laid down in the Royal Decree of 22 September 1994.[111]

With the changes introduced by the two Royal Decrees, Belgium on the whole seems to be complying with Community legislation on the public service exception. However, it is difficult to state this categorically. As we have seen in paragraph 6.5.1, there are areas within the public service (i.e. O.C.M.W.s) which were not opened up to EU citizens until 1999. There may be other such public bodies which have also not officially been opened up as required by Community law. It is, therefore, impossible to state with a degree of certainty whether or not Belgium has fully complied.

Lastly, it is worth noting here that although contractual posts are available to all non-Belgians (including third-country nationals), civil servant posts are not.[112] Appointments as civil servants (*statutair ambtenaar*) are open to European Union citizens only. This has the result of limiting the opening up of civil servant posts to non-nationals to that which is strictly required on the basis of Community law. This is a different approach from that which has been chosen by the Dutch legislator.[113]

---

111 Royal Decree concerning general principles of the rules governing the federal civil service employees of the Communities and Regions, *B.S.*, 1 October 1994, Article 1, paragraph 3, 1°.

112 See paragraph 4.

113 See Chapter 7, paragraph 2.

CHAPTER 9

Access to Public Service Employment in the United Kingdom

1 Introduction

One of the most notable features of the legal framework governing the civil service in the United Kingdom is the scarcity of statutory regulation. There is no comprehensive statutory code governing the terms and conditions of civil service employment. Some aspects are covered by statute, but most continues to be governed by royal prerogative. This, therefore, remains the main source of authority of the State as the employer.

The Royal prerogative is defined as 'the residue of discretionary or arbitrary authority, which at any given time is legally left in the hands of the Crown.'[1] In other words, the authority to control the civil service is a pure executive power. The royal prerogative should be seen as an age-old source of authority, that can be described as a body of powers, rights and immunities and duties which belong to the Crown and which are not based in statutes.[2] The prerogative is traditional and can ultimately be traced back to the relationship between the ruler and the subject, one which demands protection from the ruler, both at home and overseas, and from the subject loyal allegiance to his state and his ruler.[3] The prerogative is exercised by the government on behalf of the Crown, or on the government's or minister's advice.

2 Nationality requirements in the United Kingdom

British citizenship applies to every existing citizen of the UK and colonies. Under the British Nationality Act 1981, citizenship is acquired in 4 ways - birth, descent, registration and naturalisation. Existing colonies have special Acts pertaining to them, e.g. the British Nationality (Falklands Islands) Act 1983 automatically conferring British citizenship.

The definition of a 'UK national' as far as EC legislation is concerned is laid down in the UK Declaration on Nationality for EC Purposes which came into effect on 1 January 1983. UK nationals are: British citizens (i.e. those who are entitled to hold a British passport), some Irish and Indian citizens with dual nationality and British Dependent Territories citizens acquiring their citizenship from a connection with Gibraltar.

There are nationality requirements for a number of posts in the UK civil service. The basic rules for posts in central government civil service are laid down in the Civil Service Nationality Rules (see next paragraph). However, in

[1] Dicey, A., *Law of the Constitution* (10th edn), (Macmillan, London, 1959), p. 424.

[2] Pollard, D. and Hughes, D., *Constitutional and Administrative Law, Text and Materials* (Butterworths, London, 1990), p. 55.

[3] Speech by Viscount Ratcliffe in: *Burmah Oil Co Ltd* v. *Lord Advocate*, [1965] A.C. 75.

the UK civil service most recruitment decisions are delegated[4] and in practice recruitment is carried out by individual Departments and Agencies. This allows them to recruit in order to meet their specific needs. These Departments and Agencies also decide on which nationality requirements (if any) are applicable, but there are guidelines which are provided by the Civil Service Nationality Rules.

In the United Kingdom most classical State functions are reserved for British and Irish citizens. In fact, since 1700 aliens[5] have been excluded from 'any office or Place of Trust either civil or military.'[6] This provision is still in force and covers those individuals who hold their responsibilities directly from the Crown, such as police officers, magistrates and judges.

In principle, aliens are also excluded from appointment to any office or place in the civil service.[7] The possibility of aliens to be employed in any civil capacity under the Crown is, however, recognised in the Aliens Employment Act 1955, which allows for the *temporary* employment of individuals or groups of aliens when the service requires this.[8] Nevertheless, there is no right of access to employment on a par with nationals.

Besides the Civil Service Nationality Rules there is also the Race Relations Act (RRA) 1976, which has a bearing on discrimination against non-nationals. The RRA prohibits discrimination against non-nationals in large sectors of the public service. Thus, unlike a first impression which may be gained on the basis of the main legislation, in practice many jobs in the local and national public service are open to aliens.[9]

The RRA is relevant to the rules on access to the public service for non-nationals because it provides that it is unlawful to discriminate on racial

---

4 With effect from 1 January 1983 all Departments were given responsibility for the selection of staff at junior levels, subject to instructions by the Minister for civil servants. As a consequence, departments became responsible for about 85 percent of all civil servants appointments. After the Civil Service Order in Council 1991 came into effect, recruitment responsibility was extended to all grades and posts below Grade 7, which meant that they controlled 95 percent of all recruitment. HC (1992-93) 390-II, p. 168.

5 Commonwealth (including British) and Irish citizens are not aliens for this purpose (see Schedule 7 to the British Nationality Act 1981).

6 Act of Settlement 1700, s. III.

7 Aliens Restriction (Amendment) Act 1919, s. 6: 'After the passing of this Act no alien shall be appointed to any office or place in the Civil Service of the State'.

8 S. 1 para. 2 states that aliens can only be employed if there are no suitable British subjects available, or in cases where such an alien possesses exceptional qualifications or experience making him specifically suitable for the post.

9 Handoll, J., 'Article 48(4) and Non-National Access to Public Employment', 13 *European Law Review* (1988) pp. 223-241, p. 226.

grounds in relation to access to and the conditions of employment.[10] According to the RRA the term 'racial grounds' includes nationality,[11] which includes citizenship.[12]

Even though racial discrimination is not the same as discrimination on the grounds of nationality, the two concepts have many similarities and as such an investigation into the Race Relations Act is relevant. Moreover, there is the fact that nationality rules can have a discriminatory effect along racial lines. It is not unheard of for racial discrimination to be disguised as discrimination on nationality grounds. Therefore, it is important to realise that covert forms of racial discrimination are not allowed under UK law and that nationality requirements for reasons other than safeguarding genuine national interests cannot be tolerated.

The non-discrimination provisions of the RRA apply in principle to most posts in government service.[13] There are, however, important exceptions. The Act does not declare any act of discrimination by virtue of any enactment or Order in Council unlawful,[14] so that the statutory provision continues to apply. Nationality conditions in the Civil Service Commission General Regulations are unaffected.[15] Also, nothing will render unlawful an act for the purposes of safeguarding national security.[16] However, where ministers or government departments make appointments to offices or posts which do not constitute employment for the purposes of the RRA, they are nevertheless under a general obligation not to act in a way which would constitute unlawful discrimination if the offices or posts in fact amounted to such employment.[17]

There are two other important restrictions to the RRA. First, the non-discrimination provisions do not apply to restrictions placed on immigrants as parts of the conditions of their entry.[18] Secondly, certain prescribed public bodies may continue to impose a nationality requirement.[19]

---

10 RRA, s. 4.

11 S. 3, which states: '"racial grounds" means any of the following grounds, namely colour, race, nationality or ethnic or national origins'.

12 S. 78, which contains the general interpretation provisions, states very concisely that '"nationality" includes citizenship'. It seems that for the purposes of the RRA the legislator did not consider the difference in concept between nationality and citizenship (see Chapter 3) to be relevant.

13 RRA, s. 75 (2).

14 Ibid., s. 41 (1).

15 Ibid., s. 75 (5).

16 Ibid., s. 42.

17 The Home Office Guide to the Race Relations Act 1976, para. 3.32, http://www.homeoffice.gov.uk/reu/racdisc.htm (August 2000).

18 RRA, s. 41 (2). Not, of course, a major problem for European Community/Union workers, since the conditions for entry are now laid down in Community law, see Chapter 2.

19 RRA, s. 75 (5). See below.

On the whole the Act prohibits discrimination against non-nationals by important public sector employers: local authorities (which include education authorities), the National Health Service, public corporations such as the British Broadcasting Corporation (BBC), and numerous commercial and industrial undertakings. The RRA also applies to prison officers and the armed forces. Since the public sector bodies mentioned above together make up a large part of the public sector, it is safe to say that a large number of posts in the public sector are, therefore, in principle open to nationals from other Member States on a par with nationals.[20]

Even though the RRA has made a number of public service posts available to non-nationals, it has in essence preserved the validity of the nationality rules governing eligibility for employment in the service of Central Government and a number of prescribed public bodies. For instance, non-British nationals cannot be employed in the civil service without a certificate.[21] The RRA in itself permits the Minister to restrict employment in the service of the Crown or any prescribed public body to persons of a particular birth or nationality, descent or residence.[22] Over the years the Minister has publicised the Civil Service Nationality Rules in order to provide guidelines as to which posts were restricted to nationals only. These rules have witnessed a drastic change over the last decades due to developments within the European Community and now the European Union.

2.1 Civil Service Nationality Rules

The Civil Service Nationality Rules refer to the Aliens Restriction (Amendment) Act 1919. This Act includes a statutory prohibition on the employment of foreigners in the civil service.[23] However, nowadays there are three legal exceptions to this prohibition. The European Communities (Employment in the Civil Service) Order (SI 1991/1221) was introduced to amend the Aliens' Employment Act 1955 in order to enable nationals of other European Community (now: European Union) Member States and certain non-EU family members to be employed in many civil service posts. It is obvious that the Order was introduced so as to comply with European law on Article 39 (4) (ex Article

[20] Handoll (1988), pp. 224-226.

[21] Aliens Employment Act 1955, s. 1.

[22] RRA, s. 75(5).

[23] The Amendment Act of 1919 was an extension of the original Aliens Restriction Act of 1914. The original Act restricted the employment of non-nationals during times of war. The 1919 Amendment extended these rules and made them applicable, after the ending of the First World War, during peacetime.

48 (4)) EC as this is specifically stated in the Explanatory Note to the Order. The European Economic Area (EEA) Act 1993 enables nationals of Member States of the European Free Trade Area (EFTA), except Switzerland and Liechtenstein, to be employed in the civil service, together with certain non-EFTA family members, on the same basis as nationals of EC Member States under SI 1991/1221. There is also a provision that, in exceptional circumstances, foreigners, other than EEA and non EEA family members mentioned above, may be employed with an Alien's Certificate under the Aliens' Employment Act 1955. In addition, under the Civil Service Order in Council dated 15 March 1995 and the Diplomatic Service Order in Council dated 5 February 1991, the Minister for the Civil Service and the Secretary of State for Foreign and Commonwealth Affairs may make nationality rules governing recruitment to the Home Civil Service and Diplomatic Service respectively.

The Civil Service Nationality Rules state the following:[24]

1 Posts in the Home Civil Service where special allegiance to the state is required are reserved for UK nationals. Most posts, however, are not in the reserved category and do not therefore require such special allegiance; they are additionally open to Commonwealth citizens;[25] British Protected persons; EEA nationals of other Member States; and certain non-EEA family members. Where there is a vacancy in the non-reserved category allowing applications from these groups, the recruitment publicity accompanying the application form should say so.
2 Very exceptionally someone who falls outside the above groups may be considered for an appointment in the non-reserved category for up to five years under the Alien's Certificate arrangements in circumstances where it appears to the Minister for the Civil Service and to the Minister of the employing Department or agency that no suitably qualified person meeting the relevant nationality criteria is available or that the individual has exceptional qualifications or experience for the appointment.
3 For posts in HM Diplomatic Service and Home Civil Service posts under the Foreign and Commonwealth Office (except the Overseas Development Administration) an individual can only be eligible if:
   a. he/she is a British[26] citizen, and
   b. the Secretary of State for Foreign and Commonwealth Affairs is satisfied that he/she is so closely connected with the United Kingdom,

[24] Office of Public Service, Nationality Section of the Security Division, 1 June 1996.

[25] Which includes British Dependent Territories citizens, British National (Overseas) citizens and British Overseas citizens.

[26] An individual holding dual nationality should check with the Head of Recruitment at the Foreign and Commonwealth Office whether holding that second nationality could cause any problems.

taking into account such considerations as upbringing and residence, that he/she may be appointed.

4 For certain appointments under the Minister for the Civil Service, the Secretary of State for Defence or the Secretary of State for Foreign and Commonwealth Affairs, other than appointments in the Diplomatic Service, the relevant criteria may apply or particular requirements may be prescribed.

It has proved difficult to discover to which posts within the civil service the Civil Service Nationality Rules actually apply in practice. Numerous inquiries (via letters, faxes and e-mails) with both the Minister for the Civil Service (i.e. the Prime Minister) and several government departments (among which are the Civil Service Commissioners and the Personnel Management and Pay Division of the Cabinet Office) have alas yielded no results. Since there is also no case law on this matter to be found, it is impossible to give a comprehensive description of the posts covered by the Rules. In paragraph 3 I will look at some of the characteristics of public service employment in the hope that they will clarify which posts have the necessary grounds to be covered by the Rules and which may be covered by Article 39 (4) (ex Article 48 (4)) EC.

2.2 Prescribed bodies according to the Race Relations Act (RRA)

As far as the so-called 'prescribed bodies' according to the RRA[27] are concerned the procedure is clearer. The Minister for the Civil Service has the power to draw up a list of prescribed bodies to which the Civil Service Nationality Rules also apply. Such a list of bodies was first drawn up in 1976 according to three criteria. The first of these is the question whether there is an intrinsic reason for restricting employment in the body by nationality, for example, that a basic indication of loyalty is required. Secondly, is there a justification based on complete indistinguishability from the civil service proper? Thirdly, there might be strong management reasons for applying the Civil Service Nationality Rules. One such reason might be that there is a substantial movement of staff from the fringe body concerned to the civil service proper, as a result of which anyone recruited to the fringe body who did not need to satisfy Civil Service Nationality Rules would thereby have a distinctly disadvantageous career expectation.[28]

---

[27] RRA, s. 75 (5)

[28] Fredman, S. and Morris, S., *The State as Employer; Labour Law in Public Services* (Mansell Publishing, London, 1989), p. 320.

This list of prescribed bodies initially contained 31 bodies. These included, amongst others, the Royal Armouries; the Bank of England; the British Museum (and other museums, such as the Science Museum); the House of Commons; the National Gallery (and other galleries such as Tate Gallery and the Victory and Albert Museum); and various research councils.[29] Until the entry into force of The European Communities (Employment in the Civil Service) Order 1991 an exception for EC citizens had not been made and until that time non-UK nationals could not be employed by these prescribed bodies. In the light of the European Court's interpretation of Article 39 (4) (ex Article 48 (4)), it was clear that the inclusion of non-defence research councils, museums and galleries infringed European law.[30] However, since the introduction of the Order it has become clear that a number of bodies on this prescribed list will have to allow employees with the nationality of one of the EU Member States. As a result a new list of prescibed bodies was drawn up in 1994. There are now only ten such bodies. These are:[31]

- Bank of England
- Board of Trustees of the Armouries
- British Council
- House of Commons
- House of Lords
- Metropolitan Police Office
- National Army Museum
- National Audit Office
- Natural Environment Research Council
- United Kingdom Atomic Energy Authority.

From the list we can see that there has been a drastic cutback from the thirty-one bodies that were on the original list. Also, most of these bodies seem at first sight to be within the public service exception of Article 39 (4) (ex Article 48 (4)) EC, although questions could be raised about the Natural Environmental Research Institute. As we saw in the European Court's case law in case 225/85, *Commission* v. *Italy*,[32] research institutes on the whole are not covered by the public service exception.

---

[29] RRA 1976 s. 75(5), SI 1984/218 as amended by SI 1985/1309 and SI 1985/1757, and the Race Relations (Prescribed Public Bodies) (No. 2) Regulations 1994, SI 1994/1986 (formerly SI 1977/1774 and SI 1994/109).

[30] Fredman/Morris, p. 320.

[31] The Race Relations (Prescribed Public Bodies) (No. 2) Regulations 1994, SI 1994/1986.

[32] [1986] ECR 2121, see paragraph 3.5 of Chapter 4.

3 The status of public service employees

In paragraph 2.1 the civil service nationality rules have been discussed. The next step is to discover to which posts these rules apply. In the next few paragraphs I want to take a look at the definition of public service and the characteristics which are deemed to be specific to public service employees, such as special allegiance and loyalty, a certain work ethos and political neutrality.

There are more than 60 departments and over 100 executive agencies making up the UK civil service. It employs around 460,000 people, making it one of the largest employers in the UK.[33] Civil servants work directly for the Crown and serve the public through the elected government of the day, although they themselves remain politically impartial. The civil service is permanent and appointed on merit.

Strange as it may seem for such a large-scale employer, the civil service is largely staffed and regulated under arrangements which are not legally enforceable.[34] For instance, it has generally been held that under common law civil servants of the Crown, and military servants also, have no legal right to their salaries and no legal protection against wrongful dismissal. There is no Civil Service Act which lays down the legal status of the civil servant, although such legislation has been advocated by a number of people.[35] There are, as a result, many different Acts of Parliament which deal with the regulation of the civil service. However, none of these acts fully and comprehensively explains the legal status, duties, obligations or rights of civil servants.[36]

It is unclear whether civil servants have contracts of employment. For example, in the Employment Act 1988, civil servants are regarded as having contracts of employment for the purposes of the law relating to industrial action alone. It has sometimes been said that a civil servant enjoys a legal status, but is not employed under contract. However, this state of affairs has not made it impossible for civil servants to recover damages for wrongful dismissal or to obtain a declaration that they are entitled to reinstatement.[37] Also, the fact that the power to appoint and regulate the conduct of civil servants is derived from royal prerogative is not in itself irreconcilable with the existence of a contract of employment, because it is obvious that the Crown can enter into binding contracts in the exercise of its prerogative functions.

---

33 http://www.cabinet-office.gov.uk/civilservice/statistics/qsr/qsr.htm (August 2000).

34 Wade, W., *Administrative Law* (Clarendon Press, Oxford, 1994) p. 68.

35 E.g. by Lewis, N., in: 'A Civil Service Act of the United Kingdom', [1998] *Public Law* (Autumn), pp. 463-488.

36 McEldowney, J., *Public Law* (Sweet & Maxwell, London, 1998), p. 104.

37 Cf. *Vine* v. *National Dock Labour Board* [1957] A.C. 488 (dock labourers); *Ridge* v. *Baldwin* [1964] A.C. 40 (chief constable).

Paradoxically, in practice the situation is just the opposite of what these legal rules would suggest. Crown service, though it legally seems to be the most insecure of all employments, is in reality the most protected.[38] Also the Crown, which is the largest employer of labour in the country, could not remain unaffected by the extensive laws on employment, labour relations and social security. The statutes that have come into existence as a result of these developments have had a major effect on the legal character of Crown service. It has changed from a relationship which was almost ignored by the law into one in which the employee now has numerous legal rights. The most radical alteration of the position of the Crown's employees under common law are the changes that bring them within reach of the provisions against unfair dismissal which were first enacted in 1971 and are now contained in the Employment Protection (Consolidation) Act 1978.[39] Under this Act Crown employees are entitled to financial compensation for unfair dismissal, as defined in the Act,[40] whether or not the dismissal is also a breach of contract.

In the UK there is no clear theory of the *fonction publique*, such as can be found in France. However, it is obvious that the civil servant is subject to a special regime, reflecting the nature of the employment, which is different from a normal employer-employee relationship in the sense that it is much more hierarchical. One can say that the (legal) position of a civil servant is certainly secondary to the needs of the public service.[41]

The values which should identify the British civil service according to a Treasury and Civil Service Committee Report[42] are 'impartiality, integrity, objectivity, selection and promotion on merit and accountability'. The Report also stated that 'the case for a permanent, politically impartial civil service is as compelling now as it has been for well over a century.'

The question that is raised by this traditional idea of what the UK's civil service is like, is whether the civil service, as the UK has known for years, is threatened by influences from outside, mainly influences from 'Europe'. Is there a need to protect the 'impartiality' and 'integrity' of the UK civil service by introducing nationality or other requirements?

This question is particularly interesting since many posts within the UK civil service in fact involve European issues. There are many European units within the UK Government. European units can be defined as 'any administrative or political unit specialising in European affairs within the department or

---

38 Wade, p. 69.

39 Act of 1978, s. 138.

40 Sections 52-62.

41 Handoll (1988), p. 225.

42 5th Report, Treasury and Civil Service Committee, 1993-93 HC 21-1, The Role of the Civil Service. Vol. 1, paras. 4-5.

elsewhere within government.'[43] EU-related posts are defined as any post within such an European unit, or posts where more than 50 per cent of the employee's time is spent on EU issues. The role of these units depends on the department of which they are a part. For example, within the Department of Agriculture there is no European unit at all, since all policy has to take European issues into account. One could almost say that the whole Department is a European unit. Other Departments have European units the size of which depends on how much European legislation has an impact on their policy making. Having some kind of European experience is important when working in one of these European units and plays a part in recruitment, as do language skills.

When more and more posts within the civil service actually involve increasing amounts of EU issues, the question of the actual need for nationality requirements also comes to the fore.

Even though there is no clear definition of the civil service, the definition which is broadly accepted is the following: civil servants are 'servants of the Crown, other than holders of political and judicial office, who are employed in a civil capacity and whose remuneration is paid wholly and directly out of moneys voted by Parliament'.[44] The Crown is formally the head of the civil service. This definition of civil servants excludes the armed forces and police officers. It also does not incorporate public servants in local government and the public corporations which are not servants of the Crown. These public servants are not paid directly from money earmarked by Parliament.

Overall Ministerial responsibility for the civil service resides with the Prime Minister, who is the Minister for the Civil Service. The day to day running of the service, however, is split between the Minister of State, the Treasury (pay and manpower); and the Minister of State, and the Privy Council Office (personnel management, efficiency and organisation).

Within the civil service two main categories of civil servant, namely industrial and non-industrial civil servants, can be distinguished. These two categories can on the whole be compared to blue- and white-collar workers in the private sector.[45]

The precise status of civil servants has never been fully resolved. The Civil Service Pay and Conditions Code states that they do not have contracts of employment.[46] However, this is not necessarily the end of the matter because the courts have never produced an authoritative ruling on a civil servant status. In civil servants' letters of appointment, though, the Crown claims the right

43 Maor, M. and Stevens, H., 'Measuring the Impact of New Public Management and European integration on Recruitment in the UK Civil Service',(1997) *Public Administration*, Vol 75, (Autumn), p. 539.

44 See, e.g., Report of the Committee on the Civil Service (Fulton Report), Cmnd 3638, 1968, appendix.

45 Fredman/Morris, p. 21.

46 Para. 14.

to unilaterally vary their conditions of service at any time. This would have to change according to labour law were they to have contractual status.

There are some groups of public service workers which are employed under contracts of employment in the same way as their private sector counterparts,[47] but the status of three major groups remain unclear. These are civil servants, police officers and parliamentary staff.

Although there are contracts for some public servants, these are often subject to greater constraints than most private sector contracts. Ultimately, control still remains in the hands of Central Government (the Crown). This is made clear by the fact that bargaining outcomes and review recommendations cannot be implemented without Ministerial consent.

On the whole it is safe to say that in the public service the concept of the contract has never become universally established. As shown above, civil servants remain 'servants of the Crown' regulated by royal prerogative, despite the fact that this is not really consistent with the reality of their role in the modern state.

The question remains as to why civil servants should be different from other public sector workers. A common argument is that the courts should not interfere in the Crown's relationship with its servants.[48] A reason for this argument could be that this would be a breach of the principle of division of power.

4 Civil servants

Among all public service employees the civil servants are most easily identifiable as a separate group. They are also most likely to have nationality requirements applicable to them since on the whole it will be civil servants' activities which will 'involve direct or indirect participation in the exercise of powers conferred by public law and duties designed to safeguard the general interests of the state or of other public authorities'.[49]

As we have seen above, a civil servant is defined as: 'a Crown servant (other than the holder of a political or judicial office or a member of the armed forces) appointed directly or indirectly by the Crown, and paid wholly out of funds provided by Parliament and employed in a Department of Government'.[50]

---

47 For example, two groups of public service employees who definitely *are* employed under contracts are local government and National Health Service (NHS) employees.

48 Fredman/Morris, p. 66.

49 Case 149/79, *Commission* v. *Belgium*, [1980] ECR 3881, para. 10.

50 Smith. S. de, and Brazier, R., *Constitutional and Administrative Law* (7th edn) (Penguin Book, London, 1994), p. 209.

In other words, it comprises all the permanent and non-political offices and posts held under the Crown, with the exception of the armed forces and the judiciary. All these officers and employees form the permanent administrative staff of the Central Government. The legal test of a civil servant is that he/she should be in the non-military service of the Crown, i.e. there must be a legal relationship of master and servant. This test excludes nationalised industries and their employees, and it excludes the great majority of public corporations.[51] The term 'civil servant' is generally also taken not to include employees of local government, the NHS[52] and university staff and police officers.

In law, all Crown servants are directly servants of the Crown itself. A civil servant is not in law the servant of his minister. Although, theoretically, the idea is that the ministers, who are elected representatives, make policy decisions and the civil servants, who are paid employees and not representative of the electorate, execute them, in reality the situation is not that clear-cut. The civil service is more than just a body of administrators for and advisers to Ministers. Many decisions, and the responsibility for taking them which rests by law with Ministers, are in practice taken by civil servants in the Minister's name, in most cases without reference to the Minister personally. This practice has been accepted by the courts[53] even when the Minister has not explicitly authorised the civil servant to make the decisions, and in cases where it concerns a type of decision which is not so vital that nothing but the Minister's personal decision will suffice. Also there are statutes that vest powers of decision directly in certain named classes of civil servants.[54] In a number of Departments numerous policy decisions will in practice be made by civil servants with the Minister's formal concurrence, a form of delegation.[55] It would be impossible for a Minister to decide everything himself. However, according to the principle of ministerial responsibility, at the end of the day it is the Minister who is answerable to Parliament for any and all decisions taken within his department. This is an incentive for ministers to at least have some control and often have the last say when it comes to policy decisions. After all, he/she will be the one who will have to defend the decisions before the Cabinet, the Treasury, the party and, most importantly, Parliament.[56]

---

[51] Wade, p. 57.

[52] The National Health Services Act 1977, schedule 5, para. 15 and the Employment Protection (Consolidation) Act 1978, s. 38(5) provide that NHS employees are *not* to be regarded as Crown employees and that their legal rights and liabilities are to be treated independently.

[53] *Carltona Ltd* v. *Commissions of Works* [1943] 2 All E.R. 560, *R.* v. *Skinner* [1968] 2 Q.B. 700.

[54] E.g. customs and excise officers and inspectors at town planning inquiries.

[55] De Smith & Brazier, p. 209.

[56] Molan, M., *Constitutional and Administrative Law Textbook* (16th edn) (HLT Publications Ltd, London, 1994), p. 169.

The civil service is regulated primarily under the royal prerogative. Formal prerogative Orders in Council relating to the civil service are few and far between, however. The main Order was enacted in 1982. Regulations, minutes and circulars issued formerly by the Treasury, between 1968 and 1981 by the Civil Service Department, and since then by the Office of the Minister for the Civil Service, have been the main substance of the law and custom of the civil service. This makes the area of legislation dealing with the civil service somewhat less than clear.

In 1968 a Senior Appointments Selection Committee was set up which helps the Head of the Home Civil Service in making recommendations to the Prime Minister for the filling of senior posts[57] within the civil service. The committee consists mainly of a number of senior permanent secretaries, a civil service commissioner, the Head of the Senior Civil Service group and the relevant permanent secretary, i.e. the permanent secretary of the department where the vacancy has arisen.

4.1 Next Steps agencies

In the 1980s many dramatic changes in the organisation of the civil service were introduced. The then Prime Minister, Margaret Thatcher, made us of private managerial techniques which were supposed to help avoid waste and to save money.

Firstly, a large number of civil service jobs were eliminated. The civil service was reduced by some 100,000 posts. Moreover, an efficiency strategy was introduced. The goal of this new strategy was to eliminate inefficiency and unnecessary areas of costs, duplication and overlap.[58] The programme of reform was continued through the 1980s and in 1988 the Next Steps Unit was set up, with the aim being to improve management and to deliver better services within available resources. It was responsible for setting up executive agencies.[59] Each of these agencies is headed by a Chief Executive who is responsible for the day-to-day running of each agency. He has to work within a framework of policy objectives and resources, based on market criteria and indicators which are set by the Minister responsible for the policy area in consultation with the Treasury.

The notion behind the Next Steps Programme is to create smaller units which can be run along more market-based managerial lines, which in turn should lead to greater efficiency. The idea is that this new organisational form

---

57 Deputy-secretary level and up.

58 McEldowney, p. 316.

59 According to the Civil Service Yearbook 1997, p. lxxxvi, by the end of 1996 there were 129 agencies which had 348,529 civil servants working for them.

should make civil servants more 'innovative, pro-active and forward thinking, rather than reactive'.[60]

In recent times the UK's civil service has been transformed 'from a staid and traditional institution to a fragmented and semi-autonomous set of units, each potentially with its own employment policies and practices.'[61]

4.2 Special allegiance and the duty of loyalty

In paragraph 2 of this chapter the nationality requirements were discussed. In the following three paragraphs I want to take a look at possible grounds for the use of nationality requirements in the public service. The first of these is the idea of special allegiance and the duty of loyalty which is supposed to be one of the pillars of the civil service.

The notion of special allegiance and a duty of loyalty to the Crown is one of the basic principles behind the idea of nationality requirements, the idea being that only nationals can have the necessary loyalty to the State that is required. Non-nationals on the whole also have a loyalty to their state of origin. These can, of course, clash, especially in the area of Foreign Affairs and Defence.

The Civil Service Management Code says that 'Civil Servants are servants of the Crown and owe a duty of loyal service to the Crown as their employer'.[62] In other words, a civil servant owes loyalty not to the public, but to his or her Minister as a member of the Crown's Government of the day.

However, this loyalty is not supposed to be blind or without limits. Parliament has on at least one occasion[63] accepted the view that there are limits to the extent to which civil servants should assist ministers in their political role. No civil servant can, for example, be obligated to carry out a clearly illegal ministerial instruction. There could also be situations in which civil servants might feel that they should resign rather than co-operate in actions which they considered to be unwise, reckless or immoral.[64]

One of the problems with the idea of a duty of loyalty in the UK is that, while civil servants remain with a government department year in year out, the Government can change from one day to the next. This can make this duty of loyalty difficult for an individual civil servant. Overnight the priorities in his department can change and so must his loyalty. This means that the idea of state

60 McEldowney, p. 333.

61 Fairbrother, P., *Politics and the State as Employer* (Mansell Publishing, London, 1994), p. 1.

62 Para. 4.1.1.

63 Report of the Select Committee on Parliamentary questions. H.C. 393 (1971/72), paras. 31-36.

64 Marshall, G., 'Ministers, Civil Servants, and Open Government', in Harlow, C. (Ed.), *Public Law and Politics* (Sweet & Maxwell, London, 1986), p. 90.

interests, which civil servants must serve, can also change from one day to the next. This is a result of the strict principle of ministerial responsibility. Only the minister is ultimately accountable for government policy and civil servants are only tools in making policy and executing it.

4.3 Political neutrality

The civil service has always been seen to be politically neutral. That is to say, it is supposed to be able to work with any government in the same efficient and responsive way. The origins of this principle of neutrality can be found in the establishment of the Civil Service Commission in 1855. A prohibition on political activities, which could give public expression to privately held political views, was introduced.[65] This notion of civil servants having a duty to the Minister of the day was emphasised in The Note of Guidance on the Duties and Responsibilities of Civil Servants. It was issued by the Head of the Home Civil Service in 1985 and revised in 1987. It stated that a civil servant should not decline to take an action because to do so would conflict with his personal opinions on matters of political choice.

As we saw in the previous paragraph, the doctrine of ministerial responsibility is of key importance to the UK's constitutional arrangements. It has a profound effect on the work of civil servants because this means that they have to preserve the appearance of political neutrality. It is the presumption underlying the organisation and management of the civil service and has as one of its consequences a high degree of centralisation. This means that civil servants cannot be politically active in the sense of commenting on public policy or stating their own opinion at to the actions of their Minister. This, of course, also means that most civil servants cannot pursue a political career while being in the civil service.

The effect of ministerial responsibility is that civil servants always speak on behalf of their ministers and, as a result, cannot voice their own ideas. They cannot comment on government policy, nor can they speak about their own conduct exercised in the service of the Crown. The prohibition on discussing of policy goes beyond Parliament itself. At public inquiries and select committees civil servants may be required to give evidence concerning departmental policy, but they may not be asked any questions directly relating to the merits of government policy.[66] The Government has always maintained that 'speaking on behalf

---

65 Civil Service Pay and Condition Code, para. 9923.

66 Bradley, A. and Ewing, K., *Constitutional and Administrative Law* (12th ed.) (Longman, London/New York, 1997), p. 317.

of the Minister' is vital if the civil service is to remain non-political.[67] The idea behind this argument is that if accountability together with responsibility were delegated it would result in a loss of civil service neutrality. Another argument is that the direct accountability of civil servants to select committees would result in the removal of all limitations upon what they would say, and thus erode the clear hierarchical relationship between the Minister and the civil servant. This would result in less comprehensive accountability.[68]

It is also the case that on the whole Ministers do not reveal the role which individual civil servants play in formulating policy. This used to be more strictly adhered to than it is these days. There is a trend towards more open government, which also has an impact on the anonymity of civil servants. More often than was previously the case, government documents now reveal the names of the civil servants who were responsible for producing them. Investigations by select committees also have the outcome of 'piercing the veil' and revealing the civil servants behind the policy document.

Overt political partisanship cannot be reconciled with the principle of official impartiality and neutrality. Most civil servants are disqualified by statute from membership of the House of Commons.[69] However, it is not the case that civil servants are ruled out from political activity altogether. For instance, workers at the Royal Mint, porters or junior clerks are not sufficiently closely related to their Minister and his policy agenda to pose a threat to the ideal of impartiality should they become politically active.

In order to allow civil servants a reasonable measure of freedom of political expression, they are divided into three main groups.[70]

Firstly, there is the 'restricted category'. This category includes the senior members of the service: civil servants in senior administrative grades, staff in executive and clerical grades whose work is associated with those giving advice to Ministers and civil servants who have direct contact with the public.[71] This category of civil servants is debarred from national political activities.[72] They

---

67 Woodhouse, D., 'Ministerial Responsibility: Something Old Something New', [1997] *Public Law* (Summer), p. 274.

68 Ibid., p. 275.

69 House of Commons Disqualification Act 1975.

70 See: the Civil Service Pay and Conditions of Service Code.

71 Molan, p. 170.

72 This includes standing as a candidate for elections to the European Parliament; holding office in party political organisations which relate to party politics in the UK or European Parliament; speaking on matters of national controversy, or expressing such views in books, articles or leaflets. Canvassing on behalf of a party or candidate in UK or European Parliament elections is also prohibited.

are, however, entitled to take part, with the permission of their Department, in local political activities, provided that they act 'with moderation and discretion, particularly in matters affecting their own Department'.[73]

Secondly, there is the 'intermediate category'. This group includes clerical officers, typists and persons charged with technical and specialised responsibilities, which do not involve questions of political policy. Members of this group may be given permission[74] by their Department to take part in both local and national political activities, except for parliamentary candidature.[75] There is a code of discretion which has to be adhered to when engaging in political activities, though.[76] Permission is likely to be refused, however, to officers who come into direct contact with members of the public in the course of participating in discretionary decisions[77] or who are closely associated, though in a subordinate capacity, with Ministers and senior policy makers.[78]

The remainder of the civil service falls within the 'politically free' category. This category is by far the largest group and consist of industrial civil servants and non-industrial civil servants in most of the minor grades. They may engage in all national and local political activities,[79] except for parliamentary candidature. The only restriction which applies is that they are not allowed to be politically active while on duty, wearing an uniform or on government premises.[80] They do, of course, have to observe the Official Secrets Act, like all civil servants, which prohibits them from making public any confidential information which they have gained as a result of their employment as a civil servant.

Crown servants, like other public servants, are not prevented by statute from joining the appropriate trade union, though. Civil servants' trade unions may be affiliated to the Trade Union Congress and most are.

As opposed to political activities, there is no binding code of conduct laid down in legislation anywhere which governs the private economic activities of civil servants. On the whole the rule is that civil servants must avoid creating conflicts between their public responsibilities and their private interests, because such conflicts could lead to embarrassment for their departments or Minister. The civil servants should always maintain the appearance of neutrality.

---

73 Over the last few years the number of politically restricted civil servants who have been given permission to engage in local political activity has been around 50.

74 Some 100,000 have been given this permission.

75 Molan, p. 170.

76 E.g. these civil servants should avoid causing embarrassment to their department and should not make personal attacks on their Minister.

77 For example, decisions on social benefits, taxation, etc.

78 De Smith & Brazier, p. 211.

79 They should, however, endeavour to avoid embarrassing their department and/or Minister.

80 Molan, p. 170.

The impartiality of the civil service is also enhanced by the fact that it has traditionally been shielded from the public gaze and protected from public enquiry. The Ministers are ultimately responsible and it has always been very difficult to discover the identity of the civil servants who were responsible for any particular policy document. This culture of anonymity was changed in the early '80s with the introduction of the permanent select committees which scrutinise government departments. In their investigations they would ask civil servants to account for their actions and in some cases they were no longer anonymous. This implies a trend towards personalisation of the civil service. Coupled with this is the increased naming of civil servants in government reports.

All this means a degrading of the strict principle of ministerial responsibility. Blame can now be seen to be trickling down. This in a way is realistic since the average department has some 90,000 civil servants and a Minister cannot be expected to know about everything that takes place. On the other hand, a strict principle of ministerial responsibility does require ministers to keep a close eye on their departments, which can never be a bad thing.

4.4 Public service ethos

Another reason for having nationality requirements can be the existence of a so-called 'public service ethos', the idea being that this ethos has specific national and cultural elements foreign to non-nationals. The question is whether there is such a thing as a public service ethos and, if so, how this should be defined. If the conclusion is that there is such a public service ethos, then the question arises whether this should be protected and if nationality requirements can play a role in that protection.

The public service ethos can be viewed as the result of the key principles on which the UK civil service is supposed to be based. A number of definitions were provided in the House of Lords Select Committee on Public Service Report.[81] Key principles that were reffered to are: integrity, political impartiality, objectivity, elections and promotion on merit and accountability through Ministers to Parliament. The public service ethos has been described as 'a portmanteau phrase which connotes not only the sense of and the pride in serving the public and the public interest but also the qualities of integrity, of dispassionateness, of freedom from corruption'.[82] The public service ethos has also

---

81 Session 1997-98, 11 February 1998, HL 55, paras. 247-298. See: http://www.parliament.the-stationery-office.co.uk/pa/ld199798/ldselect/ldpubsrv/055/psrep01.htm (August 2000).

82 Lord Armstrong of Ilminster in a Special Report for the House of Lords Select Committee on Public Service, HL Paper 109, p. 2.

been described as having the following characteristics: 'motivation primarily non-financial; subordination of private to ministerial opinions; party political neutrality, demonstrably permitting an official to serve any government; ability to see both sides of an argument but to make choices; loyalty to both the minister and the public interest, even where these are irreconcilable; willingness to offer frank and if need be unwelcome advice without regard to personal consequences; acceptance that however high he is promoted, the official will remain the servant and the political chief his master; abstention from the use of official position or information for private gain; rigorous and demonstrable propriety in the conduct of official business; resistance to the temptation to cut corners, make generous gestures, relax discipline, take risks or experiment or innovate except within clearly authorised ministerial policy; acceptance of obligations of confidentiality, security, and often anonymity.'[83]

With the introduction of agencies and the farming out of public services to private companies the fear has arisen that the public service ethos may have eroded. Witnesses before the Select Committee felt that no irreparable damage had been done, but that the public service should not be taken for granted, but rather nurtured and protected.[84] The Committee concluded that the most important factor leading to the preservation or alternatively the erosion of the public service ethos was the esteem in which it is held and that therefore it need to be constantly fostered. The Committee also underlined that the role of Ministers is important, it being up to Ministers to affirm the value of the public service ethos in maintaining standards of conduct and service in the public interest.[85] At a ministerial level, the overall responsibility for protecting ethos and morale lies in the first place with the Minister for the Civil Service (i.e. the Prime Minister) and under him the Chancellor of the Duchy of Lancaster as the Head of the Office of Public Service.

The United Kingdom's civil service has always been known for its public service ethos and politically neutral relationship with Ministers. However, since the 1990s these values are no longer accepted without question as being the most important. The introduction of Next Steps Agencies has changed the civil service. It is no longer in any meaningful sense a single uniform civil service. Within the new specialised units efficiency and market-oriented thinking have become as important. Also, the staff of these agencies are explicitly encouraged to develop a sense of loyalty to their own particular institution, rather than to the civil service as a whole. This will have an influence on the way of thinking and working within the civil service.

---

83 Sir Brian Barber, ibid., p. 215. For further definitions of the public service ethos see the House of Lords Select Committee on Public Service Report, op cit.

84 House of Lord's Public Service Report, para. 268.

85 Ibid., paras. 289-292.

In addition to the introduction of more entrepeneurial values into the civil service due to the changes over the last two decades, there is also another trend which could lead to an erosion of the public service ethos, namely, the fact that being a civil servant is no longer seen as a lifelong career. More and more high-ranking civil servants leave the civil service to take up posts in industry with whom they had contact while being employed in the civil service. Sometimes there is no more than six months between their retirement from public service and the start of their new post.[86] Also there is increasing use of contract staff. These employees often come from the commercial sector and work within the civil service on a temporary basis, before then returning to the commercial sector.

5 The impact of European law on the UK public service

The work of most departments in the UK Government has been severely affected by the UK's accession to the European Communities in 1973 and subsequently its membership of the European Union. Many of the statutes under which these departments work are statutes which arise from European directives or have to be made consistent with European law.

In a more practical sense European Community law grants European Economic Area (EEA) nationals a right to live and work in the United Kingdom. This is called a 'right of residence'. An individual has a right of residence if he is an EEA national and:

- he is working in the United Kingdom, or
- he is not economically active in the United Kingdom *and* has sufficient funds to support himself throughout his stay without needing assistance from the United Kingdom's public funds.[87]

Individuals with a right of residence do not need to apply for a residence permit or register with the police. However, if someone wishes to do so anyway, he/she can apply to the Immigration and Nationality Directorate for a residence permit. This piece of paper simply confirms that he/she has a right of residence in the United Kingdom under European Community law. An individual *does* need to apply for a residence permit if he has family members who wish to apply for a residence permit. A residence permit is normally valid for five years. An

[86] Greenaway, J.,' Having the Bun and the Halfpenny: Can Old Public Service Ethics Survive in New Whitehall?' (1995) *Public Administration*, Vol 73, (Autumn), pp. 361/362.

[87] The Immigration Rules require that all those coming to live in the United Kingdom can be supported and accommodated without claiming certain state benefits known as Public Funds. These are: Housing and Homelessness Assistance, Income Support/Job Seekers Allowance (JCA), Child Benefit, any Disability Allowance, Housing Benefit and Council Tax Benefit.

individual who has a right of residence may be joined by his family members as defined by European Community law.[88]

The principle of non-discrimination on the ground of nationality as laid down in Article 39 (ex Article 48) of the EC Treaty has of course also had an effect on the public service. Areas of the public service that do not fall within the public service exception of Article 39 (4) (ex Article 48 (4)) had to be opened up for non-nationals. These developments have had their effects on the Civil Service Nationality Rules.[89]

The number of bodies to which the Civil Service Nationality Rules apply[90] have also declined due to the European Court's interpretation of Article 39 (4) (ex Article 48 (4)) EC.

6 Other categories of public service employees

Apart from civil servants there are other government or public body employees who can be classified as public service employees. For these categories of workers it is less likely, though of course not impossible, that they fall within the definition of the public service according to Article 39 (4) (ex Article 48 (4)) EC as they do not work for the Central Government. However, this does not preclude them from being covered by the public service exception, so we will look at their characteristics in the next few paragraphs.

6.1 Decentralised authorities

Local government can be seen as a form of decentralisation of power from Central Government. It is a more effective form of government when it comes to issues which require special local knowledge and regulations on the basis of local wants and needs. Also, local government means local democracy. They are the closest contact citizens have with democracy and it gives them the possibility of playing a role in the administration of their local area.

---

88 An EU national's family members are defined by Community law (for instance in Regulation 1612/68, Article 10) as:
- spouse,
- the individual's or spouse's children or grandchildren (if they are under 21 years of age or, if over 21, dependent on the EU national),
- dependent relatives in the ascending line.

89 See paragraph 2.1.

There has been continual change in the structure of local government over the last four decades. Over and above the changes in local government structure generally, there is a trend towards devolution in Wales and Scotland. Now that Scotland has its Parliament and Wales its own Assembly, more and more decisions will be taken in Edinburgh[91] and Cardiff,[92] respectively, and not in London.[93]

To complicate matters further, the structure of local government differs between the counties of the UK: England, Scotland, Wales and Northern Ireland. All this makes the local authority structure rather confusing.

Each local authority is a body corporate, created by statute and each has a legal personality of its own, separate from that of every other government authority. 'Local government' is not an unity in the sense that Central Government is.[94]

Local government has no other powers than those which are conferred on them by Parliament. According to the legislation concerned, local authorities deal with a number of public services. These services include, amongst others, schools, sanitation, street lighting, traffic control, housing, environmental planning and certain welfare services (for example, child care). A few local public service are provided or regulated by *ad hoc* authorities composed wholly or mainly of members of the local authorities in the area. A local authority's power to operate these services is not conferred by the Local Authorities Act 1972, but by the separate statutes dealing with those different services. The powers that are delegated to these local authorities differ enormously from one statute to another. In addition to powers awarded to them by public general statutes, individual local authorities have obtained private Acts of Parliament conferring further rights on them.

---

[90] The so-called prescribed bodies of s. 75 (5) of the RRA laid down in the Race Relations (Prescribed Public Bodies) (No. 2) Regulation, SI 1994/109, see paragraph 2.1.

[91] The Scottish Parliament has powers in the following areas: agriculture, fisheries and forestry, economic development, education, the environment, food standards, health, home affairs, law and the courts, police, fire services, local government, sports and the arts, transport, training, tourism, research and statistics, and social work. The total budget that the Scottish Parliament has to spend is £ 14 billion annually.

[92] The Welsh Assembly has powers in the following areas: economic development, agriculture, forestry, fisheries and food, industry and training, education, local government, health and personal social services. housing, the environment, town and country planning, transport and roads, arts, culture and the Welsh language, the heritage, sports and recreation, tourism, water and flood defence. The total budget that the Welsh Assembly has to spent is £ 7 billion annually.

[93] In this dissertation I have not investigated the consequences of the devolution processes as far as nationality requirements are concerned.

[94] Foulkes, D., *Administrative Law* (Butterworths, London, 1995), p. 22.

The general functions of local authorities, and public corporations conducting the affairs of the remaining nationalised industries, are not performed as servants or agents of the Crown. They enjoy a substantial degree of independence from the Crown, and their functions are not unambiguously within the area of activity and responsibility of Central Government.

From a political point of view, the single most important fact concerning local authorities is that their members are elected by the population at large. The basic rules governing local elections procedure are similar to those for parliamentary elections. The qualifications for voters are almost identical.[95] To be qualified for election as a councillor in a certain area there are some requirements connected to residence: a person must either be on the local register of electors or have been resident or have occupied property or have had his/her principal place of work within the area of the local authority for the twelve months preceding nomination day and the date of the election.[96] As a result of EC legislation, local elections are now also open to EU citizens.

There are a number of differences between parliamentary and local elections as regards the list of disqualifications.[97] The main disqualification is tenure of an office of profit at the disposal of the local authority or any of its committees; this disqualifies not only council officials, but also schoolteachers. Bankruptcy, surcharge by a local government auditor, a conviction for corrupt and illegal practices, and incurring a sentence of three months' imprisonment within five years of an election, also disqualify.

Central Government has a number of possibilities for intervening in the affairs of local authorities. These forms of control are determined by statute, and specific intervention is legally valid only when it falls within the powers given by the statute to Central Government to do so. The degree and method of control by the Central Government over local authorities differs from one service to another. For instance, the relationship between Central and local government is quite different in education from what it is in transport.

Central Government also has extensive financial controls over local government. Although local authorities' income is derived directly from council tax and from payment for the services its provides, these two sources of revenue are only a small portion of the income required. The remainder of the income needed for local government (around 80%) is made up of Central Government grants. Through the means of attaching certain conditions to the eligibility for grants, Central Government has a powerful intervention tool.

---

95 The one difference being that Peers may vote in local elections, whereas they may not do so in parliamentary elections.

96 Local Government Act 1972, s. 79.

97 Subject to certain exceptions, Local Government Act 1972, ss. 80 (2), (3), 81 (4).

6.2 Police officers

The most notable fact about the British police is that, except in London, they are not under the direct control of Central Government. They are organised in local forces maintained by local authorities, rather than Central Government. The independence of the police force from Central Government is shown in the fact that the Crown has no powers to give orders directly to local forces. The local chief constables especially have a high degree of independence from any kind of political control.[98]

Although the police have many statutory powers, their primary powers and duties as peace officers have long been based upon common law rather than legislation. Their general powers of arrest without warrant were, however, made statutory by the Criminal Law Act of 1967,[99] and it has been held that their ordinary functions are 'statutory powers or duties' because the Police Regulations 1971 require them to perform all duties and to attend to all matters within the scope of their office.[100]

The employment status of the police is closely connected with their constitutional status as being independent from Central Government control. At common law, individual police constables are considered to be 'independent' officers, exercising 'original authority' derived directly from the legal powers inherent in their office.[101] But, they have also been described as being in some context 'servants of the Crown'.[102] However, they are paid by local police authorities and are under the 'direction and control' of the chief constable,[103] who, as we saw above, is for the most part independent from political control. It is clear that they are not Crown servants in the way that civil servants are: they do not take orders from a Minister and there is no direct line of accountability from the police force to Parliament via a Minister.

Constables are police officers. It can be argued that they are Crown servants, because when they are appointed, they must declare that they will well and truly serve the Queen. For certain purposes a police officer is undoubtedly an officer of the Crown;[104] and the maintenance of law and order, the preservation of the

---

98 Wade, p. 148.

99 Section 2.

100 *George* v. *Garland* [1980] RTR 77.

101 *Fisher* v. *Oldham Corporation* [1930] 2 KB 364; *Attorney-General for New South Wales* v. *Perpetual Truster Co.* [1955] A.C. 477, PC.

102 Viscount Simonds in *Attorney-General for New South Wales* v. *Perpetual Truster Co.* [1955] A.C. 477, PC.

103 Police Act 1964, s 48 (1).

104 See the review of authority and principles in *Att-Gen. for New South Wales* v. *Perpetual Trustee Co.* [1955] A.C. 457; and also see *Fisher* v. *Oldham Corporation* [1930] 2 K.B. For the purpose of the Official Secrets Act a police officer is a person holding office under the Crown: *Lewis* v. *Cattle* [1938] 2 K.B. 454.

peace, is seen as a being function of executive government.[105] It is one of the classical functions of the state.

A police officer is not paid directly out of Central Government funds, and except in the Metropolitan area he/she is neither appointed nor dismissable even indirectly by the Crown. He/she is appointed and dismissable by the chief constable of a local police force and paid by the local police authority. He/she is under the command of the chief constable, who is appointed by the local authority and can be removed by that authority on prescribed grounds.

A chief constable is nobody's servant, but an independent officer upon whom powers and duties are directly granted by law for the benefit of the public.[106] A police officer holds a public position, that of peace officer. The chain of command terminates at the chief constable and not, for instance, with a Minister. As we have seen, the chief constable is in effect an independent authority,[107] and must act free from all political influence, whether national or local.[108]

The rank and file of the police force obviously do not enjoy the degree of autonomy that the chief constable enjoys, but it is not possible to identify any single person or body as their employer and for this reason they can still be regarded as 'independent' public officers rather than employees of any specific authority.

Members of a police force cannot become Members of Parliament[109] or indeed 'take any active part in politics'.[110] This is to preserve the principle of independence between central government and the police force. Moreover, that officers below the rank of superintendent cannot join a trade union.[111]

6.3 Parliamentary staff

Parliamentary staff are a legally distinct category, separate from the civil service. Their specific status is derived from parliamentary privilege, or the right of the Houses of Parliament to run their own affairs without interfer-

---

[105] De Smith & Brazier, p. 418.

[106] See *R. v. Metropolitan Police Commissioner, ex. p. Blackburn* [1968] 2 Q.B. 118 at 135-6, 138, 148-149.

[107] See the Royal Commission's Report, Cmnd. 1728, para. 106.

[108] Wade, p. 153.

[109] House of Commons Disqualification Act 1975, s. 1.

[110] Police (Discipline) Regulations 1985, S.I. 1985, No. 518.

[111] Officers of that rank, and above, are represented, respectively, by non-statutory bodies, the Superintendents' Association and the Association of the Chief Police Officers, Police Act 1964, s. 44 (6). Officers below this rank are represented by the Police Federation which, although not legally a trade union as such, fulfils similar functions.

ence from the courts.[112] This is another example of the principle of separation of powers, this time between the executive and the parliamentary, coming into play.

Clerks in the House of Lords and Assistant Clerks in the House of Commons are officers of the Houses, not civil servants. They serve Parliament and not the government of the day.

Since both Houses of Parliament are on the List of Prescribed Bodies,[113] nationality requirements are applicable to their employees.

6.4 The judiciary

Judges may be regarded as servants of the Crown in the sense that they are 'Her Majesty's judges', holding offices granted by the Crown and bound by oath well and truly to serve the sovereign in those offices.[114] On the other hand, it is axiomatic that judges are independent: the Crown has no legal right to give them instructions as this would violate the principle of separation of powers between the judiciary and the executive. They do not therefore satisfy the test of the relationship of master and servant at common law and are not civil servants in that sense. It is nevertheless obvious that judges in administering justice supply one of the most important services of the Crown.

6.5 Public bodies

With the growth of the welfare state in the twentieth centuries more and more areas came to fall under government influence. Since it was impossible to govern all these areas, public bodies were set up to regulate and control a certain area within the public sphere. As we shall see in the following paragraphs, these public bodies take many forms.[115] In order to obtain a better idea of what a public body is, a look at the definition of 'public body' for the purposes of judicial review could prove helpful.

Judicial review is only available for testing the decisions taken by public bodies. When deciding whether or not a body whose decision is being challenged is in fact a public body, the court will look at its functions. The test that is applied is not whether the body in question is a government body as such,

---

[112] See Article 9 of the Bill of Rights.

[113] See para. 3.1.

[114] Promissory Oaths Act 1868, s. 4; Supreme Court Act 1981, s. 10(4).

[115] For a list of non-departmental public bodies and agencies, see: http://www.homeoffice.gov.uk/agency.htm (October 2000).

but whether it exercises powers which are equivalent to those of government bodies.[116] In *R* v. *City Panel on Takeovers and Mergers ex parte Datafin Ltd.*,[117] Lloyd LJ stated that often the source of power of a body is decisive in deciding whether it is a public body or not. That is to say, whether or not a body is set up under statute or by delegated legislation. However, Lloyd LJ stated that there could be cases where the matter would remain unclear and in cases like that it was necessary to look beyond a body's source of power and to scrutinise the 'nature of power' being exercised. The exercising of public law functions or functions which has public law consequences can be decisive and may allow judicial review.

What we can see here is another example of a functional approach. The legal form of the bodies is not all that decisive, it is the functions that they perform which will be of most importance.

6.5.1 Agencies

The term 'agency' covers numerous institutions, and the actual names of these bodies may vary greatly. They perform governmental functions, though not within the traditional departmental framework which is representative of Central Government.[118] Examples of agencies are: the Prison Service Agency and the UK Passport Agency.

Following the Fulton Committee's Report in 1968[119] it became clear that the organisational structure of the civil service needed changing. Two major themes were evident in the Committee's Report. One was the need for improved efficiency within the traditional departments, and this entailed a structure in which different units had clearly defined authority for which they could be held responsible. The other theme was that it should be reassessed precisely which activities required to be taken within the department at all, in other words there was a drive towards delegation of activities. The proposals by the Fulton Committee had some effect and were one of the catalysts for moving a number of functions away from the traditional department and towards newly created agencies. This trend was only enhanced after the establishment of the Rayner Unit in 1979 (now known as the Efficiency Unit) by the then Prime Minister, Margaret Thatcher.

---

116 Barnett, H., *Constitutional and Administrative Law* (2nd edn) (Cavendish Publishing, London, 1998), p. 318.

117 [1987] 2 Q.B. 815.

118 Craig, P., *Administrative Law* (3rd edn) (Sweet & Maxwell, London, 1994), p. 81.

119 Report of the Committee on the Civil Service 1966-68, Cmnd. 3638 (1968).

Once the drive for efficiency was established, and once the existing departmental structure had been challenged, it was natural to ask whether it really was desirable for activities to be performed in departments.[120] As a result, large parts of the civil service were assigned elsewhere and now have agency status.

The specific names of the institutions which are classified as agencies vary enormously: commission, directorate, inspectorate, authority, service and office are all common denominations, as is of course the name agency itself. Another common name that covers all these institutions is 'quango', which is an abbreviation of the term 'quasi-autonomous non-governmental organisation'.

The allocation of government functions to largely autonomous bodies has become an important feature of the UK's public administration. For instance, none of the remaining nationalised industries is run by a government department, though Ministers retain a restricted range of powers and duties in relation to them. Aside from the nationalised industries there are miscellaneous other bodies performing what can on the whole be described as functions of Central Government, but which lie outside the reach of specific ministerial control.

There are also a mixed bunch of bodies and trying to make sense of them and their status is difficult. For instance, most of them are statutory creations, but then again, a number are non-statutory; some are incorporated and some are not. None of these bodies is headed by a civil servant, but some are staffed by them. Their sources of income vary enormously too. Whereas some have executive powers,[121] others have advisory functions only,[122] and still others even have both. All in all there is no common pattern to these bodies, their form of organisation and their status.[123] Their powers may involve the provision of a public service,[124] the regulation and management of a public service,[125] or the regulation or promotion of private and public activities.[126]

Then there is an assortment of bodies staffed mainly or entirely by civil servants, but without any ministerial form of management. Even so, a Minister

---

120 Craig, p. 84.

121 Such as: the Commission for Racial Equality and the Police Complaints Authority.

122 For example, the Advisory Council on the Misuse of Drugs and the Central Fire Brigades Advisory Council.

123 De Smith & Brazier, p. 193.

124 For example, the British Broadcasting Corporation, the Forestry Commission, the National Museums and Art Galleries.

125 For example, the Independent Television Commission, The Radio Authority, the Countryside Commission.

126 For example, the Civil Aviation Authority, the Commission for Racial Equality, the Development Commission, the Arts Council, the British Tourist Authority.

can sometimes be answerable to Parliament for some or all of their activities.[127] For the most part these bodies have been kept at arm's length from the original departments for a variety of reasons. Some of these reasons are the following: the bodies in question perform specialised functions which are not seen as being politically controversial and therefore not in need of direct Parliamentary control; because some of the functions of such bodies are considered to be outside the political sphere (for example, because they are judicial or equivalent to judicial, such as the Criminal Injuries Compensation Board and Police Arbitration Tribunal) and should, therefore, remain separate from Central Government. Lastly, the body in question might originally have been created outside the framework of a political department and there was never perceived to be a sufficiently strong reason for bringing it within Central Government.[128]

On the whole, it will be the Minister of the Department under whose control the organisation exists who will appoint the staff to run these agencies. However, appointments are not left completely for the uncontrolled discretion of the relevant Minister. The Public Appointments Unit of the Civil Service Department maintains a central list of potential members of public bodies. The Minister is accountable to Parliament for the appointments which are made, and he or she has to consult the Prime Minister concerning major posts. So there is a form of Parliamentary control there, even though it is not very direct.

6.5.1(a) The National Health Service (NHS)

The creation of the NHS was provided for by the National Health Service Act 1946.[129] Section 1 of the Act imposed on the Minister of Health the duty to promote the establishment of a 'comprehensive health service' and for that purpose to providing or secure the effective provision of certain services.

The NHS was reorganised in 1980 and again in 1990. The position now is that in England and Wales[130] District Health Authorities (DHAs) are responsible for proving certain services in their area; in England there is also a higher tier of Regional Health Authorities (RHAs) with responsibilities for planning those

[127] For example, the Chancellor of the Exchequer is answerable to Parliament for (amongst others) the Central Statistics Office and the Treasury Solicitor; the Secretary of State for Defence for the Meteorological Office, the Secretary of State for Health for the General Register Office, etc.

[128] De Smith & Brazier, pp. 193/194.

[129] The current legislation can be found in the National Health Service Act 1977, as amended, especially by the National Health Service and Community Care Act 1990.

[130] For Scotland see: National Health Service (Scotland) Act 1978 as amended. For Northern Ireland see: SI 1972/1265 (NI 14).

services best administered on a wider, regional basis. Both types of authority are bodies corporate. They used to be financed almost entirely out of general taxation raised by Central Government and allocated by it to them.[131] However, nowadays a National Health Service Trust does have a certain degree of authority to rais its own (commercial) finances.

The legal relationship between the three tiers - Secretary of State, RHAs and DHAs - is that the Secretary of State may direct RHAs to exercise on his behalf such functions relating to the health service as are specified in a direction, and it is the duty of the RHAs to comply with these directions. RHAs can then delegate certain functions to the DHAs.

Health authorities used to be Crown bodies, and their hospitals regarded as Crown properties. However, section 60 of the National Health Service and Community Act 1990 now provides that 'health service bodies' (which includes health authorities) are no longer Crown bodies. The same act also brought some structural changes. National Health Service Trusts (NHSTs) were created. Section 5 of the Act provides that the Secretary of State may by order establish NHSTs whose function is to assume responsibility for the ownership and management of hospitals previously managed by RHAs and DHAs. Facilities owned by a NHST have thus been removed from of the ownership of the Secretary of State and of the management of the RHA and DHA. They have what is called 'opted-out' of the hierarchical Secretary of State - RHA - DHA system of ownership and management. Each NHST is a body corporate and not a Crown body. It has a board of directors consisting of a chairman and non-executive and executive directors, the former group being appointed by the RHA or Secretary of State, the latter by the NHST itself, being its employees. A NHST is to carry out its functions 'effectively, efficiently and economically'; it must achieve the financial objectives set for it by the Secretary of State. The Secretary of State can give a NHST directions on a considerable range of matters and it must submit and annual report to him. A NHST can be dissolved by ministerial order.

In short, apart from that last point, NHSTs are very like the boards which run nationalised undertakings.[132]

6.5.2 Public corporations and nationalised industry

As a legal organism the public corporation has many uses. So many in fact, that it abounds at all levels of the governmental system. It is employed wherever it is convenient to confer corporate personality. However, they are most widely used as vehicles for the Government's involvement in

---

[131] Foulkes, p. 26.

[132] See the next paragraph.

industry. The problems with these corporations lie largely in finding the right balance of power between them, the Government, and Parliament.

Whenever Parliament is willing to grant a measure of autonomy, the public corporation is often what is created as a result. Public corporations have been the principal vehicle in the nationalisation of industry. The public corporation has a legal existence of its own, and can be given certain statutory functions. Public corporatoins can operate outside the normal organisation of the service of the Crown. According to Wade, '[i]t offers scope for many kinds of governmental experiment, under which central control, local control, and independence can be blended in any desired proportions.'[133] It can also be said that the public corporation is sometimes used as a device for embarking upon some administrative activity outside the range of administrative law.

After the Second World War the nationalisation of industry really took flight. It was designed to bring important industries into public ownership. In this way they could be operated for the benefit of the public rather than for the sole interest of shareholders. However, making them government departments was not an option, as an industry cannot function while under constant parliamentary investigation and criticism, nor can it successfully be run along civil service lines. The solution was to place the nationalised industries in the hands of statutory corporations, intended to enjoy managerial liberty subject only to Ministerial control in case the corporation's policy should conflict with the public interest.[134]

The interests of the public as customers were to be represented by statutory consumer councils or users' councils, entitled to be consulted and to make their wishes known to the corporations.[135]

There are numerous nationalising statutes. Though they have many differences, there is a common pattern to all of them, namely key provisions concerning the power of appointment and the removal of members of the corporation. This power is vested in the Crown or a Minister. There are also provisions that lay down that the Minister may give the corporation 'directions of a general character'. This rather vague formula is intended to express the distinction between the control over general policy in the public interest, for which some Minister is responsible to Parliament, and the ordinary business management of the industry, in which the corporation is supposed to be free from interference.[136] Any directions given under this power must be published in the corporation's annual report, which has to be laid before Parliament. However, the Minister

[133] Wade, p. 163.

[134] Ibid., p. 164.

[135] E.g. Electricity Act 1974, s. 7; Post Office Act 1969, s. 14; Gas Act 1372, s. 9. All, or nearly all, of the members of these bodies are appointed by a Ministers.

[136] Wade, p. 165.

is also given the power to suppress publication if in his opinion it is contrary to the national interest.

On their own these powers are enough to place the Minister in a commanding position. However, besides these, he also has important financial powers which by themselves give him the possibility to steer a corporation's policy. For instance, any programmes which involve substantial capital expenditure, such as reorganisation or development programmes, are subject to his approval. He also has control of the corporations borrowing powers.[137] All in all, the Minister has many different possiblities of interfering in the running of nationalised industries.

There are not that many formal directions. However, to judge Ministerial influence by those directions is misleading, because in reality interference is frequent and pervasive. The important financial powers can be exercised informally, and in the background are the more general powers, which cast a deep shadow over the corporations' precarious independence. The Minister has a powerful lever within his control in that he is responsible for the appointment and tenure of the chairman and members. A chairman who is appointed for short term, perhaps several years, and who hopes for the renewal of his appointment, is in no position to resist pressure from the Minister, however informally applied.

Public corporations as such have no direct responsibility to Parliament. Ministers who have powers of control over them are responsible to Parliament in the normal way in so far as they have exercised, or failed to exercise, their statutory powers. Public corporations are, of course, subject to the ordinary law, e.g. concerning corporate powers, taxation, and liability in tort, unless they enjoy some statutory exception.

Where the corporation has a sufficient degree of independence, neither the corporation nor its employees are legally servants of the Crown. The corporation's independence in law, if not in fact,[138] breaks the chain of command leading down from the Crown. As we have seen when we defined Crown servants,[139] the legal relationship of master and servant demands that the master shall have complete control over what the servant does. This test is not satisfied when it comes to public corporations or nationalised industries, merely because the Minister may appoint and dismiss the members, or give directions 'of a general character', or because he can give any kind of directions. This is not in itself sufficient to be able to speak of a master-servant relationship.[140]

---

[137] Ibid., p. 166.

[138] See, for example, the Minister's powers to interfere with the running of public corporations above.

[139] Para. 4.

[140] Wade, pp. 176/177.

Since 1979 a large number of these nationalised industries have been denationalised. It was thought that the system did not live up to its expectations. The most profitable industries were transferred back to the private sector and their assets were placed back in companies of the ordinary kind.

The main bodies conducting the affairs of the remaining nationalised industries are British Coal, British Shipbuilders, the United Kingdom Atomic Energy Authority, the Post Office, a complex network of inland transport authorities, and the BBC.

6.5.2(a) The British Broadcasting Corporation (BBC)

The British Broadcasting Corporation (BBC), constituted by Royal Charter in 1926, provides all non-commercial radio and television services. The BBC is not a Crown body, the fact that a corporation is created by the exercise of Crown prerogative does not in itself make the corporation a Crown agent.[141] Whether or not it is such depends on its relationship to the Crown. Its functions are prescribed by its charter, the current licence and agreement[142] under which it operates, and any directions issued by the Home Secretary in pursuance of powers conferred on him by the governing instruments. Under the agreement he is empowered to require the Corporation to refrain from broadcasting any matter or class of matter at any time. If the BBC fails to comply with the valid direction he may revoke the licence.[143] The fact that the BBC has in effect a contractual relationship with the Crown, in which the BBC is an independent contractor of sorts, suggests that it is not an agent for the Government.

7 Conclusions

In the United Kingdom there are clear nationality requirements for a number of posts in the UK civil service. The basic rules for posts in Central Government civil service are laid down in the Civil Service Nationality Rules.

Even though the rules themselves are clear, which posts they apply to is less so. Within the UK civil service most recruitment decisions are delegated and in practice recruitment is carried out by individual departments and agencies. The departments and agencies also decide on which nationality requirements (if any) are applicable, but they have to act within the guidelines which are provided by the Civil Service Nationality Rules. This practice of delegation and individual

---

[141] *British Broadcasting Corporation* v. *Johns*, [1964] 1 All ER 923.

[142] Cmnd 8233 (1981) sets out the present licence and agreement.

[143] Licence, clauses 13 (4), 23.

recruitment practices for different departments and agencies amounts to a less than crystal-clear overall policy when it comes to nationality requirements.

The Civil Service Nationality Rules allow for access to post within the public service to certain categories of foreigners (but not all foreigners)[144] if the post is not in the so-called reserved category, or if the post does not require special allegiance. It has proved difficult, if not to say impossible, to determine which posts are in fact reserved.

Non-reserved posts within the UK civil service are open to Commonwealth citizens,[145] British Protected persons, EEA nationals of other Member States and certain non-EEA family members. This means that the UK government has chosen not to open non-reserved posts within the civil service to all foreigners. It has limited itself to certain groups. In choosing to include, besides EU nationals, nationals from EEA Member States and Commonwealth citizens, the UK civil service is thereby open to a wider group of non-nationals than is the case in Belgium. However, in contrast to the situation in the Netherlands, the posts in the UK civil service which do not require UK nationality are, for the most part, not open to third-country nationals other than those included in the categories mentioned above.

According to Section 75 (5) of the Race Relations Act, the Minister for the Civil Service has the power to draw up a list of prescribed bodies to which the Civil Service Nationality Rules apply, based on three criteria. The first of these is the question whether there is an intrinsic reason for restricting employment in the body by nationality, for example, that a basic indication of loyalty is required. Secondly, is there a justification based on complete indistinguishability from the civil service proper? Thirdly, there might be strong management reasons for applying the Civil Service Nationality Rules. One such reason might be that there is a great deal of movement of staff from the fringe body concerned to the civil service proper, as a result of which anyone recruited to the fringe body who did not need to satisfy Civil Service Nationality Rules would thereby have a distinctly less adventageous career expectation.

It has proved difficult to determine whether the UK is in compliance with Community law as far as Article 39 (4) (ex Article 48 (4)) EC is concerned, because it is very difficult to gain an impression of to which posts the Civil Service Nationality Rules apply. For a start, there is the difficulty of the absence of a written constitution. It is in the constitution where the basis for public service exceptions can often be found. Despite these difficulties, no examples of violations of the public service exception in the UK have come to light during my investigation of this subject matter.

---

144 Irish nationals and nationals from (former) Commonwealth Countries have special privileges over other non-nationals, as do nationals from EEA Member States.

145 Which includes British Dependent Territories citizens, British National (Overseas) citizens and British Overseas citizens.

CHAPTER 10

Summary and Conclusions

1 Summary

Central to this thesis is one of the exceptions to free movement of persons within the EU. As we discovered in Chapter 2, the exceptions are to be interpreted narrowly. Direct and indirect discrimination on the basis of nationality is prohibited, except when covered by one of the exceptions laid down in Article 39 (ex Article 48) EC. Only exceptions based on grounds of public policy, public security and public health according to paragraph 3 of Article 39 (ex Article 48) EC are allowed. Paragraph 4 of that same Article adds one more possible exception, namely the so-called public service exception. Article 39 (4) (ex Article 48 (4)) proclaims the provisions of that Article not to apply to 'employment in the public service'. This thesis focuses on the definition of this exception. Which posts are covered by this exception, and why?

The Treaty provisions as such offer relatively little specific elaboration on the basic right of freedom of movement of persons within the Community. Article 39 (2) (ex Article 48 (2)) EC specifies the 'abolition of any discrimination based on nationality between the workers of the Member States as regards employment, remuneration and other conditions of work and employment'. This is an extension of the basic Treaty rule forbidding any discrimination on grounds of nationality within the scope of the Treaty, which is contained in Article 12 (ex Article 6) EC. The rights as laid down in Article 39 (ex Article 48) EC are elaborated in secondary legislation.[1]

As stated above, the right to free movement is, of course, not unlimited. Public interest criteria come into play. In Article 39 (3) and (4) (ex Article 48 (3) and (4)) EC, respectively, it is laid down that the right may be limited 'on grounds of public policy, public security or public health' and does not apply to 'employment in the public service'. Because these provisions are exceptions to a basic principle of Community law, i.e. free movement of persons, they are subject to the same interpretation that applies to all provisions that are hostile to the basic principles of free movement. That is to say, the barriers to the free circulation of persons (and also goods, services and capital, for that matter) within and between the territories of the Member States must be interpreted narrowly so as not to damage the *effet utile* of Community law. This also means that their scope cannot be unilaterally determined by each Member State, but that their interpretation is subject to control by the institutions of the Community, most notably the Commission and the Court.

Chapter 3 focused on the concept of citizenship and nationality. Even though both terms are often used as if they are interchangeable, in fact they are two different concepts entirely.

---

1 Regulation 1612/68, Directive 68/360, Regulation 1251/70 and Regulation 1408/71.

Citizenship denotes a status of social and political belonging. There is one element that binds all the different meanings of citizenship together and that is the notion of an individual's membership of a political community, whatever form that community may take. The term citizen refers to the social status within the political/legal organisation

Nationality, on the other hand, represents a legal relationship between an individual and a state according to which the individual is subject to the public authority and the legal order of that nation state. Nationality, traditionally, means being subject to the government of a particular state and can as such serve as a demarcation against foreigners.

In this thesis I have chosen to define the concept of citizenship as the relationship between the state and an individual in terms of rights (and also duties) which make it possible for the individual to have an active role in the shaping of the political/legal organisation. That is to say, for that person to participate in the decision-making process within the nation state and to be part of the debates within the public sphere which deal with general interest within the nation state. As such it has a more internal character, because such rights and duties create a relationship between the nation state and its citizens. Nationality, on the other hand, I have defined in terms of the position of passive submission of a subject to the state, which was its historical definition. Nationality also has a more external character, as it is a person's nationality which gives him/her a form of identity (and as a result certain rights, e.g. diplomatic rights) when abroad. Nationality is often a condition for exercising certain rights.

Over the years, the number of people who have been given rights within the internal legal order has increasingly grown. We no longer condone slavery or discrimination against women, for example. The extension of citizenship rights to most (adult) nationals of modern states, means that in practice the concept of nationality and citizenship have become inextricably linked and the lines of demarcation between the two concepts have become somewhat blurred.

However, we can also see an extension of the use of the concept of citizenship beyond national boundaries. Such is the case with European citizenship as laid down in the EC Treaty in Articles 17 to 22 (ex Articles 8 to 8e) EC.

The wording of Article 17 (1) (ex Article 8 (1)) of the EC Treaty and the Declaration on Nationality (which was annexed to the Maastricht Treaty) indicate a desire on the part of the Member States to retain the autonomous power to determine who is to be a Union citizen. However, whilst the definition of nationality remains a matter for the Member State, the nature of the link between the Union citizen and the Union is a more direct one, working through directly effective rights as laid down in Community legislation. The Commission has also cautiously argued that a direct link has been forged between the citizens of the Member States and the Union through the election of the EP. This right was designed to foster a sense of identity with the Union. One could say that the indirect political link which already existed between the individual and the Community, enjoyed through citizenship of the individual Member State, has been joined by a direct link.

In terms of positive decision-making powers, the frontier between Member State and Community power has not been fixed. Over the years the boundaries have shifted in favour of the Community. This has been the result of the case law of the European Court which involved wide interpretations of express powers with an eye very much towards *effet utile*, the acceptance of a broad theory of implied powers, as well as the acceptance of the doctrine of pre-emption. This dynamic process has been diminished by the introduction in the EC Treaty of a number of principles by the Maastricht Treaty. The most talked about of these is the principle of subsidiarity in areas of shared competence, which is laid down in the second paragraph of Article 5 (ex Article 3b) EC. The first paragraph of that same Article encorporates the principle of limited attribution of powers to the Community. On top of those more general principles, which are applicable to all areas within Community competence, there are the clearer delineations of Community and national powers in specific policy areas, such as education and culture. Last, but not least, Article 6 (1) (ex Article F (1)) of the TEU lays down the principle of the recognition of national identities.

Union citizenship can best be seen as a *sui generis* status entitling a Member State national, being a Union citizen, to enjoy a number of rights and obligations in certain areas covered by the EC Treaty. The citizenship provisions are designed to make the Union more relevant to the individual, by reinforcing existing, and creating new, rights and duties. By giving EU nationals these, and hopefully in the future additional, rights the hope is that more of a sense of belonging to a European Community outside their own national Community will come into being.

The European Union citizenship rights go beyond the set of the well-known EC market freedoms. For instance, the voting rights and the right to consular protection possess what can be called a *'communitarian'* dimension and go beyond what is necessary to ensure an effective working of the Common Market. These rights point to the existence of a European community which goes beyond merely adding of the peoples of Europe. One could say that it is the start of the formation of a new community. A new community to which every citizen of the Member States belongs and contributes, and by which he/she is has certain rights based on Community legislation irrespective of his/her nationality of any one Member State.

Article 191 (ex Article 138a) of the EC Treaty, which states that political parties at the European level contribute to forming a European awareness and to 'expressing the political will of the citizens of the Union' is the only direct reference to the constitutive nature of Union citizenship. A more implied reference can be found in Article 189 (ex Article 137), which in defining the role of the European Parliament, states that the European Parliament is to 'consist of representatives of *the peoples of the States* brought together in the Community' [JEB: emphasis added]. At this moment in time it is obvious that the Community/Union in no way replaces the Member State as the primary state unit as far as Union citizens are concerned. There are certain elements in Union citizenship which point to the beginnings of constitutive elements of citizenship. For example, Union citizens can exercise the right to vote and stand for EP elections on the basis of residence rather than their nationality. However, there is no constitutive Union citizenship on a par with the national citizenship existing in individual Member States.

The continued central importance of national citizenship has been accepted and, indeed, reinforced in the Maastricht and Amsterdam Treaties. What is also clear is that further progress in the area of Union citizenship rights, through Treaty amendment, is dependent on national citizens of the Member States mandating their governments and endorsing changes in this field. The importance of national governments receiving the support of their national electorates was clearly seen in the processes for ratifying the Maastricht Treaty. However, receiving the support of the national electorate which is required in order to extend citizenship rights beyond their current status does not seem likely to occur in the near future, since it has become clear that most citizens of Europe are not particularly enthusiastic about the European Union as it now stands and most people seem to consider 'everything going on in Brussels' as being complicated, far removed from their surroundings and not directly related to their own lives. As a result, it does not seem likely that it will be the nationals of the Member States who will press for greater European unity at this point in time.

Chapter 4 looked at the public service exception. The reasons for the public service exception in Article 39 (4) (ex Article 48 (4)) are not difficult to comprehend. Every Member State is concerned, to a greater or lesser degree, that certain activities carried out by or in the name of that State should be performed only by the State's own nationals. The idea behind this is the assumption that its own nationals have a better understanding of what is required and they are invariably more likely to be loyal to their own State.

Article 39 (4) (ex Article 48 (4)) EC provides that the freedom of movement does not apply to employment in the public service. In other words: whereas it is forbidden to discriminate on the grounds of nationality in other areas of employment (except when any of the other exceptions of Article 39 (ex Article 48) apply),[2] it is still permitted to discriminate against non-nationals when it comes to employment in the public service. However, the Treaty does not define

[2] Article 39 (2) (ex Article 48 (2)) EC: 'limitations justified on grounds of public policy, public security or public health'.

the term 'public service'. It was left up to the European Court to determine its boundaries.

From what we saw in Chapter 4, the Court's case law on Article 39 (4) (ex Article 48 (4)) EC gives primacy to the principle of free movement of workers. As a result, the exception to this free movement, i.e. the public service exception, is interpreted narrowly. The Court has refused to apply the exception in the fields of education, health, scientific research and operational services in local government.

According to the Court, only posts 'which involve direct or indirect participation in the exercise of powers conferred by public law and duties designed to safeguard the general interests of the state or of other public authorities'[3] are covered by the public service exception.

Though it is apparent that the interpretation of this exception is narrow, it is not totally clear which posts do and do not fall within this definition. With the definition being rather vague and the Court adopting a case by case approach, this has led to confusion on the parts of Members States as to whether certain posts fall within the definition.

One reason which could explain the Court's *ad hoc* approach could be that it avoids giving an abstract definition or a list of what may constitute posts involving the exercise of public authority. The result of this approach is a flexible tool for the Court to work with. In practice a post-by-post evaluation of whether or not it is covered by the exception is required.

The Court has also not provided a definition of 'exercise of powers'. The test may be whether the public servant exercises a power, discretionary or otherwise, which affects the position of individuals, whether legal or natural persons. This is still a very vague definition and could be interpreted both narrowly and widely. Looking at the Court's emphasis on effectiveness of Community legislation, however, a wide interpretation is unlikely to be employed either by the Court or the Commission.

What we can conclude is that when it comes to interpreting the meaning of the public service exception the aim is to reduce the cases in which the public service exception can be used by interpreting emanations of the state very narrowly. Such a narrow approach has been chosen with the aim of achieving effective Community law. It is obvious that when it comes to an exception to one of the main principles of European law, e.g. to the principle of free movement of persons, the provision in question should be interpreted narrowly, as is the case with the public service exception. If such a provision includes a definition of 'the state' then that definition should be interpreted narrowly.

The European Court's approach when if comes to the public service exception does have its drawbacks, however. It is at times difficult for Member States

[3] Case 149/79, *Commission* v. *Belgium*, [1980] ECR, 3881, para. 10.

to apply the provisions correctly and coherently. Because the different interpretations are vague and often ambiguous, States are not always certain whether they apply in an individual case or not. This can also be an excuse for Member States not to adhere to Community law. They can use the uncertainty as an excuse for not complying with Community law. As long as no one (i.e. the Commission or a Community citizen) makes a point of bringing such cases before a court, then Member States can 'get away' with non-compliance for quite some time. This problem is compounded by the fact that it is difficult for individuals to be certain of their rights when to them the rules are also totally confusing. Situations like this do not help to make Community law more effective. The pertinent question is the following: where does the Court's approach start losing its effectiveness because of the confusion it generates?

The main conclusion that can be drawn from the differences in approach used by the Court, is that it focuses on the effectiveness of a specific provision or set of provisions, without much regard for the effectiveness of Community legislation as a whole. Citizens of the Union are often quoted on the basis of polls and questionnaires, as complaining that they do not understand the goings-on 'in Brussels'. Since one of the aims of the European Union after the coming into force of the Maastricht Treaty was to bring it closer to 'the people', i.e. its citizens, maybe the Court should re-evaluate its decisions and instead of aiming for maximum effectiveness on an *ad hoc* basis, instead concentrate on elucidation and more coherence in the use of important definitions which form the basis of Community law. Or, at the very least, it should make clear that definitions of concepts such as 'the state' or 'emanations of the state' vary drastically from provision to provision and it should thereby explain why it finds the need for such differing definitions.

In contrast to the narrow definition of public service as laid down in Article 39 (4) (ex Article 48 (4)) EC, we saw in Chapter 5 that the European Court of Justice wants to interpret the concept of 'the State' very broadly when it comes to the direct effect of directives. Also when we look at the interpretation of 'the State or regional or local authorities' in the Public Procurement Directives, this concept is widely interpreted. Both methods of interpretation seem to be rooted in the idea of effective EC law or *effet utile*.

If a provision of Community law is to have maximum effect, e.g. directives and the provisions dealing with public procurement, then it is to be interpreted broadly. If such a provision includes a definition of the state, then this definition is also to be interpreted broadly. When it comes to the public service exception, the Court talks of the exercise of official authority and the true interests of the state, whereas in cases of direct effect and public procurement control by the state or a state body seems to be the major issue. As we saw in Chapter 5, the European Court takes a functional approach to Community legislation. It looks at the goal the legislation in question wishes to achieve and then interprets it with that in mind. As a result, when it comes to the direct effect of directives, the Court interprets 'emanations of the state' very broadly[4]. It does so in order to give directives maximum effect since they can only be relied upon against the state and state bodies. When it comes to deciding whether or not a body is in fact an 'emanation of the state' the Court focuses on who controls such a body, either through financial control (e.g. awarding of subsidies under certain conditions) or through the power to appoint the management.

In the *Foster* case the Court stated that for the purposes of direct effect 'the state' includes bodies 'providing a public service under the control of the State'.[5] The Court followed the Advocate General's Opinion in the *Foster* case. Advocate General Van Gerven considered that, in the light of the case law of the Court of Justice, the concept of 'the state' should be interpreted broadly. He referred to 'the criterion of actual control' which he then defined as being a 'dominating influence and the possibility on the part of the authorities to give binding directions, regardless of the manner in which such control is exercised'.[6]

Alternatively, when it comes to the public service exception, the Court does not focus on who controls a body, but more on the duties and tasks a public body performs. It looks at whether there is an exercise of official authority, or whether general interests of the state are involved. There is no mention of control over a public body when deciding whether or not a post with such a body is covered by the public service exception.

All these interpretations are based on the principle of *effet utile*. Since the public service exception is a deviation from the principle of non-discrimination it needs to be interpreted restrictively. Direct effect legislation and public procurement legislation needs to be interpreted broadly for EC law to have the greatest impact on national law and to avoid Member States shirking of their duties.

After looking at two areas of Community law in Chapter 5, namely that of the direct effect of directives and public procurement, and that of the public service exception in Chapter 4, it is safe to say that the idea of what 'the state' is depends on which area of Community law one is dealing with. More often than not, the European Court takes a functional approach. It looks at the purpose and ideas behind a certain piece of legislation and interprets it with that in mind. It is clear that the thought behind this functional approach is to make European law more effective.

Looking at other areas of European law, as was done in Chapter 5, may help to explain why the interpretation of the public service exception as laid down in Article 39 (4) (ex Article 48 (4)) EC is a rather vague definition. The Court obvi-

4 See e.g.: *Marshall* (case 152/84, [1986] ECR 735); *Johnston* (case 222/84, [1986] ECR 1651); *Costanzo* (case 103/88, [1989] ECR 1839); *Foster* (case C-188/89, [1990] ECR I-3133).

5 Case C-188/89, [1990] ECR I-3133, para. 20.

6 Ibid., para. 16.

ously wants to keep its options open and at the same time it is striving towards making Community law more effective, or at least as effective as possible.

Chapters 2 to 5 of this book have a general and more descriptive character. They deal with the provisions which lay down the rights of free movement of workers, EU citizenship rights, concepts of 'the state' in various other parts of EU law and they describe in detail the public service exception of Article 39 (4) (ex Article 48 (4)) EC and the case law dealing with the public service exception. In order to obtain a more detailed understanding of how the public service exception is interpreted by the Member States of the EU, looking at national legislation is required. This more specific research into the public service exception can be found in Chapters 6 to 9.

The conclusions that can be drawn from the general study in Chapter 6 is that the Member States have different interpretations of the public service exception and have also chosen different ways in which to implement the legislation dealing with this topic. On the whole national legislation is often clearly influenced by Community provisions as is the case in Italy, Portugal, and Luxembourg. The Austrian legislator chose to make a direct link with Article 39 (4) (ex Article 48 (4)) EC by mentioning the said Article in its Civil Service Code, namely in the section dealing with general appointment requirements, thereby directly incorporating all Community legislation and the case law of the European Court.

There are four ways in which national requirements are laid down in national legislation. The first option which one encounters is to lay down a general criterion which designates a post as falling within the public service exception. This form has been chosen by the Austrian legislator, for example. Alternatively, a list of posts may be drawn up which are covered by the public service exception and which can only be filled by nationals. This is the so-called negative list. However, if a list of excepted posts does exist, as is the case in Finland, for example, then there is, over and above this list, also the possibility for some government official or institution to declare that a particular post requires the nationality of that Member State. As such, the systems used by the Member States are not 'pure'. A third system uses a positive list. It lists the posts which are open to non-nationals. This system used to be present in Italy, but is no longer in use today. Lastly, there is a mixed system, where both a general criterion is used and at the same time there is a list which states which areas of the public service are open to nonationals, as is the case in Luxembourg.

Three European Union Member States have been investigated in greater detail. These are the Netherlands, Belgium and the United Kingdom. The reasons for this choice are the following. As this is a Dutch study, the choice of the Netherlands is obvious. The two other countries were chosen because they were equally interesting when it comes to the public service exception, because all three countries have very different civil service systems, but also for more the practical reason of language ability. Since Belgium was the subject of the first real investigation by the European Court into the public service exception it seemed a good choice. The United Kingdom was chosen mainly for the practical reason of my versed in the English language, as well as my having connections in the UK, but also because its legal system is very different from that on the continent of Europe.

In the Netherlands there seem to be few, if any, problems concerning the openness of the Dutch public service to non-nationals. Overlooking the nationality requirements as laid down in Dutch legislation the main conclusion that can be drawn is that on the whole the Dutch public service is open to non-nationals, except for posts which are clearly covered by the public service exception. The number of posts which require Dutch nationality have been kept to a minimum.

The posts which do require Dutch nationality according to Dutch legislation are all covered by the public service exception as laid down in Article 39 (4) (ex Article 48 (4)) EC. Therefore, one can conclude that the Dutch legislation dealing with nationality requirements are in accordance with Community law.

During the course of my research it has become evident that the definition of what constitutes the public service in the Netherlands is not always clear. There are many semi-public and also private law bodies of which it is not immediately apparent whether they fall within the public service. However, this not a problem as far as the public service exception is concerned. There are no specific nationality requirements which apply to these bodies, nor is it likely that a position requiring confidentiality would be part of such semi-public or private bodies. As such, the fact that the distinction between public service and non-public service bodies is not always clear is interesting, but not really relevant as far as the public service exception is concerned.

In Belgium access to public service employment for non-nationals was historically limited. A broad institutional approach was used when laying down nationality requirements. Under the influence of Community legislation, and more specifically the Court's judgment in *Commission* v. *Belgium*[7], this approach had to be abandoned.

The Constitution in Article 10 states that only Belgians can be appointed to posts in the public service and military. The Article does provide for exceptions to be made in special cases which have to be laid down in legislation. A non-national can only be appointed to a post in the public service if there is an Act which specifically provides for this possibility.

Nowadays it is clear that as far as EU citizens are concerned the meaning of 'public service' has to be considered narrowly, in accordance with what the European Court has determined to be public service for the purposes of Article

7 Case 149/79, [1980] ECR 3881.

39 (4) (ex Article 48 (4)). This restriction to the Constitution's Article has been recognised, but has not led to any amendment of the provision itself.

Nationality requirements for public sector workers employed under contract were for the most part abandoned by the implementation of a Royal Decree in 1991. The rule to be applied is the following: Belgian nationality is required when the post involves direct or indirect participation in the exercise of public authority and this includes activities designed to safeguard the general interests of the state. This definition is very similar to the the European Court's interpretation of Article 39 (4) (ex Article 48 (4)). Posts not covered by this exception are open to Belgians and European Union citizens alike. It is worth noting here that posts as civil servants (*statutair ambtenaar*) are not open to all non-nationals, only to European Union citizens, thereby limiting its effect to that which is strictly necessary on the basis of Community law. However, posts as contractual employees are open to all non-nationals, including third-country nationals.

In the United Kingdom there are nationality requirements for a number of posts in the UK civil service. The basic rules for posts in Central Government civil service are laid down in the Civil Service Nationality Rules. However, in the UK civil service most recruitment decisions are delegated and in practice recruitment is carried out by individual departments and agencies. The departments and agencies also decide on which nationality requirements (if any) are applicable, but there are guidelines which are provided by the Civil Service Nationality Rules. This, however, renders the overall policy somewhat less than crystal clear when it comes to nationality requirements.

The Civil Service Nationality Rules allow for access to posts within the public service to certain categories of foreigners (but not all foreigners)[8] if the post is not in the so-called reserved category, or if the post does not require special allegiance. It has proved difficult, if not impossible, to determine which posts are in fact reserved.

As far as the so-called 'prescribed bodies' according to Section 75 (5) of the Race Relations Act, to which the Civil Service Nationality Rules also apply, are concerned, the procedure is somwhat clearer. The Minister for the Civil Service has the power to draw up a list of prescribed bodies to which the Civil Service Nationality Rules apply, based on three criteria. The first of these is the question whether there is an intrinsic reason for restricting employment in the body based on nationality, for example a basic indication of loyalty is required. Secondly, is there a justification based on complete indistinguishability from the civil service proper? Thirdly, there might be strong management reasons for applying the Civil Service Nationality Rules. One such reason might be that there is a great deal of movement of staff from the fringe body concerned to

8 Irish nationals and nationals from (former) Commonwealth Countries have special privileges over other non-nationals, as do nationals from EEA Member States.

the civil service proper, as a result of which anyone recruited to the fringe body who did not need to satisfy Civil Service Nationality Rules would thereby have a distinctly less adventageous career expectation.

2 Conclusions

The main problem with the public service exception as it now stands in Article 39 (4) (ex Article 48 (4)) EC is that it is worded in such a way as to appear to be a very broad exception to the principle of free movement of workers within the EU, especially when compared to the exception in Article 45 (ex Article 55) EC which deals with the exception to the right of establishment. The exception in Article 45 (ex Article 55) makes use of much narrower wording and directly refers to the exercise of 'official authority'. When compared with the public service exception in Article 39 (4) (ex Article 48 (4)) one could be forgiven for assuming that this exception has more far-reaching consequences than it does in practice.

Of course, the fact that the public service exception has limited impact is mainly due to the European Court's narrow interpretation of the exception. From the very first cases dealing with the public service exception as laid down in Article 39 (4) (ex Article 48 (4)) the Court made it clear that, because it is an exception to one of the fundamental principles of EC law, it should be interpreted narrowly.

In my opinion, the problem with the Court's interpretation is not its intent. I feel that the Court's objective is sound, namely a narrow interpretation of the public service exception, but the Court's case-by-case approach to the subject matter does not mean an easy application of the said provision by the Member States. The two conditions referred to by the European Court as making the public service exception applicable, namely 'safeguarding the national interests of the state' and 'exercise of official authority', are in themselves not crystal clear and open to different interpretations. There is also still some confusion on the part of the Member States as to whether the two conditions are to be applied cumulatively or alternatively.[9]

Since it is not evident which posts are covered by the two conditions, the range of this exception is still unclear and will not become much clearer as long as the Court persists on dealing with these matters on a case-by-case basis.

---

9 Though, personally, I think that the Court has shown a clear preference for the cumulative approach. Case 225/85, *Commission* v. *Italy*, in which the Court seemed to apply the criteria alternatively, may be considered as a one-off abberation.

3 The Way Forward

After having looked at the public service exception from different angles, namely that of the European Court and Commission and that of the Member States, it is now time to focus on how the interpretation of the public service exception should progress.

One could say that as the integration of the Member States increases with the introduction of more and more extensive powers at the European Union level, the need for the public service exception will decrease. Increasingly fewer public policies will be purely national in character and therefore may no longer require loyalty and concern for national interests on the part of its civil service staff. However, it is unlikely that national policies will disappear altogether, not even in the distant future.[10] I believe that there will always be certain posts which require the nationality of the nation state in question, primarily for national security reasons, but also for cultural reasons. Protection of the national identity in cultural terms will become more important as the powers of the European Union expand. As such, the public service exception, in one form or another, will probably remain in existence.

The question is whether the public service exception, as laid down in Article 39 (4) (ex Article 48 (4)) EC, is still useful in its current form and whether it will remain so in the future.

In my opinion there are a number of ways out of this problem, all of which have practical problems of their own. The first would be a more strictly formulated interpretation of the exception, or a newly worded exception to replace Article 39 (4) (ex Article 48 (4)) EC. However, this would be an inflexible tool and difficult to apply to the very different systems of public service that are present in the fifteen Member States. It would also be extremely difficult to come up with a wording that is applicable to all the different public services of all Member States and which would have the same effect in all those Member States.

Another option would be a wide-scale inventory of public service posts in all Member States, for example, by national governments. The national governments could decide post-by-post or category-by-category as to whether certain posts are covered by the exception. Such a list could then be put before the national parliament and, once approved, could go to the Commission in the form of a notification procedure. The Commission would then have a set period to respond to the list via a Reasoned Opinion, in which it states whether or not it concurs with the posts listed as being within the scope of the public service exception. Lastly, there would be the possibility of a ruling on the matter by

---

10 The slow progress within the second pillar of the EU, namely the Common Foreign and Security Policy, is perhaps illustrative of this point.

the European Court of Justice as to whether the posts on the lists are in fact consistent with the criteria as laid down by the Court in its case law concerning Article 39 (4) (ex Article 48 (4)) EC.

Although such a solution would solve the problem, it would only do so temporarily. New public service posts are created and old ones disappear on a regular basis. Such lists would require regular updates and would be very expensive to create in the first place and also to be subsequently maintained.

A third solution, and in my opinion the most workable in the short term, would be to codify the Court's case law in the EC Treaty. By referring to the two criteria, namely 'exercise of official authority' and 'safeguarding the general interests of the state', and clarifying in the wording chosen that these two are to be applied cumulatively, some of the confusion might be alleviated. At least it would make the the public service exception's legitimate field of application clearer to the European citizens as well as to the governments of the Member States, which have a duty to interpret the public service exception correctly and to implement its effects in their national legislation.

When it comes to human rights which are the be protected, the European Court looks towards national constitutions when deciding whether or not a right is in fact a widely accepted human right in all (or most) Member States and therefore worthy of protecting and maintaining. Maybe the Court could do the same when it comes to deciding which are the 'general interests of the state' and which posts involved with the protection of these 'general interests' are covered by the public service exception. Or perhaps this could even be codified in a new paragraph in the EC Treaty?

I propose that the following changes be made to Article 39 (ex Article 48) EC. This provision's fourth paragraph should be replaced by:

'The provisions of this Article shall not apply to employment in the public service when this employment involves the exercise of official authority and the safeguarding of general interests of the state which are guaranteed in the national constitution.'

I would also propose that the following distinctions be made when defining the term 'public service' for the purposes of Article 39 (4) (ex Article 48 (4)) EC. Firstly, there are office holders (*ambtsdragers* in Dutch) who have been elected to their posts, either directly of indirectly, or whose appointments are political. For example, Ministers and mayors. Office holders often exercise public authority directly. Secondly, there are civil servants (*ambtenaren*), and some of whom exercise public authority, although most of the time indirectly, some of which do not. Thirdly, there are public servants who do not have the status of a civil servant, for example contractual employees.

Looking at these distinctions, I would like to suggest that posts which fall within the category of office holders, i.e. those which represent the political element within a democratic state, should be covered by the public service exception, as should those civil servants who exercise public authority. Both categories should be allowed to have a nationality requirement under Community law. The remainder of the posts within the public service should be open to other EU citizens who are not nationals of the Member State in question.

I realise that the difficulty with this approach lies with the second category, namely that of the civil servants who do or do not exercise public authority. Like the current public service exception the main problem lies with the definition of what 'public authority' actually is. However, until the whole of the public service is opened up to non-nationals, this problem will remain and be at the heart of whatever form of public service exception is chosen to be applicable and it seems to me that this problem is unavoidable.

Lastly, the European Court could decide to use a different criterion altogether when deciding whether a post is covered by Article 39 (4) (ex Article 48 (4)) EC. Maybe it is time to switch to a more practical criterion, one which is already used in the area of public procurement.[11] Such a criterion could be formulated as follows:

> *'Public service covers activities which due to their nature could not be performed equally well by a private individual or company.'*

The nature of such activities which would make it impossible for them to be performed by a private individual or company could, for instance, be the fact that they involve the exercise of sovereign power (e.g. policy decisions), the use of force (the police, armed forces) or that they involve sensitive information vital to the interests of the state (e.g. foreign policy, defence, protection of privacy). This would rule out such posts as members of a national orchestra, teaching posts and railway workers from being within the scope of the public service exception.

Even if changes are made to the public service exception, there will still be the practical problem of realising the full openness of that public service which is not covered by the public service exception. In practice it is very difficult to gain an impression as to whether or not a public service is truly open (or being opened up) to non-nationals in the way it should be. In an individual case it is very difficult, if not almost impossible, to prove that a non-national has not been appointed into the public service merely because of his nationality. The authorities can easily claim that a different candidate was more suitable for the post in question, which is very difficult to disprove because of the many subjective factors involved in the appointment and dismissal of personnel. Only when (a specific part of) the public service consistently appoints only nationals,

---

[11] See Chapter 5, paragraph 3.

even though qualified non-nationals keep applying for posts, will an allegation of discrimination have a chance of success as things now stand. In cases which are part of a pattern of discrimination it could be more easily proved in a court of law that discrimination against non-nationals is a fact. A national ombudsman or an anti-discrimination body could be of assistance in bringing patterns of discrimination out in the open.

One way to solve this matter is to reverse of the burden of proof.[12] Laying the burden of proof on the public body would mean that it would have to justify more clearly its decision not to appoint a non-national. The introduction of such a reversal would make it easier for the individual to prove discrimination and, at the same time, more difficult for public bodies to consistently discriminate against non-nationals. A reversal of the burden of proof could be combined with a limited number of arguments which could justify discrimination against non-nationals, such as national security and confidentiality, but also the protection of national cultural identity.

Reversal of the burden of proof in a discrimination case would not be new in Community case law. The European Court has decided in favour of it in the past, namely in cases *Danfoss*,[13] *Enderby*[14] and *Royal Copenhagen*,[15] where it decided that with an eye on the effective legal protection of victims of discrimination the burden of proof (which normally lies with the victim) can be reversed.[16] Reversal of the burden of proof is also introduced in discrimination cases in Article 8 of Directive 2000/43/EC of 29 June 2000 implementing the principle of equal treatment between persons irrespective of racial or ethnic origin.[17]

My hope is that the public service will be opened up to more and more non-nationals in the future. This, in my opinion, becomes increasingly likely with the extension and broadening of Community powers. As ever more national legislation has its roots in European directives, regulations, etc., national interests will become less and less pronounced. General interests of the state will become European interests. Why should European citizens who are not national of a Member State then be denied entry to a post on the basis that it deals with safeguarding national interests?

Finally, I want to mention a possible problem which might surface with the opening up of the public service to non-nationals, and this is the problem of promotion. When someone initially commences a career in the public service

---

12 See also: Leenders, M., *Bewijsrecht en discriminatie bij de arbeid* (W.E.J. Tjeenk Willink, Deventer, 1997), pp. 157ff.

13 Case 109/88, [1989] ECR 3199.

14 Case C-127/92 [1993] ECR I-5535.

15 Case C-400/93, [1995] ECR I-1295.

16 Jans, J.(*et al.*), *Inleiding tot het Europees Bestuursrecht* (Ars Aequi Libri, Nijmegen, 1999), pp.312-314.

17 OJ L180, p. 20.

and rises to higher positions, there may come a point when he/she becomes eligible for promotion to a post which is covered by the public service exception and is open to nationals of the Member State only. Both the civil servant in question and his/her superiors are then faced with a dilemma. Should this person be denied the promotion outright? Should he/she be made to choose between, on the one hand, the promotion subject to obtaining the Member State's nationality, or on the other, dismissal or stagnation as regards his/her career? These are practical problems which will more often come to the fore once the admission of non-nationals into the public service becomes increasingly prevalent. I suggest that Member States should start thinking about the consequences and consider setting up a policy which is applicable in these cases.

Selective Bibliography

ADAMS, M. AND WINTGENS, L. (EDS.)
Wetgeving in theorie en praktijk (MAKLU, Antwerpen/Apeldoorn, 1994)

AKKERMANS, P. AND KOEKOEK, A.
De Grondwet: een artikelsgewijs commentaar (W.E.J. Tjeenk Willink, Zwolle, 1992)

ALEN, A.
Algemene beginselen en grondrechten van het Belgisch Publiek Recht; Boek 1 De Instellingen (Story-Scientia, Brussel, 1988)

ALEN, A. (ED.)
Treatise on Belgian Constitutional Law (Kluwer, Deventer, 1992)

ALEN, A., TILLEMANS. B. AND MEERSSCHAUT, F.
'Decentralised Authorities', in Alen, A. (Ed.), *Treatise on Belgian Constitutional Law* (Kluwer, Deventer, 1992) pp. 160-174

ANTONSEN, M. AND JØRGENSEN, T.
'The "Publicness" of Public Organizations', 75 *Public Administration* (1997) (Summer) pp. 337-357

ARNULL, A.
'Legal Order of the ECSC', 15 *European Law Review* (1990) pp. 321-326

ARNULL, A.
'Judging the New Europe', 19 *European Law Review* (1994) pp. 3-15

ARNULL, A. AND JACOBS, F.
'Applying the Common Rules on Free Movement of Persons', in Schermers, H. (et al.) (Eds.), *Free Movement of Persons in Europe* (Martinus Nijhoff Publishers, Dordrecht, 1993) pp. 272-285

ARROWSMITH, S.
The Law of Public and Utilities Procurement, (Sweet & Maxwell, London, 1996)

BARAV, A.
'Court Recommendation to Deport and the Free Movement of Workers in EEC Law', 6 *European Law Review* (1981) pp. 139-161

BARENTS, R.
'Het Verdrag van Amsterdam: een eerste indruk', *Nederlands Juristen Blad* (1995-28) pp. 1261-1268

BARNETT, H.
Constitutional and Administrative Law (2nd Edn) (Cavendish Publishing, London, 1998)

BEKKE, H., PERRY, J. AND TOONEN, T. (EDS.)
Civil Service Systems in Comparative Perspective (Indiana University Press, Bloomington/Indianapolis, 1996)

BENSE, M. AND ZIJLSTRA, S.
'Het begrip bestuursorgaan - Betekenis en strekking van artikel 1:1 eerste lid, Algemene wet bestuursrecht', *Nederlands Tijdschrift voor Bestuursrecht* (1994/9) pp. 253-270

BERGE, J. TEN
Besturen door de overheid (W.E.J. Tjeenk Willink, Deventer, 1996)

BERGE, J. TEN
Bescherming tegen de overheid, (W.E.J. Tjeenk Willink, Deventer, 1999)

BERGE, J. TEN, DAALDER, E. AND NAEYÉ, J.
De Nationale Ombudsman, VAR-reeks 106 (Samson H.D. Tjeenk Willink, Alphen aan den Rijn, 1991)

BERGE, J. TEN AND ZIJLSTRA, S.
De publiekrechtelijke rechtspersoon in ontwikkeling (Preadvies NJV 2000) (W.E.J. Tjeek Willink, Deventer, 2000).

BETLEM, G.
Civil Liability for Transfrontier Pollution; Dutch Environmental Tort Law in International Cases in the Light of Community law (Graham & Trotman/Martinus Nijhoff, London/ Dordrecht/Boston, 1993)

BETLEM, G.
'Medium Hard Law - Still No Horizontal Direct Effect of European Community Directives After *Faccini Dori*', Vol. 1, No. 3 *Columbia Journal of European Law* (1995) pp. 469-496

BOELES, P.
'Kroniek van het migratierecht', *Nederlands Juristen Blad,* (1997-31) pp. 1476-1483

BOER, J. DE
'Niet-openbare werving van overheidspersoneel in strijd met de Grondwet', *Nederlands Juristen Blad* (1990-11), p. 425

BOES, M.
'The Central Administration and the Decentralized Agencies', in Craenen G. (Ed.), *The Institutions of Federal Belgium; An Introduction to Belgian Public Law* (Acco, Leuven, 1996) pp. 131-148

BOGNADOR, V.
'Britain and the European Community', in Jowell, J. and Oliver, D. (eds.), *The Changing Constitution* (Clarendon Press, Oxford, 1994) pp. 3-31

BONO, R.
'The International Powers of the European Parliament, the Democratic Deficit and the Treaty on European Union', 12 *Yearbook of European Law* (1992) pp. 85-138

BRACKE, N.
'Horizontale Werking van richtlijnen?', *RegelMaat* (1994/5) pp. 205-208

BRADLEY, A. AND EWING, K.
Constitutional and Administrative Law (12th ed.) (Longman, London/ New York, 1997)

BRASZ, H.
'Toegankelijkheid van overheidsdienst voor vreemdelingen', *Tijdschrift voor Overheidsadministratie* (1984 -8) pp. 163-166

BREDERVELD, E.
Gemeenterecht (W.E.J. Tjeenk Wilink, Deventer, 1996)

BRENNINKMEIJER, A.
'Case note AB/474, ABRS of 3 October 96' (Schiphol) *Jurisprudentie Bestuursrecht*, 321

BRINK, M. VAN DEN, AND VIERHOUT, R.
'Democratic Control without Frontiers? The European Parliament and Free Movement of Persons', in Schermers, H.G (et al.) (Eds.), *Free Movement of Persons in Europe* (Martinus Nijhoff Publishers, Dordrecht, 1993) pp. 379-390

BURKENS, M. AND KUMMELING, H. (EDS.)
EG en grondrechten - Gevolgen van de Europese Integratie voor de nationale grondrechtenbescherming (Tjeenk Willink, Zwolle, 1993)

BUTLER, R.
'The Evolution of the Civil Service - a Progress Report', 71 *Public Administration* (1993) (Autumn) pp. 395-406

CHAPMAN, R.
'Change in the Civil Service', 72 *Public Administration* (1993) (Winter) pp. 599-610

CHAPUS, R.
Droit Administratief Général (Montchrestien, Paris, 1997)

CLAPHAM, A.
A Human Rights Policy for the European Community', 10 *Yearbook of European Law* (1990) pp. 309-366

CLARK, D.
'The Modernization of the French Civil Service: Crisis, Change and Continuity', 76 *Public Administration* (1998) (Spring) pp. 97-115

CLARKE, P.
Citizenship (Pluto Press, London/Boulder, 1994)

CLOSA, C.
'The concept of Citizenship in the Treaty on European Union', 29 *Common Market Law Review* (1992) pp. 1137-1169

CLOSA, C.
'Citizenship of the Union and Nationality of Member States', 31 *Common Market Law Review* (1995) pp. 487-518

CLOSE, P.
Citizenship, Europe and Change (Macmillan, London, 1995)

COPPEL, J. AND O'NEILL, A.
'The European Court of Justice: Taking Rights Seriously?', 29 *Common Market Law Review* (1992) pp. 669-692

CRAENEN, G.
'Belgium: General Background and Legal Charecteristics', in Craenen G. (Ed.), *The Institutions of Federal Belgium; An Introduction to Belgian Public Law* (Acco, Leuven, 1996) pp. 11-28

CRAENEN, G. (ED.)
The Institutions of Federal Belgium; An Introduction to Belgian Public Law (Acco, Leuven, 1996)

CRAIG, P.
Administrative Law (3rd edn) (Sweet & Maxwell, London, 1994)

CRAIG, P. AND DE BÚRCA, G.
EU law: Text Cases and Materials (2nd edition), (Oxford University Press, Oxford, 1998)

CURTIN, D.
'The Province of Government: Delimiting the Direct Effect of Directives in the Common Law Context', 15 *European Law Review* (1990) pp. 195-223.

CURTIN, D.
'The Decentralised Enforcement of Community Law Rights; Judicial Snakes and Ladders', in Curtin, D. and O'Keeffe, D. (Eds.), *Constitutional Adjudication in European Community and National Law* (Butterworth (Ireland) Ltd, Dublin, 1992) pp. 33-49

CURTIN, D.
'The Constitutional Structure of the Union: A Europe of Bits and Pieces', 30 *Common Market Law Review* (1993) pp. 17-69

CURTIN, D. AND MEIJERS, H.
'Openbaarheid in Europa - Geheim bestuur door "Schengen" en "Maastricht"', *Nederlands Juristen Blad* (1995-5)

DAHRENDORF, R.
'The Changing Quality of Citizenship', in Steenbergen, B van (Ed.), *The Condition of Citizenship*, (Sage, London, 1994) pp. 10-19.

DASHWOOD, A.
'Community Legislative Procedures in the Era of the Treaty on European Union', 19 *European Law Review* (1994) pp. 343-366

DENYS, C.
'Grote schoonmaak in de overheidssector', *Nederlands Tijdschrift voor Europees recht*, 1996/10, pp. 221-224

DEVROE, W.
'Privatizations and Community law: Neatrality versus Policy', 34 *Common Market Law Review* (1997) pp. 267-306

DICEY, A.
Law of the Constitution (10th edn), (Macmillan, London, 1959)

D'OLIVEIRA, H.
'European Citizenship: Its Meaning, its Potential', in Monar, J., Ungerer W. and Wessels, W. (Eds.), *The Maastricht Treaty on European Union: legal complexity and political dynamic* (European Interuniversity Press, Brussels, 1993)

DURAND, A.
'European Citizenship' 4 *European Law Review* (1979) pp. 3-14

EVANS, A.
'The Political status of Aliens in International, Municipal and European Community law', 30 *International and Comparative Law Quarterly* (1981)

EVANS, A.
'Nationality Law and European Integration', 16 *European Law Review* (1991) pp. 190-215

EVERLING, U.
'Will Europe Slip on Bananas? The Bananas Judgment of the Court of Justice and National Courts', 33 *Common Market Law Review* (1996) pp. 401-437

EVERSON, M. AND PREUSS, U.
Concepts, Foundations, and Limits of European Citizenship, ZERP-Diskussionpapier 2/95

FAIRBROTHER, P.
Politics and the State as Employer (Mansell Publishing, London, 1994)

FIORILLO, L.
in Carince, F. (ed.), *Il lavoro alle dipendenze della amministrazioni pubbliche* (Giuffré, Milano, 1995)

FOSTER, N.
'Equal Treatment and Retirement Ages', 13 *European Law Review* (1988) pp. 222-229

FOULKES, D.
Administrative Law (Butterworths, London, 1995)

FREDMAN, S. AND MORRIS, S.
The State as Employer; Labour Law in Public Services (Mansell Publishing, London, 1989)

FRISSEN, P. (ET AL.)
Verzelfstandiging van het openbaar bestuur (VUGA, 's Gravenhage, 1992)

GARDNER, J. (ED.)
Hallmarks of Citizenship; A Green Paper, (London, The British Institute of International and Comparative Law, 1994)

GERVEN, W VAN
'Horizontal Effect of Directive Provisions Revisted', in Curtin, D. and Heukels, T. (Eds.), *Institutional Dynamics of European Integration, Essays in Honour of Henry G. Schermers* (Nijhoff, Dordrecht, 1994)

GOORDEN, C.
'Het aanwijzingsbesluit bestuurorganen Wob en WNo', *Nederlands Tijdschrift voor Bestuursrecht* (1994/3) pp. 61-67

GREENAWAY, J.
'Having the Bun and the Halfpenny: Can Old Public Service Ethics Survive in New Whitehall?', 73 *Public Administration* (1995) (Autumn), pp. 357-374

GRIEF, N.
'Direct Effect of Directives and Organs of the State', 16 *European Law Review* (1991) pp. 136-143

GROENENDIJK, C.
'Nationality and Access to Employment in the Public Service: Law and Practice in the Netherlands', 36 *Netherlands International Law Review* (1989-2) pp. 107-129

GROENENDIJK, C.
'Three Questions about Free Movement of Persons and Democracy in Europe', in Schermers, H. (et al.) (Eds.), *Free Movement of Persons in Europe* (Martinus Nijhoff Publishers, Dordrecht, 1993) pp. 391-402

GROOT, G. DE
'De Toekomst van het Nederlanderschap', in Donner J, Groot, G. de, Holterman, Th. *Toekomstperspectieven van het Nederlandse Vreemdelingenrecht* (Tjeenk Willink, Zwolle 1994)

GROOT, G. DE AND BOLLEN, C.
'Netherlands Nationality Law', in Nascimbene, B. (ed.), *Nationality Laws in the European Union* (Butterworths/Giuffrè Editore/ Milano, 1996) pp. 545-597

GUNSTEREN, H. VAN, (ET AL.)
Eigentijds Burgerschap (WRR, s-Gravenhage, 1992)

GUNSTEREN, H. VAN
'Four Conceptions of Citizenship', in Steenbergen, B. van (Ed.), *The Condition of Citizenship* (Sage, London, 1994) pp. 36-48

HABERMAS, J.
'Citizenship and National Identity', in Steenbergen, B. van (Ed.), *The Condition of Citizenship* (Sage, London, 1994) pp. 20-35

HALL, S.
'The European Convention on Human Rights and Public Policy Exceptions to the Free Movement of Workers under the EEC Treaty', 16 *European Law Review* (1991) pp. 446-488

HALL, S.
Nationality, Migration Rights and Citizenship of the Union (Martinus Nijhoff Publishers, Dordrecht, 1995)

HANDOLL, J.
'Article 48 (4) and Non-National Access to Public Employment', 13 *European Law Review* (1988) pp. 223-241

HANDOLL, J.
Free Movement of Persons in the European Union (Wiley & Sons, Chichester, 1995)

HARDING, A.
Public Duties and Public Law (Clarendon Press, Oxford, 1989)

HEEDE, K.
European Ombudsman: redress and control at Union level (Kluwer Law International, The Hague, 2000)

HESSEL, B. AND MORTELMANS, K.
EG-regelgeving voor decentrale overheden (Kluwer, Deventer, 1997)

HESSEL, B. AND MORTELMANS, K.
Het recht van de Europese Gemeenschappen en de decentrale overheden in Nederland (W.E.J. Tjeenk Willink, Deventer, 1997)

HIRSCH BALLIN, E.
'Soevereiniteit in de Europese Unie', *Nederlands Juristen Blad* (1997-44) pp. 2005-2010

HOEFNAGEL, F.
Bibliotheken en omroep als publieke zaak; Een analyse van de Welzijnswet en de Mediawet (HRWB, s Gravenhage, 1988)

IERSEL, J. VAN
'Free Movement of Persons - Democratic Control', in Schermers, H. (et al.) (Eds.), *Free Movement of Persons in Europe* (Martinus Nijhoff Publishers, Dordrecht, 1993) pp. 369-378

JANS, J.(ET AL.)
Inleiding tot het Europees Bestuursrecht (Ars Aequi Libri, Nijmegen, 1999)

JANVIER, R.
Contractanten in overheidsdienst (Mys en Breesch, Gent, 1997)

KAKOURIS, C.
'Dp the Member States Possess Judicial Procedural "Autonomy"?', 34 *Common Market Law Review* (1997) pp. 1389-1412

KALBERG, S.
'Cultural Foundation Of Modern Citizenship', in Turner, B. (Ed.), *Citizenship and Social Theory* (Sage Publications, London/Thousand Oaks/New Delhi, 1990) pp. 91-114

KAPTEYN, P, AND VERLOREN VAN THEMAAT, P.
(3rd Ed. edited by Gormley, L.), *Introduction to the Law of the European Communities* (Kluwer Law International, London/The Hague/Boston, 1998)

KICKERT, W.
'Public Governance in the Netherlands: an Alternative to Anglo-American "Managerialism"', 75 *Public Administration* (1997) (Winter), pp. 731-752

KONIJNEBELT, W. (ET AL.)
Hoofdlijnen van administratief recht, (LEMMA, Utrecht, 1994)

KORTMANN, C.
De Grondwetsherzieningen van 1983 en 1987 (Kluwer, Deventer, 1987)

KOVAR, R. AND SIMON, D.
'La citoyenneté européenne', *Cahiers de droit européen* (CDE), 3-4, 1993

LANGE, R. DE
'Paradoxen van Europees burgerschap', *Recht en Kritiek* (1995/3) pp. 278-197

LANGE, R. DE
'Paradoxes of European Citizenship', in Fitzpatrick, P. Nationalism, *Racism and the Rule of Law* (Alderhot, Dartmouth, 1995)

LANGE, R. DE
'Burgerschap en inkleuring: the language of the master,' Inleiding Leuven, 7 december 1995

LANGE, R. DE
'Openbare lichamen, rechtspersonen en bestuursorganen: kortsluiting in het publiekrecht', in Vucsán, R. (ED.), *De Awb-mens: boeman of underdog* (Nijmegen, Ars Aequi Libri, 1996)

LANGE, R. DE
Europees burgerschap, Congres 'Licht op Maastricht' te Utrecht, 13 februari 1996

LAYTON-HENRY, Z.
'Citizenship or Denizenship for Migrant Workers', in Layton-Henry, Z. (Ed.), *The Political Rights of Migrant Workers in Western Europe* (Sage, London, 1990) pp. 186-195

LEENDERS, M.
Bewijsrecht en discriminatie bij de arbeid (W.E.J. Tjeenk Willink, Deventer, 1997)

LENNAERTS, K.
'Fundamental Rights to be Included in a Community Catalogue', 16 *European Law Review* (1991) pp. 367-390

LENZ, B.
'The Public Service in Article 48 (4) EEC with Special Reference to the Law in England and in the Federal Republic of Germany', *Legal Issues of European Integration* (1989) pp. 75-122

LEWIS, N. AND LONGLEY, D.
'Ministerial Responsibility: The Next Steps', [1996] *Public Law* (Autumn) pp. 490-507

LEWIS, N.
'A Civil Service Act of the United Kingdom', [1998] *Public Law* (Autumn) pp. 463-488

LONBAY, J.
'Education and Law: The Community Context', 14 *European Law Review* (1989) pp. 363-387

LUNSHOFF, H.
'De ontwikkeling naar een Europees staatsburgerschap', in Burkens, M. and Kummeling, H. (Eds.), *EG en grondrechten - Gevolgen van de Europese Integratie voor de nationale grondrechtenbescherming* (Tjeenk Willink, Zwolle, 1993) pp. 189-218.

LYONS, C.
'Citizenship in the Consitution of the European Union: rhetoric or reality?', in Bellamy, R. (Ed.), *Constitutionalism, Democracy and Sovereignty: American and European Perspectives* (Avebury Press, Aldershot, 1996)

MANCINI, G.
'The Free Movement of Workers in the Case-Law of the European Court of Justice', in Curtin, D. and O'Keeffe, D. (Eds.), *Constitutional Adjudication in European Community and National Law* (Butterworth (Ireland) Ltd, Dublin, 1992) pp. 67-77

MAOR, M. AND STEVENS, H.
'Measuring the Impact of New Public Management and European integration on Recruitment in the UK Civil Service', 75 *Public Administration* (1997) (Autumn) pp. 531-551

MARIAS, E.
'From Market Citizen to Union Citizen', in Marias, E. (Ed.) *European Citizenship* (European Institute of Public Administration, Maastricht, 1994) pp. 1-23.

MARSHALL, G.
'Ministers, Civil Servants, and Open Government', in Harlow, C. (Ed.), *Public Law and Politics* (Sweet & Maxwell, London, 1986)

MARSHALL, T.
Citizenship and Social Class (Cambridge University Press, Cambridge, 1950)

MARTIN, D. AND GUILD, E.
Free Movement of Persons in the European Union (Butterworths, London/Edinburgh, 1996)

MARTINEZ, J.
'Law versus Ethics; Reconciling Two Concepts of Public Service Ethics', 29 *Administration & Society* (1998-6) pp. 690-722

MAST, A., ALEN, A. AND DUJARDIN, J.
Overzicht van het Belgisch Administratief Recht (Kluwer Rechtswetenschappen, Antwerpen, 1996)

MCELDOWNEY, J.
Public Law (Sweet & Maxwell, London, 1998)

MEEHAN, E.
Citizenship and the European Community (Sage, London, 1993)

MEIJ, J. DE, AND VLIES, I. VAN DER (ET AL.)
Inleiding tot het staatsrecht en het bestuursrecht (W.E.J. Tjeenk Willink, Deventer, 2000)

MICHIELS, F.
'Woorden die beginnen met een b.', *NTB-special* (1994) p. 19.

MINISTERIE VAN BINNENLANDSE ZAKEN EN KONINKRIJKSRELATIES
Arbeidsrapportage Overheid 1999, mei 1999

MINISTERIE VAN BINNENLANDSE ZAKEN EN KONINKRIJKSRELATIES
Rijkspositie rijksambtenaar 1998, mei 1998

MOLAN, M.H
Constitutional and Administrative Law Textbook (16th edn) (HLT Publications Ltd, London, 1994)

NAPEL, H.
'De rechtsmacht van het Hof van Justitie van de Europese Gemeenschappen', *Nederlands Juristen Blad* (1998-2 pp. 67-71

NICOLAÏ, P. TROOSTWIJK, H. AND HAZEWINDUS, W.
Bestuursrecht (Uitgeverij Factotum, Amsterdam, 1997)

NIJHOF, M.
De concessie in Europeesrechtelijk perspectief: een onderzoek naar de plaats van de concessie in het Europese recht en het Nederlandse bestuursrecht (Dissertation, Universiteit Utrecht, 2000)

OBRADOVIC, D.
'Political legitimacy and the European Union', 34 *Journal of Common Market Studies* (1996), pp. 191-221

O'KEEFFE, D.
'Equal Rights for Migrants: the Concept of Social Advantages in Article 7(2), Regulation 1612/68', 5 *Yearbook of European Law* (1985) pp. 93-123

O'KEEFFE, D.
'The Free Movement of Persons and the Single Market', 17 *European Law Review* (1992) pp. 3-19 (1992a)

O'KEEFFE, D.
'Judicial Interpretation of the Public Service Exception in Article 48, paragraph 4 of the EEC Treaty', in Curtin, D. and O'Keeffe, D. (Eds.), *Constitutional Adjudication in European Community and National Law* (Butterworth (Ireland) Ltd, Dublin, 1992) pp. 89-106 (1992b)

O'KEEFFE, D.
'Union Citizenship', in O'Keeffe, D. and Twomey, P. (Eds), *Legal Issues of the Maastricht Treaty* (Chancery Law, London, 1994) pp. 87-107

O'KEEFFE, D.
'The Emergence of a European Immigration Policy', 20 *European Law Review* (1995) pp. 20-36

O'LEARY, S.
'Nationality Law and Community Citizenship: A Tale of Two Uneasy Bedfellows', 12 *Yearbook of European Law* (1992) pp. 353-384

O'LEARY, S.
'The Relationship between Community Citizenship and the Protection of Fundamental Rights in Community Law', 32 *Common Market Law Review* (1995) pp. 519-554

O'LEARY, S.
The Evolving Concept of Community Citizenship: From the Free Movement of Persons to Union Citizenship (Kluwer Law International, The Hague/London/Boston, 1996)

O'LEARY, S.
'The Free Movement of Persons and Services', in Craig, P. and de Búrca, G. (Eds.), *The Evolution of EU Law*, (Oxford University Press, Oxford, 1999) pp. 377-416

PACTET, P.
Institutions Politiques; Droit Constitutionnel (Armand Colin/Masson, Paris, 1996)

PARKER, J.
Citizenship, Work and Welfare; Searching for the Good in Society (Macmillan Press, Houndmills/Basingstoke/ Hampshire/London, 1998)

PAUL, K.
Ambtenarenrecht (H. Nelissen, Baarn, 1996)

PEERS, S.
'Towards Equality: Actual and Potential Rights of Third-Country Nationals in the European Union, 33 *Common Market Law Review* (1996) pp. 7-50

PEETERS, P.
'The Federal Structure: Kingdom, Regions and Communities', in Craenen G. (Ed.), *The Institutions of Federal Belgium; An Introduction to Belgian Public Law* (Acco, Leuven, 1996) pp. 55-70

PEETERS, P. AND ALEN, A.
'The Executive', in Alen, A. (Ed.), *Treatise on Belgian Constitutional Law* (Kluwer, Deventer, 1992) pp. 84-94

PEIJPE, T. VAN, AND RIPHAGEN, J.
Schets van het Nederlands Ambtenarenrecht (Kluwer, Deventer, 1994)

PESCATORE, P.
'The Doctrine of "Direct Effect": An Infant Disease of Community Law' 8 *European Law Review* (1983), p. 155

PLENDER, R.
'The Free Movement of Persons in Europe - The role of the National Judiciary', in Schermers, H. (et al.) (Eds.), *Free Movement of Persons in Europe* (Martinus Nijhoff Publishers, Dordrecht, 1993) pp. 286-297

PLIATZKY, L.
'Quangos and Agencies', 70 *Public Administration* (1992) (Winter) pp. 555-563

POLLARD, D. AND HUGHES, D.
Constitutional and Administrative Law, Text and Materials (Butterworths, London, 1990)

PRECHAL, S.
'Remedies after Marshall', 27 *Common Market Law Review* (1990) pp. 451-473

PRECHAL, S.
Directives in European Community Law (Clarendon Press/ Oxford Press, Oxford, 1995)

PREUSS, U.
'Problems of a Concept of European Citizenship', 1 *European Law Journal* (1995) pp. 267-281

RAHM, G. DE
'Naturalisation: The Politics of Citizenship Acquisition', in Layton-Henry, Z. (Ed.), *The Political Rights of Migrant Workers in Western Europe* (Sage, London, 1990) pp. 158-185

RATH, J.
'Voting rights', in Layton-Henry, Z. (Ed.), *The Political Rights of Migrant Workers in Western Europe* (Sage, London, 1990)

RAWORTH, P.
'A Timid Step Forwards: Maastricht and the Democratisation of the European Community', 19 *European Law Review* (1994) pp. 16-33

RICHARDS, D.
'Appointments to the Highest Grades in the Civil Service - Drawing the Curtain Open', 74 *Public Administration* (1996) (Winter) pp. 657-677

RIESENBERG, P.
Citizenship in the Western Tradition. Plato to Rousseau (The University of North Carolina Press, Chapel Hill/London, 1992)

RIMANQUE, K. AND WOUTERS, J.
De betekenis van de Grondwet voor de Europese Rechtsorde (Preadvies Vereniging voor de vergelijkende studie van het recht van België en Nederland) (W.E.J. Tjeenk Willink, Deventer, 1998)

ROEST, O. VAN DER
Ambtenarenprocesrecht in de praktijk (VUGA, 's Gravenhage, 1986)

ROSAS, A.
'Nationality and Citizenship in a Changing European and World Order', in Suksi M. (Ed.), *Law Under Exogenous Influences* (Publications of Turku Law School, Vol.1, 1994) pp. 30-59

ROUBAN, L.
The French Civil Service (La Documentation Française, Paris, 1998)

RUZIE, D.
Citoyenneté et nationalité dans l'union européenne. Paper for the 2nd ECSA-World conference: *Federalism, subsidiarity and democracy in the European Union*, Brussels 5-6 May 1994 p. 10.

SCHOONHOVEN, M.
Provinciérecht; Een algemene Beschouwing over huidig en toekomstig provinciérecht (Koninklijke Vermande, Lelystad, 1991)

SCHRIJVERS, P. AND SMEETS, H.
Staats- en bestuursrecht (Wolters Noordhoff, Groningen, 1998)

SCHROTEN, K.
De overheidsstichting op het niveau van de centrale overheid (W.E.J. Tjeenk Willink, Deventer, 2000)

SEVENSTER, H. AND BIESHEUVEL, M.
'Kroniek van het Europees Recht', *Nederlands Juristen Blad* (1997-41) pp. 1434-1438

SIKKES, J. (ED.)
Ambtenarenrecht in beweging; Beschouwingen over de rechtspositie van het overheidspersoneel in de jaren tachtig (VUGA, 's Gravenhage, 1985)

SMITH, J.
'The Public Service Ethos', 69 *Public Administration* (1991) (Winter) pp. 515-523

SMITH. S. DE, AND BRAZIER, R.
Constitutional and Administrative Law (7th edn) (Penguin Book, London, 1994)

SOHRAB, J.
'The Single European Market and Public Procurement', 10 *Oxford Journal of Legal Studies* (1990) pp. 522-538

SPENCER, S. (ED.)
Strangers and Citizens. A positive Approach to migrants and refugees (IPPR/Rivers Oram Press, London, 1994)

STAPLES, H.
The Legal Status of Third Country Nationals Resident in the European Union (Kluwer, Den Haag, 1999)

STEENBERGEN, B. VAN
'The Condition of Citizenship: An Introduction', in Steenbergen, B. van (Ed.), *The Condition of Citizenship*, (Sage, London, 1994) pp. 1-9

STEWART, F.
'Citizens of Planet Earth', in Andrews, G. (Ed.), *Citizenship* (Lawrence & Wishart, London, 1991) pp. 65-75

STEYGER, E.
'De neveneffecten van het vrij verkeer op specifiek nationale beleidsterreinen, *Social Economisch Weekblad* (1996-6) pp. 226-233

SZYSCCZAK, E.
'Case Law: Foster and Others v. British Gas plc.' 27 *Common Market Law Review* (1990) pp. 859-871

THOMAS, R.
'The Duties and Responsibilities of Civil Servants and Ministers: A Challenge Within British Government', 52 *International Review of Administrative Sciences* (1986)

TILLEMAN, B. VAN HAEGENDOREN, G AND ALEN, A.
'Legal Position of Aliens', in Alen, A. (Ed.), *Treatise on Belgian Constitutional Law* (Kluwer, Deventer, 1992) pp. 236-244

TIMMERMANS, C.
'Free Movement of Persons and the Division of Powers between the Community and Its Member States - Why do it the intergovernmental way?', in Schermers, H. (et al.) (Eds.), *Free Movement of Persons in Europe* (Martinus Nijhoff Publishers, Dordrecht, 1993) pp. 352-368

TRIMIDAS, T.
'The Role of the Advocate General in the Development of Community law: Some Reflections', 34 *Common Market Law Review* (1997) pp. 1349-1387

TRIMIDAS, T
'Horizontal Effect of Directives: a Missed Opportunity?' 19 *European Law Review* (1994) pp. 621-636

TROTABAS, L. AND ISOART, P.
Manuel Droit Publique (L.G.D.J. Paris, 1996)

TWOMEY, P.
'European Citizenship and Human Rights: Actual Situations and Future Perspectives', in Marias, E. (Ed.) *European Citizenship* (European Institute of Public Administration, Maastricht, 1994) pp. 119-133

VERSCHUEREN, H.
Internationale arbeidsmigratie; De toegang tot de arbeidsmarkt voor vreemdelingen naar Belgisch, internationaal en Europees gemeenschapsrecht (Die Keure, Gent, 1990)

VERSCHUEREN, H.
'De toegang tot de openbare dienst voor EG-onderdanen: macht en onmacht van het Europese Gemeenschapsrecht', *Rechtskundig Weekblad Antwerpen*, nr. 13, 30 nov. 1991, pp. 425-435

WADE, W.
Administrative Law (Clarendon Press, Oxford, 1994)

WATSON, P.
'Free Movement of Workers and Social Security', 14 *European Law Review* (1989), 415-422

WEATHERILL, S & BEAUMONT, P.
EC Law (Penguin Books, London, 1993)

WEBER, M.
Economy and Society: An Outline of Interpretive Sociology (University of California Press, Berkeley/Los Angeles/London, 1964)

WEISS, F.
'Public Procurement in the EEC - Public Supply Contracts', 13 *European Law Review* (1988), 318-334

WEISS, F.
'Public Procurement in European Community Law', *European Community Law Series* (volume 4) (The Athlone Press, London & Atlantic Highlands, NJ, 1993)

WHITE, R.
'A Round-up of Cases on Free Movement of Workers', 12 *European Law Review* (1987) pp. 147-153

WHITE, R.
'Equality in the Canteen', 19 *European Law Review* (1994) pp. 308-313

WILLIAMS, D.
'The Influence of European Union Law upon United Kingdom Administration', in Richardson, G. and Glenn, H. *Administrative Law & Government Action* (Clarendon Press, Oxford, 1994) pp. 231-247

WINTER, J.
'Public Procurement in the EEC', 28 *Common Market Law Review* (1991) pp. 741-782

WISSEN, G. VAN
'De vreemdeling in openbare functies', in Honée, E. (et al.), *Minderheden in een dominante cultuur* (Tjeenk Willink, Zwolle, 1988) pp. 51-70

WISSEN, G. VAN
Grondrechten (Tjeenk Willink, Zwolle, 1992)

WOODHOUSE, D.
'Ministerial Responsibility: Something Old Something New', [1997] *Public Law* (Summer) pp. 262-282

WOUTERS, J.
'European Citizenship and the Case-Law of the Court of Justice of the European Communities on the Free Movement of Persons', in Marias, E. (Ed.) *European Citizenship* (European Institute of Public Administration, Maastricht, 1994) pp. 25-61

WYATT, D. AND DASHWOOD, A.
European Community Law (3rd Ed.) (Sweet & Maxwell, London, 1993)

WYATT, D.
'Article 48 (4) EEC: Scope of Public Service Proviso' 6 *European Law Review* (1981) pp. 459-463

ZIJLSTRA, S.
'Het aanwijzingsbesluit bestuurorganen Wob en WNo (reactie op C.P.J. Goorden)', *Nederlands Tijdschrift voor Bestuursrecht* (1994-5) p. 132

ZIJLSTRA, S.
Noot bij silicose-uitspraak, *Nederlandse Jurisprudentie Administratieve Beslissingen*, 1996/136

ZIJLSTRA, S.
Zelfstandige bestuursorganen in een democratiche rechstsstaat (VUGA, 's Gravenhage, 1997)

ZUTPHEN, A. VAN
De rechtspositie van de rijksambtenaar (VUGA, 's Gravenhage, 1991)

ZUTPHEN, A. VAN
'Het begrip openbare dienst in de Ambtenarenwet 1929; Een verkenning op de grens van het bestuursrecht', *Nederlands Tijdschrift voor Bestuursrecht*, (1998/4) pp. 119-127

ZWAAN, J. DE
'Institutional Problems of Free Movement of Persons; The Legal and political Framework for Cooperation', Schermers, H. (et al.) (Eds.), *Free Movement of Persons in Europe* (Martinus Nijhoff Publishers, Dordrecht, 1993) pp. 335-351

ZWAAN, J. DE AND BULTENA, A.
'Kroniek van het Europees recht', *Nederlands Juristen Blad* (1998-32) pp. 1441-1447

Table of Cases

European Court of Justice

List of Abbreviations

AB	Nederlandse Jurisprudentie Administratief Rechtelijke Beslissingen
A.C.	Appeal Cases
AG	Advocate General
Appl(s)	Application(s)
Awb	Algemene wet bestuursrecht
AWGB	Algemene Wet Gelijke Behandeling
BAT	Bundes-Angestelltentarifvertrag
BBC	British Broadcasting Corporation
BDG	Beamten-Dienstrechtsgesetz
BRRG	Beamtenrechtsrahmengesetz
B.S.	Belgisch Staatsblad
Bull.	European Commission, Bulletin of the European Union
BV	Besloten Vennootschap
BVD	Binnenlandse Veiligheidsdienst
BW	Burgerlijk Wetboek
CAO	Collective Arbeidsovereenkomsten
CDE	Cahiers de droit européen
CMLR	Common Market Law reports
CMLRev.	Common Market Law Review
CNR	Consiglio Nazionale delle Ricerche
CRvB	Centrale Raad van Beroep
DHA	District Health Authority
Doc.	Document
EC	European Community
ECHR	Convention for the Protection of Human Rights and Fundamental Freedoms
ECR	European Court Reports
Edn	Edition
Ed(s).	Editor(s)
EEA	European Economic Area
EEC	European Economic Community
EFTA	European Free Trade Area
EIPA	European Institute of Public Administration
ELR	European Law Review
EP	European Parliament
ETS	European Treaties Series
EU	European Union
GemW	Gemeentewet
GG	Grundgesetz
GW	Grondwet
HC	House of Commons
HL	House of Lords

HM	Her Majesty's
HR	Hoge Raad
ICCPR	International Covenant on Civil and Political Rights
ICJ	International Court of Justice
I.L.O.	International Labour Organisation
IPPR	Institute for Public Policy Research
JB	Jurisprudentie Bestuursrecht
Jur.	Jurisprudentie van het Hof van Justitie van de Europese Gemeenschappen
KB	Koninklijk Besluit
K.B.	King's Bench
KLPD	Korps Landelijke Politiediensten
LJ	Lord Justice
MID	Militaire Inlichtingendienst
NHS	National Health Service
NHST	National Health Service Trust
NJ	Nederlandse Jurisprudentie
NJB	Nederlands Juristenblad
nr.	number/nummer
NTB	Nederlands Tijdschrift voor Bestuursrecht
NV	Naamloze Vennootschap
O.C.M.W.	Openbaar centrum voor maatschappelijk welzijn
OJ	Official Journal
Para(s)	Paragraph(s)
Pw	Provinciewet
Q.B.	Queen's Bench
quango	quasi-non-governmental-organisation
RHA	Regional Health Authority
RRA	Race Relations Act
R.v.St.	Raad van State
s.	Section
SEW	Sociaal-Economische Wetgeving
S.T.A.	Supremo Tribunal Amministrativo
STE	Stichting Toezicht Effectenverkeer
Stb.	Staatsblad
Supp.	Supplement
TAR	Tijdschrift voor Ambtenarenrecht
T.A.R.	Tribunale amministrativo regionale
TEU	Treaty on European Union
TK	Tweede Kamer
UK	United Kingdom
VAR	Vereniging voor Administratief Recht

WPQ	Written Parliamentary Question
Wte	Wet Toezicht Effectenverkeer
ZBO	Zelfstandig bestuursorgaan
ZERP	Zentrum fur Europäische Rechtspolitik, Bremen

Index